KISSING OUTSIDE THE LINES

A TRUE STORY
OF LOVE AND RACE
AND HAPPILY
EVER AFTER

DIANE FARR

SEAL PRESS

KISSING OUTSIDE THE LINES

A TRUE STORY OF LOVE AND RACE AND HAPPILY EVER AFTER

Copyright © 2011 by Diane Farr

Published by
Seal Press
A Member of the Perseus Books Group
1700 Fourth Street
Berkeley, California

Library of Congress Cataloging-in-Publication Data

Farr, Diane.
   Kissing Outside the Lines: A True Story of Love and Race and Happily Ever After / by Diane Farr.
       p. cm.
   ISBN-13: 978-1-58005-390-7
   ISBN-10: 1-58005-390-4
1. Intermarriage—United States. 2. Interracial marriage—United States. 3. Inter-ethnic marriage—United States. 4. Ethnicity—United States. I. Title.
   HQ1031.F37 2011
   306.84'50973–dc22

                            2011003087

9 8 7 6 5 4 3 2 1

Cover design by Abby Weintraub
Interior design by Domini Dragoone
Printed in the United States of America
Distributed by Publishers Group West

FOR SEUNG YONG.

A lesser man would have muzzled me right from the start.
Sarang-ay-o, Big Daddy.

AUTHOR'S NOTE

All stories herein are true,
as told from my perspective.
All of the couples who appear in the book exist,
they are not composites.
In some cases, names and places
have been changed to preserve privacy.
And "timing is everything" as an actor,
but not as an author,
so the timing of events has been changed
in some cases, as well.

TABLE OF MIXED CONTENTS

WE ALWAYS HOPED OUR DAUGHTER WOULD NOT MARRY OUTSIDE OF OUR RACE

ONE YEAR INTO my marriage, my mother looked at my husband and said, "We always hoped that Diane would not marry outside of our race."

My mother felt the silence in our living room. Her glance swung between my husband's eyes and mine. Looking at them did not give her pause so I had to interject. "Mom, you realize Seung and I are different races?" My mother grunted a laugh. "No, you're not."

My husband is Korean. He was born in Seoul and immigrated to the United States as a child with his parents. I am a second-generation American, of Irish and Italian descent. And my mother, at fifty-eight years old, did not realize that my husband and I are different races because she, above everything else, is a New Yorker. And to a New Yorker, there are only two races, it seems: black and not black.

I would say black and white, but every time my husband's family refers to me as "white," my mother, and the rest of my family, laughs out loud. My mother claims I am not white. You may be thinking my mother is not all there from the previous quote, but she's right about my skin. My coloring is olive. My hair is dark. I'm taller than most American women, and my body frame is small. You could argue that I look Brazilian or Russian, with the body of a Swede or a sub-Saharan African, depending on your frame of reference. But when my Korean in-laws look at me I am most importantly not Asian. Therefore, I am white.

While I do not own a set of pearls or a single knee-length skirt, nor have I ever been to a derby of any sort, we could assume the Koreans mean I am "culturally white." But if this is acceptable logic, even an appropriate generalization, then why is my mother's belief that my husband and I are of the same race wrong? Seung and I grew up watching the same TV shows. His sister and I had the same dolls and similar restrictions on eyeliner. He played all the same sports as my brothers and was also told that boys don't cry. These similarities are all that my mother sees when she looks at my husband. Does the fact that my mother did not see my Korean-born husband as different from us make her more or less racist? Specifically, more or less racist than my husband's parents, who categorize me with a culture I have little in common with except that it's not theirs?

Or are both of our parents' misnomers just a generational mistake? Should every age be given license to use antiquated, incorrect language just because "they don't mean it that way"? Should we also excuse young people in pockets of this country who use "regional" terms for race and religion just because their parents did? Or is there a larger question? Why don't any of these people, of either generation, just consider themselves to be American—the most obvious and common bond between them all?

The plain answer in my story is because the Koreans in this family trust Korean Americans more than other Americans. Not because they have an inherent dislike of anyone but because they feel most comfortable with their own race. As do many Americans, recent to this country or not. On the other hand, my mother felt that specific groups of Americans—having nothing to do with her heritage and only to do with her very regional experience—would not fit in her family. She may love all people as friends and neighbors and business partners, but she just didn't see a comfortable fit at her holiday table for some. Neither of these prejudices is a blanket statement of hate. Both may even have validity. However, they become an issue when the parent expects the child to subscribe to (what is at the very least) their narrow-mindedness.

IMMIGRATION TO THE UNITED STATES, today, usually leads to über-embracement of the society left behind. There is so much revelry afforded to the old country now that Americans whose ancestors have been in this country for two hundred years are seeking out and embracing foods, holidays, and clothing of people they presume a relation to and have often never met. So if many old and new Americans are burning a torch for a way of life that has nothing to do with their current residence, is the homage just alienating us from other Americans?

It is this refusal to assimilate that stokes the argument to keep the others out of this country. But Jews and Greeks (here and in their homeland) require a bloodline for membership. So do the governments of Qatar, several African nations, and America for an American Indian classification. Most Laotians hate for their own to mix with Chinese, and many Cubans feel the same about Dominicans. And Tibetans will not let other races adopt their orphans. So why does my stomach turn when I hear an American radio station talk about a purebred white bloodline? Perhaps because these other nationals are at risk of losing their culture to a neighbor threatening to overtake them, yet I don't feel America's white man's majority, or at least his dominance, is in any real jeopardy. Yes, Kwanza is celebrated in our preschools and Yom Kippur shuts down the cities of L.A. and New York and Spanish-only radio stations are found across the country. And you might wonder if the fanatical descendants of Plymouth Rock have a point about their country changing too much or too fast.

Until you recall that this is the point that birthed America. It was not built as a refuge for just a few. These states were united for anyone suffering under a government that no longer took care of them. Our land, minus the unsustainable portions we gave back to the people who are really from America, is full of people who came from elsewhere, including the Anglo descendants of King James. There is no "seniority clause" in our constitution that gives more privileges to those who fled here the earliest. At this time in our history, when large portions of the world are so angry at the seeming entitlement of America, you would think our country might come together. But for all the social progress we have made over the last thirty years in public—in education and real estate, and business and friendship even—forward movement has not fully crossed over into the privacy of people's homes. Many good people in this country, including my husband's parents and mine, are still drawing a line at who is acceptable for love—and who is not. Many adult Americans alive today have been told by someone in their family that all people are created equal but still, "You can't love one of them." Maybe there was also a seemingly reasonable argument as to why whole groups of people are not "right" for your affections. Maybe these theories still make some sense but leave you to wonder if they fit with how you live the rest of your life—or if you would teach these sentiments to children. Yours or anyone's . . .

MY MOTHER'S LIMITED experience with race was the smallest issue I faced when marrying a man whose hair is one shade darker than mine, as his family's idea of a wife for him was never me. I'd love to think I could just walk you along my path to marriage and believe this could solve any problem between every Hatfield and McCoy of varying shades in America. But my experience is only one—of a racial mix that isn't even that foreboding—and still it took a village full of advice for me to arrive at my union. So instead of pretending I'm a genius pioneer who scaled every racial speed bump America has to offer by my lonesome, this tale includes the most riveting couples I've met on my journey to making a family.

With the help of all their insight, I finally constructed a road map to the destination I was originally looking for: the time and place in America where multicolored love stories live happily ever after. Where love really does trump race. And once I discovered it, I was no longer seeing this place solely from the perspective of my family. I was thinking about it from yours.

YOU AND I ARE FOREVER ENTWINED. We are countrymen. My experience as an American has to inform yours for it to mean anything for my children—just as yours must inform mine. As much as I fear the nosy lady in the supermarket with her inappropriate questions about my children's race and the ignorant person behind me at the DMV who is soliciting a judgment about my marriage, I have inadvertently been both of them to other people. Over time I have learned that as unique as another couple might look or as colorful as another family might seem to me, it's not out of the ordinary to them. It's just their family.

As each of the couples in *Kissing Outside the Lines* worked to overcome America's generational, regional, religious, ethnocentric, color-centric, egocentric, gender-biased, and ageist take on the acceptable line for love, our country has evolved. It has evolved to some extent because of these couples as they are birthing new shades of Americans. I hope the thru-line of all those documented here brings solace or guidance to anyone with their heart at stake in, on any side of, a multiracial love story. And that my personal journey—over one year to love, one year to marry, and one more year to making my own family—in all its humanity and recurring stupidity, helps everyone laugh at things that might otherwise break their heart.

My first child was born in 2007. He was born in California and is, therefore, American. He has three last names, each of a different ethnic descent, as well as two full sets of grandparents who don't have a common language between them. He was joined by two sisters, who surprised us all when they arrived one year later in tandem and identical. These three babes are my personal trinity in number and ethnicity. Luckily, they have all gotten to know their one great-grandparent. She is the immigrant in my family and the proudest American I know. She has taught me and hopefully will get to tell all of my children to love all people regardless of how similar or different they are from the people in your house. And that you should kiss these people often—as well as tell anyone who sees you different from how you see yourself, to kiss your ass.

CHAPTER 1

EURO GIRL FALLS

FOR KOREAN DUDE

IN CALIFORNIA

*"How many sake bombers does it take
for a white girl to score an Asian guy?"*
—THE WOMAN WHO INTRODUCED
ME TO MY HUSBAND

MET SEUNG (pronounced like "sing" a song) at my good friend's engagement party shortly after my own engagement debacle. I had only been engaged for six weeks but extricating myself from the union took ten times as long. Six months later, I might as well have tattooed Gloria Gaynor's "I Will Survive" through a heart on my shoulder and worn a cut-off muscle T-shirt, as these details were the only thing missing from my swinging sailor demeanor as I entered this party. I was in no place to have a relationship. I could say that maybe my engagement faux pas led me to attend this friend's pre-wedding soiree as drunk as I was. But when I arrived and saw the posse of hot women I hang out with every weekend lapping it up on the dance floor, the pool table, and even the buffet, my first thought was: *I need to drink more and catch up*. And so, catch up I did.

Hours later, totally in the bag, I noticed the soon-to-be groom's friends staring in astonishment at his fiancée's girlfriends. For smart, successful, attractive women, we were all partying like members of the armed forces on leave. I was standing on the dance floor, doing some kind of gyration no doubt, with my friend Christine break-dancing on the floor literally beneath my skirt—when I looked over and saw this giant Korean guy. I thought he was cute. So I stopped dancing, cocked my head to the side, put an index finger into the air, and summoned him over. I remember him looking . . . afraid. So I raised a brow at him, implying: *Are you really gonna say no to this? There is an actual party going on underneath my skirt.* I indicated with my one finger again. Now The Giant Korean turned back to look around, wondering who I could possibly be talking to. There was only the bar behind him. But to be sure, when he turned back to look at me one last time from a distance, I took both index fingers and pulled on my eyelids, making the international sign for "Yes, Charlie Chan . . . I mean you," and then waved him over again.

How on earth Seung found the courage to come over after that, or why he had any interest to, is a testament to the man I would later marry. But first, I had some hoops for both of us to jump through.

I was pretty charming, aside from the slant-eye reference that is, in my drunken state. I immediately said something about Korea being the only place in Asia I hadn't been yet and maybe he could show me around someday. Seung was so flabbergasted that I knew his origins, probably because I seemed moronic so far, that I just kept going with the "I feel your people" theme. I commented on his size (knowing that most Asians over six foot two are Koreans), but explained that his shoulders were the dead giveaway. Shoulders as wide as his reside only above the Mekong because his ancestors had to work the land without the help of a river. I ran my finger over his face, saying that his amazing cheekbones were so prominent because Koreans are direct descendants of the Mongols—northern Russians to be exact—and therefore his cheeks are Western like mine. I stepped in a little closer to prove that his eyes are actually bigger than mine, even without a fold, for much the same reason. One inch from his face I whispered, "My green eyes are like wee little peas next to yours."

I'm telling you, I was a drunken sailor with rap honed to perfection. The Giant Korean didn't stand a chance.

By night's end I said to my betrothed friend hosting this party, "I'm going home with one of three guys that your fiancé is friends with. I'm too drunk to know who's cool, so you have to pick." My mother is so proud reading this right now. I pointed out Seung and two other guys dispersed in the room. My friend was totally freaked out. Not because I was picking a date in this manner at age thirty-four, but because she really didn't know her man's friends very well and was afraid to pick the wrong guy. I reminded her that I wasn't looking for a life partner at this moment. The fiancé finally said, "Oh, just go with Tim then. I don't think he is your type but he's smart so at least you'll have something to talk about." Again, talking was not the goal, but Tim it was.

Before leaving I had some explaining to do. I went over to The Giant Korean and softly said, "I'm going now but I'd like to give you my number in case you make that trip to Malaysia and want some travel advice." He looked me in the face and said, "I'll call you, but not for travel advice." I giggled, feigning innocence long gone in me, and stepped up to the bar to fetch a napkin for digits. My friend

Gregg and his girl were sitting at the bar, drunk as skunks, as well. Joking with Gregg, I wrote on the napkin:

TRAVEL yes—DATE no.

Diane

and my phone number here . . .

I handed this napkin of love to Seung and sauntered off. This, ladies and gentlemen, may have been the stupidest thing I've ever done. Or perhaps not, considering how broken and desperate I felt inside and what a pain in the ass I would have been had I spoken to this earnest man beyond my rehearsed routine at that juncture in life—I'm sure I would have ruined us. It doesn't matter how you look at it, though, because fate was on my side.

When I woke in the morning, my first thought was, *What is that giant pain in my head?* Soon I realized I was having it because someone was talking. Someone whose name I eventually had to get from the bride-to-be. The uncontrollable desire to shut this person up led me to turn and see Tim, almost like it was for the first time.

I immediately lifted the covers to make sure my clothing was still intact. Not only was all my clothing on but so were my shoes. My friend did pick the perfect guy for me as he is so talkative, he acted like a gentleman even when I was incapable of behaving like a lady. Still, Tim was never to be seen in my bed again.

Six months later, my engaged friend was still planning her wedding and had no time to fete her fiancé's birthday. She called all the girls and asked us to rally for a last-minute karaoke night. I stopped by this impromptu gathering, after rehearsing the sitcom I was on at that time, in sweatpants and a ponytail. I bellied up to the bar next to the same hot, party-animal women from the engagement party whom I still call my closest friends. Looking around at the rest of the guests, I had to ask one of my girlfriends what the birthday boy did for a living. "He works in video games, I think," said Christine (who was dancing under my skirt when last you heard about her). I couldn't help but laugh. "Are you just saying," I asked, "that you think all these guys work in video games just because they're Asian?" There were at least two dozen Asian men in the room amongst us white, olive, brown, and black girls. And Christine was not making a bad joke; they were all in video games. So we ordered up some sake bombers and it became the theme of the night. The ladies and I, and our tray of drinks, were headed off to find a booth when a woman grabbed my arm.

At the booth next to the bar was Seung, sitting with his cousin and his cousin's girlfriend. Seung had just told his table of our last meeting. He summed up our story with his getting my number and being subsequently blown off. The girlfriend at the table said, "I know her! We just worked together and she totally looked after me." Seung, the cousin, and his girlfriend who knew me made a fast plan for the girlfriend to lure me in and give The Giant Korean a running start at more than my number this time.

It took me a moment to remember Breanna, the actress who had just guest-starred on my sitcom. As the lightbulb went off, so did another—illuminating how I knew Seung, who was sitting across from her. My drunken behavior came back first, then the napkin note. I wanted to run. In a moment of fleeting maturity I stayed, though, and smiled until some confidence came back to me. I chatted with them for a few minutes in hopes of seeming more presentable than when last we'd met.

Humbly exiting to my table of alcohol-filled girlfriends, I sat next to the engaged one. I laughed at myself and whispered that I still thought The Giant Korean was cute. And that he didn't seem too put off by my last showing. My dutiful friend was about to say some really nice things about Seung, which she was going to make up because she still didn't know Seung very well, when the "Asian Ken doll" came in. To imagine Asian Ken, picture this: perfect, silken, shoulder-length black hair; broad shoulders; and a deep voice. This guy was one of the more beautiful humans I have ever seen. His father was Scottish and American Indian and his mother was Korean and Japanese. The jokes at our booth went like this:

"I'm removing my IUD under this table in hopes of conceiving that man's child in the bathroom of this bar." "Which one of you will consider a threesome and never talk about it again—if it will help us capture that perfect creature?" "How many sake bombers does it take for one white girl to . . . " You get the point. And *Cosmo* thinks women sit around wondering if they are wearing the "right" bra to *catch a man*. Ha.

While the ladies made secret-evil plans to lure Asian Ken over to the table, I snuck away and asked him if he would sing a karaoke song with me. Two seconds later we were onstage. AK (as I went on to call him) sang wonderfully while simultaneously trying to under-stand why a gaggle of women were hissing at us. Three hours deeper and another buzz on, I was headed to the bar to get another napkin of love to give AK my number. For the record, it's about three sake bombers. I sidelined myself by stabbing a few olives, as dinner, before grabbing a cocktail napkin. With a mouth full of Greek delights, I discovered The Giant Korean was next to me.

"How are you, Diane?" said Seung.

"Really busted!" I wanted to say. And a little intimidated, too.

The Giant Korean is six foot two and has shoulders twice the size of mine. I felt like a bean out of my pod next to him and I'm almost six feet tall myself. *How come you're never mad when you catch me flirting with you and then picking up other guys?* I thought about this but all I squeaked out was, "Fine, and you?"

Seung gave me a big smile with a pause that I didn't understand. He then humbly spoke like I was one of many ladies he was happy to exchange pleasantries with that night. "I'm good. I'm Seung, if you can't remember my name." I didn't know his name, because I never use a guy's name until I'm sure he's sticking around. But this name came flooding back fast. "Seung—like 'sing' a song—I remember." I smiled and Seung turned away. *Oh, maybe he is annoyed after all,* I thought, then, *No! He's turning back!*

"Did you need one of these?" Seung handed me the napkin I had reached for when my desire for olives outweighed my desire to write AK my number. I thanked him and scampered away laughing. The Giant Korean had just called me out. Cool guy.

AK and I hung around each other for a couple of months. He was sweet and beautiful but young. I was afraid I might pull one of the petals off of his beautiful soul, accidentally, if I let the relationship go anywhere beyond occasional kissing. So for the two times my future husband witnessed me hooking up, I never even got laid. How on earth would I ever explain that?

It was another six months before this damn engaged couple would get married. A solid year lived between their engagement party and the nuptials I wondered if Seung would attend. I left one TV show and started another in New York City. I had also started my first relationship in over a year, which didn't begin at a bar with one of my close-this-deal-quick pickups. I was almost healthy again after having had my heart so badly broken the winter before. But would I take my new guy to the very first wedding in my party crowd?

Nope. Too big a risk. Because, being the first to call their single days adjourned, Mr. & Mrs. Friends-of-Mine were planning an event like nothing I had ever seen before or since. Fifty friends were flown to Zihuatanejo, Mexico, and put up in villas along the beach. We were asked to drink shots of tequila as a wedding toast, just before we all jumped into the ocean together—and that was just the rehearsal dinner. The weekend was destined to be epic. I couldn't risk it on a new person. And besides, the big guy, with the shoulders and the cheekbones and all the rest was going to be in the house. . . .

Before leaving, we knew that the women outnumbered the men for this hot-tamale love-fest. The groom, always astounded that his girl's friends were all single and ready to party, was inviting people he met along the way (in the airport lounges and random cities in Mexico) to just "stop by" because a gathering of his future wife's friends was like a Miss America pageant with points given out for cocktailing abilities. As a team captain (read: "bridesmaid"—and there were, like, eleven), I decided the safest way for all these fabulous ladies to get along was for every woman to "call" a guy before landing on foreign soil.

On the Thursday night flight to Mexico, I stood in the aisle and asked every unaccompanied woman to say out loud whom she was interested in hooking up with. This way there could be no feigning ignorance if you stepped on someone else's Mexi-weekend fantasy. Shockingly, there was not one man-overlap in the preplan. Which I was especially thankful for because I had broken up with the "almost guy" in New York on Monday, in order to arrive Tuesday in Los Angeles unencumbered and up to the standards I used to hold myself to before being tossed like a Caesar salad by the ex-fiancé. After hearing all the ladies' confessional crushes at thirty thousand feet, I added, "Mine is the giant Korean. You'll know him because he's the biggest Asian you have ever seen."

The deal was, any woman who called a guy had him on reserve through the rehearsal dinner and wedding ceremony. If you hadn't closed your deal by Saturday's reception, your man was back on the open market. Clearly I hadn't abandoned all the military training I had gathered over the past eighteen months of singlehood. I was just acting more like an officer now.

* SEUNG AND I KISSED FOR THE FIRST TIME AFTER the rehearsal dinner and I fell for him fast. As a bridesmaid I had access to the seating chart for the wedding and I rearranged all the tables to accommodate the hook-ups of the night before (particularly mine). The wedding was lovely, but it paled in comparison to the magic I shared with Seung all weekend. En route to the airport on Sunday evening, I hinted and hinted that there would be no "alone time" once we deboarded at LAX because my father was picking me up. Yet Seung Chung never asked for my phone number. Not in the air, not through customs, not at the baggage carousel, and not even after he shook my father's hand outside the international terminal. Of course there were people to get it from, but I worried as I watched Seung roll his suitcase away from mine. I worried that my heart was going to shrink back to its normal size, after having expanded so much in one weekend.

I woke at 5:00 AM for a photo shoot in New York the next day, without needing an alarm clock because I hadn't slept all night, wondering why this man didn't want to see me again. I spent six hours on the plane ride to New York, also not sleeping, mostly wondering if the wedding weekend was just payback for the two times I had tortured Seung the year before. But by the time I landed at JFK in NYC, Seung had left me a message.

He was asking me to dinner. He was asking for tonight. I ran to the United Airlines counter before I even returned the call, to change my flight to return to Los Angeles as soon as possible. I called Seung from a taxi as soon as I got outside. "How did you get my number?" was the first thing I wanted to ask. But I held my cool—for five seconds—and said hello first and then asked. Seung said I gave it to him. "When?"

"When I first met you. At the engagement party."

Seung never asked for my phone number when we left Mexico because he had saved it for over a year, waiting until he thought I was actually interested in him before calling me. Hearing this made my spine turn to cheese dip. I slid down the well-worn cab seat into my own puddle of happiness. Seung Yong Chung owned me now, even though I couldn't correctly pronounce any of his three names.

Seung and I both had to work in different cities for the next few days. As each of us finished the business day, we got back on a plane to spend another night together in Los Angeles. By Wednesday, Seung was flying back to the same city in the mornings just to share a meal and a cuddle with me each night. All totaled, I spent every night with Seung from the wedding rehearsal on, for about six months.

I LIKE TO FALL IN LOVE. And I like to give with all my heart—especially in the beginning to see how much depth the other person has to give back. As I shed each layer of my cool-girl facade, Seung more than met me halfway. He was infinitely kind and not afraid to share. And he is an amazing disco dancer. The search was over.

One morning we walked from his beachside apartment to a breakfast eatery in the sand. There was a beautiful Asian lady having coffee outside. As we settled at our table, I was fishing for a compliment when I asked, "Are you gonna leave me for an Asian girl someday?" Seung said nothing for just a moment too long.

"No, but this is gonna be a problem for my parents."

I had unknowingly hit the $64,000 question. Seung let out a volume of fears that I had no idea he had been carrying around for weeks. He began by saying, "I am supposed to marry a Korean girl." I didn't really understand what that could mean. Did he mean in theory, or was there an actual wedding in his future, to an actual Korean female? Seung continued, "My parents have been very clear about that my entire life." And this didn't make much sense, either. Did Seung Chung—a football-loving fraternity brother who could recite all the lyrics in any rap song from 1985 on—have an arranged marriage waiting in the wings? Was that even legal in America? "They are not going to easily accept this relationship. I'm most afraid they will never accept you."

The questions in my head stopped. It didn't matter what all this meant because I could now see Seung was willing to fight for me. And that he was being torn in half by the idea of hurting me or hurting his parents. Whatever the outcome would be, I didn't want the beautiful experience I was having with this man to be ruined by people I had never even met. Seung's last sentence implied that if there was a Miss Korea lined up to marry him, he was opting out. So I opted to take care of him and understand the details later.

I told Seung I was sorry. So sorry for what an awful feeling it must be to have this great love and a simultaneous fear of telling other people you love about it. I meant it when I then said the only problem I could foresee was for him, because at thirty-five years old I did not need his parents to accept me. They lived thousands of miles away, we were not nor would we ever be financially dependent on them, and I would be respectful to them whenever he needed me to be because I respected the great man they made. I had no interest in fighting civil rights with the aging people Seung loved most. So, if he wanted to pursue our relationship, he could take my need for a second mommy and daddy off his list of things to worry about. Seung smiled and said, "That's good to know. Because I have a plan."

UNBEKNOWNST TO ME, Seung Chung already has an elaborate plan to make his parents like/accept/love/not kill me. And aren't I great that I will support him. And aren't I even greater for not caring about Ma and Pa Chung feeling disappointed by me without even knowing me. Yeah, maybe I'm not *that* great.

I mostly find it ironic that the Chungs would judge me for not being from the same country they *left*. After Seung goes to sleep this night, probably relieved to have shared with me the cross he has been asked to bear, I toss and turn. *What do you mean your immigrant parents—who gave up everything to be in this country, in hopes of gain for their children— won't like me? Didn't your mommy and daddy just win the lotto that you fell in love with an American girl who desperately loves you back?* I know I could make this argument, but truthfully, the situation is so unfathomable to me that I'm kind of digging the drama. It, strangely, makes me feel sexy—in a "forbidden" sort of way. However, as a New Yorker, I also have an instinct to get some backup. Meaning, I'm dying to call my family and line them up to support the "white cause."

"This boy's parents are being mean to me, Mom—because I'm white! And by the way, how come you never called us 'white'? I thought you were so stupid when you told me not to fall in love with a black man because our children would never be accepted. Could you be right, Mom? Why didn't you mention that other races hate white people? And would you help me with a little quid pro quo and please sweat my boyfriend a bit? Maybe acting as if he's not up to par (even though he has a master's degree, owns a home, a company, has a retirement package already, and is infinitely honest)? Mom?"

Yeah, I never actually make this call. I instinctively know better than to have any conversations with my parents about my feelings "almost" being hurt. I feel comfortable in my skin—even if I am being judged for it—so I don't really need confirmation that I am "an okay race" to love. So instead, I call a girlfriend because this is the exact conversation that girlfriends exist for. I call many girlfriends, in fact, and between us we decide that I need to seek some counsel from people who have lived through the prejudice of one American falling in love with another, whose parents see themselves as something other than American first and foremost. All my friends are sure that there must be some boundaries or steps I should be aware of before I move further in.

This will become the understatement of the next decade in my life.

LIKE MOST PEOPLE MY AGE, I have friends who are dating someone of another race. I also have friends who are married to or have children with people of another race. Yet these are not the friends I want to lay all of my *possible* in-laws' baggage on, because up until now I have judged these friends' parents for their prejudices. I have secretly wondered how much the parents' negative influence affects their romantic union and also the children of those unions. At times I have even judged my friends for not standing up to their parents enough and just telling them to take a walk out of their lives. The last thing I want to do is expose my beautiful boyfriend's ugly family drama to my world. I need some anonymous advice. How handy for me that aside from being blessed with girlfriends to confide in, I also have unlimited access to email.

I'M SENDING A CASUAL NOTE to a few friends, in cities other than Los Angeles, asking if they know people raising mixed-race kids whom I might talk to about their experiences. Sort of implying: EVERYTHING IS PERFECTLY FINE in my relationship—I'm just curious about the future. This leads to many more emails explaining that I am not pregnant.

After convincing the masses that there is no mini-Seung on board, someone throws out: "Of course—you're writing a book on mixed-race couples. That's so you." *Oh yes.* Smile and pause. *So me!* Now laugh. Eventually, after all these half truths, I collect the names and email addresses of couples that have scaled racial speed bumps and survived. Someone I've emailed asks if I will be recording my conversations with their friend for "the book." First

I run to the electronics store and buy a recording device for the phone. Then I return the email, saying yes, I will be recording *the interview.*

I'm well aware that it's premature to write a book about being part of a mixed-race couple when I am not even known to be a couple by the guy's family—but I'm keeping my tape recorder. Because having this $25 device on gives me a justified reason to ask real questions that you can't normally ask people about their relationships. With my three-button, handheld machine and a list of strangers' email addresses, I am going to wrap up this little "your race versus my race" dilemma in no time.

Along with the cyber addresses, my people have given me CliffsNotes versions of the friends they are recommending I speak to. One of the selling points about Lisa and Dave, besides their two sons, is that Lisa's mother was "really angry when she was going to marry a black man." An injustice with a side of pain and suffering, which seems to have a happy ending since this couple is still together, is perfect! I ask my friend to set up a time when I can call Lisa. Sooner, rather than later, because I'm really excited to talk to her. Until I realize I have no idea how to do this.

"So, I hear your mother doesn't like black people?"
Yeah, that's not going to get me far.

As an actress I've been interviewed a lot. When famous people I work with are doing something deviant and I get a call from a reporter, the last thing I want to give that reporter is a shocking comment to be used out of context against someone I know. That's the loyalty I feel for a coworker I've known for a year or so. I am attempting to ask Lisa intimate and embarrassing questions about her mother and the father of her children.

"So, how old were you when you were told you weren't allowed to date 'the blacks'?"

That won't do, either. Lisa may not be interviewed regularly, but I know from Seung and me that you learn to couch your family's shortcomings into the tidiest version of the problem. Maybe I can bond with Lisa over our mothers' shared shortcoming?

"Hey, I'm Diane and my mother also told me to stay away from black guys!"

Just not gonna work. Should I just tell Lisa the truth and address the point that we have in common as couples? What do I have to lose on a perfect stranger?

"I need some advice because my husband's family is not thrilled about him falling in love with someone of my race and I know that your family didn't want you to be with . . . "

But this is her family I'm asking about, not her husband's, so there is no "in-law bashing" to be shared. And more to the point, Lisa and I are not having the same exact experience. I'm in love with an Asian guy. That's a little interesting. At worst, maybe it's off-putting to some older Asian people (in addition to Seung's family). It does not carry the taboo that still exists in a variety of social circles for a white woman and a black man. If I'm attempting to have a forthright discussion about race in America, I think I should be as truthful as possible, at least with myself. Looking at Seung and me and wondering how we are a couple might make me think you're a dummy. But looking at a black man and a white woman in love and being horrified is a slap this girl has felt. And that slap was from her mother, so I'm guessing it has left a mark.

Now I'm really scared. What right do I have to ask this woman anything? And if I take her psyche apart while digging around for the truth about bringing someone unwanted into a family, don't I have a responsibility to put her back together? I don't know how to do that, either! Oh God. And now if I blow this off, I'm the chick who was too cool to even call when Lisa agreed to tell all her deepest secrets to a total stranger for the benefit of love. My $25 phone-recording device does not have directions on how to be an investigative journalist!

IN THE END, LISA MAY THINK I am the most narcissistic person in the world because when I failed to find a way in, I came clean and simply blurted out everything about my relationship and myself. Yes, I was that savvy actress and published author said to be working on an important subject—who started crying during my second sentence on the phone with my first interviewee. And then I couldn't stop crying.

I was confused by my own display of emotion. Was I just shocked to say this out loud to someone? That my boyfriend's family didn't like me because I am a different race than him? Was I having flashbacks of junior high school, where one day you were cool and the next day you were out—with no understandable reason or remedy within grasp? Was I just now realizing that this relationship could fail over this? Or was I just plain old sad that I had to confide in a total stranger?

I still don't know. All I can say for sure is that I shocked myself by how much insecurity and fear were underlying my intention to have an intellectual and fact-finding phone call about interracial dating in

America when one family does not approve. But Lisa was not shocked. Lisa seemed to know exactly what I was feeling just as I was only first becoming conscious of this little pinhole in my heart, which without proper attention could grow into a gully.

Somewhere amidst the waterworks, mostly due to my embarrassment of turning this into telephonic therapy, I invited Lisa to jump in with her own story. She began with how she and Dave met.

CHAPTER 2.

WHITE FRESHMAN

LOVES BLACK SENIOR

IN PENNSYLVANIA

"My mother had this horrible reaction. She said something like, 'This is disgusting.' At the time, I wondered
what she was thinking. And assumed she would just kind
of get it, eventually. But she didn't."

—LISA TYLER

LISA AND DAVE were in college. They started dating her junior year, when Dave was living in the apartment below her. Lisa described the scene as a "collegiate Melrose Place." She was dating someone else and immediately dumped him when she met Dave. His humor and big heart won Lisa over right away. She was a little surprised, however, when her roommates reacted to Dave with, "Why?"

"It wasn't that they were specifically negative, but many didn't see the appeal." The appeal of a black man to a white woman, that is, says Lisa, with as much grace as that statement could possibly have. Lisa didn't have any hesitations, though. As students, she and Dave weren't very different. Dave was in an all-white fraternity. He was a senior but on a "six-year plan," so he and Lisa would graduate together. "We spent all of our time together and became boyfriend and girlfriend right away."

Friends came around quickly, but Lisa and Dave left their families out of their time together. Her parents did meet Dave briefly once, at a parents' weekend. They thought the coupling was "funny," Lisa says flatly. "They thought it was a phase. And continued to think this . . . until the day I got married."

NOW I HAVE TO ASK the hard question, because this is the part I don't exactly understand. But since I just finished bawling to Lisa, I'm also not feeling exactly confident to pretend to be a professional and probe her with questions. But Lisa seems kind, so I cross my fingers, close my eyes, and use a soft voice as I say, "Do you remember why you knew your mother wouldn't approve?"

"Well, my younger sister went to a dance with a black kid when she was young. My mom had a really hard time with this and told us so."

This answer feels rehearsed. I am about to ask another soft-voiced question when Lisa digs deeper herself. "But even earlier was the situation with my father's sisters."

Lisa's dad has two sisters, who both married black men. Lisa remembers meeting her aunts and their families when she was in middle school. After a terrific day with her cousins, Lisa was waving goodbye from her family's car, when her mother *went off.* "My mother had this horrible reaction. She said something like, 'This is disgusting.' At the time I wondered what she was thinking. And I assumed she would just kind of get it, eventually. But she didn't."

Then and now, Lisa's mom argued that a biracial relationship would be unfair to a child. This is something I also heard my parents espouse, many years ago during my childhood, and I can't ask Lisa fast enough if she feels her mom truly believes this or if she might have been looking for a way to couch her own prejudice, in a seemingly intellectual way. Lisa says she believes that her mother was worried about her. "And the way people would treat me if I was in a relationship with a black person . . . and how they would treat her."

Lisa's mother was also quick to let her daughter know that her grandparents would never approve, either. Lisa's grandfather stated, "Black people and white people together are like squirrels and raccoons mixing." For further clarification he added, "It's just not biologically right." With these statements said out loud at home, I'm not sure how Lisa even had the confidence to leave her Melrose Place apartment during college, with the pending threat of a rabid coed approaching her on the wild streets of Philadelphia.

Yet, despite all these discussions, Lisa pursued her relationship. Two years later, she and Dave finished college together and were each moving back to their parents' homes. They both grew up in northern Virginia—which isn't quite the South but isn't far from it. Their mothers' houses were only forty minutes apart, but were in many ways worlds away.

For example, Dave is the youngest of six kids. Such a large family is always defining, but having brothers and sisters who attended public school during the 1950s and '60s—in Virginia—is a radically different set of experiences within one family. My first thought as Lisa started to give me some background was that some of Dave's siblings must have attended segregated schools.

Dave's brothers and sisters were bused to class, across the county in fact, even though there was a school at the end of their street. During this time, one bus would travel to five or more towns retrieving all the black kids. The classroom these children were exiled to was often an hour away from where they lived. On top of a two-hour journey every day, even for a six-year-old, this also meant there was no way for these children to play with their school friends. And there was little chance they would be cavorting with the white kids on their block because they were clearly being told not to when they were separated every morning.

After the *Brown v. Board of Education* ruling in 1954, a Virginian senator then organized the Massive Resistance movement, which included the closing of schools rather than desegregating them. The Tyler family lived through both of these benchmarks, as well as many more education fashions that are now, thankfully, obsolete. Eventually Dave, being the youngest of his large family, got to begin his education at that school right on his street. And because of it, Dave ended up socializing at the other extreme, as his class was almost entirely white. Which also seems to have left scars.

Lisa feels that Dave has regrets about the circles he chose to run in as a kid. They might best be described as self-doubts that Dave may have "copped out" by not aligning enough with his race. But by college, Dave's social wiring was set. Thus the all-white fraternity and Lisa, who was not the first white woman Dave dated. After Dave graduated and headed home, though, his family was one place where he was immersed in black culture—as was Lisa.

Lisa spent weekends at Dave's parents' house for two years following college. "I had never experienced being the only white person in a large crowd before the Tyler family. And it took time to get used to." Dave's family was happy to give Lisa whatever she needed to get comfortable, though, because they believed Dave might have been a "college frat guy" forever, had it not been for her. And perhaps, having lived through thirty-plus years of child rearing, Dave's parents knew that many of the things student life gave Lisa and Dave in common were about to end.

It took Dave a solid year to find a job after college. Lisa worked full-time and began her MBA. When Dave finally landed work, it was in New Jersey—which put four hours between them. Yet the distance only inspired them to commit further. "I eventually quit a really good job so I could finish school full-time and move in with Dave."

While living together in New Jersey, talk of engagement came up, which finally prompted Lisa's mom to address *the phase,* which had now lasted seven years. "My mom finally said she didn't support the union. She quoted her parents, saying, 'We live in our town and the blacks live in theirs and that's all fine, but you're not supposed to stray.'"

AFTER ONLY MY FIRST phone call with Lisa it is glaringly obvious that she will do anything to avoid confrontation. Yet she is not a doormat, nor does she blow smoke to distract from the conversation at hand. I am already admiring her technique of dodging a fight, and preventing one between her family and the person she loves . . . but I can't quite figure out how she is doing it.

"I cared, but I didn't feel like I had to jump up or down. I'm very independent-minded and I knew I was going to be with Dave. I did downplay the relationship a bit, but that was also because Dave had a lot of anger and I didn't want to egg him on. I didn't want to cause super-bad behavior in anyone."

What was that about Dave's anger?

"Dave's dealt with a lot of prejudice from all the women he's dated. I mean, from all their families. Way worse than my family." Lisa's calmness is catching, and I'm finding my way to asking her all the questions that may yield me an understanding of how to navigate this love versus race battlefield—but I'm also seeing my own picture now of a very brave and pioneering, younger woman in Lisa. At this point in their relationship, Lisa is twenty-five years old. She loves Dave but knows the "white girl's" family has hurt him before and that her family may hurt Dave again. And without a lot of real-life experience under her belt, Lisa is trying to keep all the people she loves from hurting each other. So if my intent is to make a game plan, I should ask Lisa what she did next at this juncture.

"Find allies."

Lisa's sister unilaterally supported her relationship with Dave. Together these two daughters had an even bigger issue with their mother, as their parents were divorcing after twenty-five years at this time. Both sisters felt their mom was in no position to judge. Lisa's father also supported her and Dave. His only advice was to make sure they had things in common, as he felt it would be important later on. Lisa took refuge in the fact that her mother (and father, in fact) didn't know any black people. There was no way they could know more about Dave than she did, or the life she might have with him, based solely on his race.

Dave was aware that Lisa's mother had complaints about them as a couple, but he also knew his girlfriend was ready for the next phase. He forged ahead and managed to surprise her with a marriage proposal, hoping to show her that the two of them were what mattered most. And Lisa was ecstatic. Dave called his parents immediately to share his excitement, but Lisa called no one. "I wanted twenty-four hours to enjoy this for myself." The next day Lisa called her mother, who said nothing "specifically" negative. "But it was not the reaction you're hoping for when you plan to get married."

Lisa and her mom had been speaking three times a day up until this point. Lisa's next disappointment came when she didn't hear from her mother the rest of the day. Or the next day. Or the day after that. "Then we just stopped talking entirely."

* MOCKING HERSELF, LISA SAYS, "DAVE AND I STARTED dating when I was nineteen and got married at twenty-six. Looking back, I don't know why I was in such a hurry, but at the time, I was really ready."

I feel nervous now as Lisa speaks. The feelings that I'm guessing she is about to share with me are what may happen to Seung if we move forward. Alienation, judgment, and self-doubt—of whether it's okay to ever tell your parents, "You're wrong and I'm going to go my own way"—are what I imagine. I want Lisa to hurry up and tell me, and I also don't want to hear it at all.

ONE WEEK AFTER LISA'S resounding "Yes!" to Dave's proposal, she began to make her arrangements. Although she had no idea how her wedding could happen while her mother wasn't speaking to her, Lisa tried. Wedding dress shopping seems to have been the most uncomfortable.

Her visits to the bridal suites come up often in my conversation with Lisa. I don't believe this is because Lisa is a mad shopper or defines herself by marriage, but rather because the first image of herself in the white dress was upstaged by the empty space beside her in the dressing room. It seems what Lisa felt most, when she first saw herself dressed for her wedding, was lonely. This remains indelible fifteen years later as we talk on the phone tonight. But at least her mother eventually called.

"After almost a month my mom came and said this wasn't worth ruining our relationship over. She acted like she was doing me this huge favor so it wouldn't affect us. Which, of course, it already had." Mother and daughter picked up their dialogue again, but the foundation for the immediate future was already set.

"She had nothing to do with my wedding other than showing up. She and my dad gave a financial contribution and little else." Lisa openly says she wished her mother had been more involved.

"Our parents met for the first time at our rehearsal dinner. It was the most stressful dinner of my life," says our bride. There were fifty people in attendance, and thankfully everyone was cordial. Not only did Dave's parents get to meet the mom who thought their son might not be good enough because he was black, but they also met Mom's raccoon- and squirrel-fearing parents. Lisa's mom also got to meet her ex-husband's new wife for the first time. All at the same meal!

The wedding moved smoothly and the reception was everything Lisa and Dave hoped—barring one incident by Lisa's grandfather, who came despite the fact that he was "against" the marriage. Lisa says, "Dave's father was his best man. His dad saved a bottle of one-hundred-year-old scotch for his youngest son's wedding. And there was my grandfather, who refused to toast with him." Lisa sadly confesses this major moment still comes up because her grandfather made it into such a point of contention.

There was no mention of Lisa's mom eliciting any disappointing behavior this day, or ever after. I don't get the sense Lisa and her mom are a *mushy* pair. But since Mom represented the largest hurdle for Lisa with Dave, no comment feels like a good start. Without that jockeying and fighting to attend to, more space was created for Lisa and Dave to focus on each other. Tonight is my second call with Lisa in as many days, and all our discussions about her mother from this point onward are reparative.

The biggest milestone came one year after their wedding. Lisa's mom came forward and told her daughter she really loved Dave. Mom quoted the exact thing that Lisa had always felt: that she just never knew any black people. "She had this idea, this prejudice of what this race is like, and then once you get to know someone of that race you're like, 'Wow! They're just like us.'" Lisa's mom also sent Dave a heartfelt card. Both Lisa and Dave were moved by the sentiment in this letter addressed to her *son*.

* OUR MUTUAL FRIEND MENTIONED LISA TO ME

only partially because her mom was upset when she married Dave. My friend had a different clincher in mind, as she saucily said, "You must talk to them! They have twin boys. One came out white and the other is black."

Lisa and Dave named their sons Justin and Nathan. They are three years old at the time of this interview. "Everyone wondered what our kids would look like. Nathan has dark wavy hair. He can pass for many things—most easily Latino, I think. Justin is pale like me, and he's kind of the more difficult one who doesn't warm up to people easily. I can just imagine the comments Dave's family makes," laughs Lisa.

She's joking. Dave's family has loved Lisa from the start, but who could resist teasing at the idea of her darker-skinned child cuddling up to his father's family while her white child is being standoffish, making his grandparents work for his affection? Everyone does work for it, though, because Justin and Nathan were a long time coming. Besides hurdling societal and familial ideas of what husband and wife must "look like," it also took Lisa and Dave a long time to conceive. During these years, they learned to discuss things. Which still didn't set them up for all the feelings their boys would bring.

"I remember trying to warn Dave that mixed-race kids get darker as they get older. That he shouldn't freak out if they look white," says Lisa. But from their first moments of life, everyone thought each boy looked mixed.

I'm tripping over my own words because I can't ask Lisa fast enough whether she gets different reactions from strangers when she takes her sons out individually. Specifically, is a white mother of a white child treated differently than a white mother of a black or mixed child?

"We haven't had any comments." *What? Nothing?* "Nothing."

Do I have to put on my soft voice again, Lisa? Lisa jumps right in with, "People are so obsessed with the twin thing, that's all they talk about. Are they twins? Are they fraternal? That's the main question." Lisa says she has never fielded any queries about adoption, either—which I find amazing and wonderful while I am simultaneously wondering, how could this be so much more refreshing than her dating experience?

Are mothers no longer judged for their sons but only for their lovers, to quote D. H. Lawrence? Have we indeed made enough social progress that all children can be accepted for who they are—and it's only when we pick a partner for love that damnation can be set? And if this is the case, can we eradicate it if our generation teaches our children that all people are truly equal, in all things, including love?

Well, Lisa?

"We don't have any issues having mixed-race kids. Our issues were about us as a couple. But we did think about where we would live with them. We both acknowledge we could never move down south. We always have to live in D.C. or farther north."

Although Lisa has not had to answer intrusive or uncomfortable questions about her offspring, as a family they have felt the wondrous stares of the masses. "We get looks. My husband always teases me that I'm oblivious to it. He, conversely, is always the first to notice. Now we're in the D.C. area, and it's better here but not as easy as when we lived in New Jersey. We were much less self-conscious there. Here, still, they look."

Both Lisa and Dave work for a technology corporation, and their boys attend preschool nearby. "Discussions about race are just now starting with basics like, 'How come my hair doesn't feel like Daddy's?' As the queries come up, Lisa follows her instincts. She has not read any literature on raising biracial kids. She feels the homework she needed to do was about her and Dave as a couple. "Dave has felt a lot of prejudice—much worse than my family's. So I read a lot on mixed relationships. It helped me understand his feelings." As an afterthought Lisa adds, "Even though I don't think I will ever really understand."

For all of Lisa's coaching prebirth that her children would get darker with age, their mixed coloring brings her husband solace. "Dave has said very many times, he wants to teach the boys to work hard. He feels he had to work harder because he is black. He is so glad they won't have to do more to be treated equally." So as it turns out, Dave is happy with their color. "He feels they're not going to have it as hard as he did. And although it's weird that they don't look like him, he is happy about it."

"That's heartbreaking," I blurt out.

On this, my third and last long-distance, hour-plus conversation with Lisa over the phone, my heart breaks for her husband. I have never met Dave or their sons, or Lisa in person for that matter, but this comment flies out of my mouth like Lisa and I are old friends. Lisa takes a moment and says, "I know," and a heavy pause lies between us.

If that sentiment—a feeling of happiness that children don't look black just to make their life "easier"—is ruminating in the mind of a black father, I know what my final question to this white mother will be. No longer employing a soft voice—because I am sure of Lisa's where-withal now and beginning to find my own confidence in her example—I ask Lisa if she worries her children will have a harder time because they are mixed.

"No," is Lisa's immediate answer, "because Justin does not look mixed and Nathan can pass for anything, which I think is really cool. *Now* it's really cool. And they're twins and two different races—what could be cooler than that?"

CHAPTER 3.

A CRASH COURSE IN
KOREAN CULTURE

"How can all these parents move to this gigantic
country and then rope off one square mile—
forbidding their children to date outside that corral?"
—YOURS TRULY

'M INSPIRED TO move forward with my Giant Korean. I'm actually so inspired as I hang up this call with Lisa that I want to fix all the ignorant fears, of the whole world, before dinner. But Lisa has just shown me that changing views on race requires time and prudence. Her living the life she knew was right for her, day after day and eventually year after year, says so much more than any perfectly coined speech about her beliefs. Especially among family members, where most of us fail to edit ourselves as much as we probably should. So I can see I'm going to have to chill out. Which feels about as possible as giving myself a lobotomy, because I'm in love! I want to do everything and anything with my man, Seung, and not knowing if his parents will cut him out of their lives feels kind of . . . pressing. And furthermore, in love or not, neither of Lisa's attributes of patience or holding my tongue are in my wheelhouse. I'm fast and funny, which seems diametrically the opposite of measured and steadfast.

Maybe I can give myself an active job, rather than the passive, annoying one of waiting silently for Seung's parents to come around. Perhaps I can do more than interracial relationship research. Maybe I can learn all there is to know about Korea! History, art, cuisine, boy bands. Maybe I can impress Seung's parents with a keen sense of everything Hanguk!

After the euphoria of Lisa's success story levels off, I remember I would have to add another *language* to that homework list since Seung's parents don't speak much English. In reality, though, this dialogue barrier may be a gift. In my heart I understand that even my best banter won't change anything about the Chungs' opinion of me. I know this because my parents have their own prejudices. Sweeping generalizations aren't about a person; they are about the idea of a person. So perhaps the language deficit is a gift because I can't do a verbal tap dance for the Chungs. Therefore, I won't be bitter when my charm fails to change sixty years of thinking.

So instead I decide to talk to hot Asian women who, like me, have slept around. Because after sleeping with more than five men in your lifetime, you start to see a pattern. Certain men like to be in charge and others want to be told what to do. Still others like a woman who can cook, and a few even want a girl who's helpless. I figured there must be a general pattern in the K-makeup, because all romantic preferences are generated by some kind of yin and yang we saw in our parents. Understanding the Asian family dynamic might just be the key I need to unlock my future. Or it could be an oversimplified generalization about the only other Asian people I know who are not related to Seung. But since I have no other information to move forward with, I'm gonna go with what I got from my fast friends.

Imagine my chagrin to discover that all it took to decipher things in at least this family was a few brazen hotties. Loose women are wonderful! Here's everything I found out about going to the next level with a Korean guy from the Asian temptresses I'm proud to call my friends:

Lesson One: Korean people respect their elders—no matter how grown the child is, or how wrong, ignorant, or stupid their elders might be in a given situation. Second to that: Men trump women, at least outwardly, on all decisions. (We will have ample time to be outraged by this later. Let's just get through the facts for a minute.) Third: Education, marriage, and hard work, followed by earning as much money as possible and having two children, are the golden path that Korean offspring must follow. As a tangent to this, Lesson Four says there are no arranged marriages in Korea today *per se*. However, moms and dads, as well as aunts and uncles, set up "teas" with acceptable partners for their children. Depending on how controlling your family is, either you *should* marry someone from these setups or you *must*. (For the record, I have yet to meet a Korean family I'd call loosey-goosey, so these teas can be rather binding. Literally and figuratively.) Further to this point is Lesson Five: At all ages and all socioeconomic levels, men do not approach women easily and women should not approach men at all. So much so that in Korean-American nightclubs, waiters are paid to make introductions between males and females. And lastly, the deadly sixth rule of K-culture: Straying outside Korean nationals for dates in Korea or anywhere else in the world might be acceptable with some Asians but is totally taboo with Japanese people. And that's all the variation allowed! Meaning, most important for me, dating non-Asians is totally and completely outside the directive.

This is like the most exciting sociology course I have ever taken, but with a death penalty for love. How can all these parents move to this gigantic country and then rope off one square mile and earnestly believe their children will date only in that corral? I get that Seung's family doesn't dislike other races. I see that they don't want their culture to die off if their son picks someone who doesn't subscribe to the K-commandments. And I see the value in, like, two of those rules. I can also fake more than half, biannually, when I see his parents. So truthfully, I'm not as incensed as you might imagine because, as I first said to Seung, I personally have very little at stake here. I mostly want to support my man because I know he is picking me. If his pitch to convince his parents that I am "good enough" fails, he is giving them up. Which breaks my heart even more, now that I know this is also failing Lesson One as a good Korean boy. So to prevent any future heartache, I am getting on the campaign trail beside Seung.

OUR LOVE AFFAIR UNFOLDS like a spy novel now. Everything has a double meaning. Seung surprises me on our first Valentine's Day with plane tickets to Hawaii! It's a beautiful retreat—aside from the underlying operation of meeting the first representative from his family who will do the "intake" meeting for the Chungs. We will meet with a "Como," which translates to "older sister of his father." Keeping Lessons One and Two from the hot hussies in mind, notice the subtle significances of this meeting: Como is older, so she has more power, but as a female, she has no authority. Como can pass on a preliminary opinion to see if a "higher-up" should meet me. You think I'm joking, but it gets worse.

First I meet Como's daughter for no reason other than she is

Seung's cousin and she is great. (Our generation has few to none of the hang-ups the parents do; they just have a Pavlovian-like instinct to please their moms and dads. Which, for the record, my parents would kill for.) I really enjoy Cousin Pauline's company, and on the last day in Honolulu I will meet her three sons and her mother—the Como.

I bow when I first see Como and she bows back. After this Asiatic moment she never looks at me again. She certainly does not speak to me. Lunch passes and Pauline's children pick flowers for me, share food with me, give me hugs, and Pauline has them call me Auntie. But Seung's Auntie only speaks in Korean and when it is time for goodbye, I bow to her but she doesn't return the gesture. I guess this means I failed. I must admit I'm a little hurt. And kinda shocked.

Have I mentioned that I'm RICH? And somewhat *famous?* And *attractive!* And I live in the country you wanted your kids to live in! What's up with this family? Seung is telling me I did fine. I don't believe him, but he is right. Como's heartless performance was mostly political. Later I will learn that she calls Seung's mother to tell her I am perfect in all things except genetics. I still can't imagine it but Seung's mother will tell me, years from now, that Como said, "The Chungs better accept this woman or they will not only lose Seung Yong, they will miss a wonderful opportunity." I can also tell you that this Como, who sang my praises to the highest order, will fly around the world to attend my wedding in the future and still will not say one word to me. I will put photos in my wedding album of her doing shots of Crown Royal with all her nephews until the bar closes at my Korean ceremony, and yet, not one word to me. I will continue to assume this is a language barrier, until one day when Como is passing through California and she summons me—

via my husband—to take my newborn son to her hotel and introduce them. Como will open her door and give me an unexpected, and kind of frightening, hug. "You are the mother of a son! There is no greater honor. And look! He is beautiful because he looks just like Seung Yong." Como will then take my baby and show him off to the other relatives as if he was her own.

Como speaks perfect English. I just have no value until I *produce*. Specifically, until I produce a male. Yeah. Go ahead and read that sentence one more time.

But back to today, pre-Como's gracing me with her fluency in English, my entire courtship moves forward just like this. Representative after representative meets me, makes some sort of a dig toward me, and then reports to Seung's parents that I am not so bad. I'm wondering now, like you, how or even why I put up with this.

I think it's kind of a game. I love Seung, we have our life, and it has nothing to do with any of these people. The more ridiculous their behavior is, the funnier I find it. Well, most of the time.

On a particularly aggressive Chung family day, Seung's favorite aunt—a woman he really admires as a mother—approaches me after a dinner she threw (for the sole purpose of getting a long look at me). She says nothing to me all night, but while waiting for her car to pull up at the valet, she opens with, "Where do your parents live?" By now I know the tiers of judgment laden upon this query. And I know I'm going to lose this round. My parents got divorced a mere five years before I met Seung, after thirty-five years together. Of course this is a shame to top all shames. It's not even in the K-playbook because it's just understood that divorce is not an option for *respectable* families. My parents live in two different cities now, which makes this a genius/

nefarious way for Kuhn Ama (translates to "wife of older brother of Seung's father") to concisely do her recon.

I tell Kuhn Ama where my parents live. As confident as I am, I can't help but try to qualify their dissolved marriage. Which leads to the second and final thing this woman says to me: "Thirty-five years is not long for a marriage."

Herein lies my problem. I like politics. I like the exchange of power even more than I like having power, but at a certain point I also like to win. This woman is one of many Korean American "work widows," as I like to call them, because her role in marriage is first and foremost to have, raise, and take care of her children. Yes, she loves her husband and she is certainly standing by him—while he lives and works thousands of miles away from her most of the year. Her emotional wants and needs seem to come second or third or . . . just go away to facilitate taking care of the kids and their education and supporting her husband to make as much money as possible. (See hottie Lesson Three for a refresher if needed.) So many Korean American parents have some version of this, including Seung's parents.[1] Today many Koreans in Korea just have Mom move to the United States with the children while Dad stays in Seoul to make the money—for the entire duration of their marriage. But when Seung was growing up, his parents' generation had both Mom and Dad move to the States to set up shop and then just Dad went back to Asia for eight to eleven months a year. Which, of course, is noble in many ways, as both parents suffer for the betterment of the family . . . on paper. I say "on paper" because I know firsthand how much Seung wanted his father in his life. And furthermore, perhaps I'm wrong, but in American culture I believe we would call living apart from your husband most of the time "separated."

And yet this Kuhn Ama is going to pass judgment on my parents? Who actually lived together during their marriage and jointly shared the pressures of parenting and making ends meet—for thirty-five years?

"Thirty-five years is certainly not a long time when your husband lives in another country," I retort back to Kuhn Ama with a smile.

If I had been a good candidate for a Korean wife, I would have dutifully nodded when Kuhn Ama insulted me. Instead, when she looks at me in shock at this answer, I move in very close to her to say good night, so we are both perfectly clear on how small she is when standing next to me. Perhaps it's my "Italian heritage" that makes me want to give her a reciprocal jab every time I see her to this day. She's damn lucky I don't mail her a horse's head.

AFTER THIS RUN-IN with Kuhn Ama, I need a breather. In one head-nod, Seung's aunt insulted my parents while simultaneously banishing me to the un-marry-able side of the tracks. And in truth, she made me doubt my man. Which is the part that is killing me, because that's her goal! But right at this second—and I'd never say this aloud—I'm not sure I see the point in this. Not because I have doubts about Seung or us as a couple, but because we both really want children. And we live in California. It's entirely likely that our children would see these unkind aunts more than they see their actual grandparents (my parents or Seung's) just due to proximity. Do I really want these people around my kids? Calling them family? Looking to them for the kindnesses children usually get to enjoy from people of grandparent age? Wait a minute—calling them Grandma, I'm just finding out?

Seung is teaching me important bits of Korean language that I need to know as I meet each family member. I had already learned that you don't call aunts and uncles and cousins by their specific names; rather, you call them by their gender and seniority ranking. Meaning, everyone is called "younger sister of my mother" or "wife of older brother of my father." Seung doesn't even know his aunts' or uncles' names! Which I found so funny about him, until I realized none of his cousins know the names of his parents, either. Seung's whole generation just knows the "age rank" of their parents' siblings and calls them that! And today—the day after my face-off with Kuhn Ama (wife of older brother of his father)—Seung is unknowingly oversharing when he explains that our children will someday call *all* his parents' siblings Grandma or Grandpa because, of course, an even younger person couldn't call these adults by a first name. This means all eight siblings of Seung's father and their spouses and all eight siblings of his mother and their spouses are called Grandmother and Grandfather. Which makes sixteen grandmas and sixteen grandpas! And at least two who are mean to the one and only mommy!

I love my grandmother. She lived with us my entire childhood, and I feel she is my third parent. This is not a title I take lightly, nor something I want my unrealized kids to miss out on because it's being wasted on thirty-two people.

This may seem insignificant compared with some of the other differences between Seung's culture and mine, but the Grandma title is the one that makes me want to jump ship. Now, for the first time, I have an instinct to get off this ride right here. Of course, I can logically see that this issue is not insurmountable, but my bitter feelings (which I'm pretending are facts) may not even be necessary. It seems that this choice just might be made for me, by something totally outside the Korean language or mandate.

AS I'M SITTING IN my home office, future-negative-fantasizing about grandmas, I receive a call from my agency. My TV show in New York just got picked up for another season. Joy, congratulations, and praise are being uttered by many agents who are all on the phone together to tell me this "great news." In the midst of which I hear, "You are shipping out in three weeks, girl, so start packing fast!"

When Seung and I began dating, I had just wrapped my first season on this job. Seung and I have only been dating for five months—in the city of Los Angeles, where I live. But now I will need to leave this city and go back to New York. Under the terms of my contract I will be *required* to be apart from him, for a longer period of time than we have even been together. The absolute minimum I will be away is six months.

I know how this separation plays out. When a woman physically leaves a relationship for a job, it does not sit well with the male ego/libido/psyche or heart for very long. I have seen this fact, combined with the increasingly long and expensive hurdles of flying around the world, crush most of my adult relationships as an actress.

My agents are still celebrating while I'm stuck thinking my mother's generation was wrong when they said women can have it all. I've tried to believe this hype since I started working regularly on television almost ten years ago, but over this decade I've seen the greedy-girl theory come up short every time.

After having my own mother pound into my head how equal I was to a man in all things, in the late 1990s I was then told,

"Women are the keepers of intimacy in a relationship." I spent two hundred episodes as the cohost of *Loveline* arguing with my dear coworker, Dr. Drew Pinsky, about this very subject because he kept telling me that along with my equality, this was true too. And I kept reiterating my belief that girls think just like guys when it comes to dating and sex. Drew told me over and over that there are hormonal secretions in women's bodies that emotionally bond them to a partner after sex, and that there are similar secretions in the male body that basically make them want to expel semen whenever and wherever they can—and society tells us both of these instincts are uncool. Thus, each sex tries a variety of behaviors between what is acceptable and what is biologically wired into them. I was twenty-seven during my tenure at *Loveline*, and nearly a decade later I can now clearly see that the good doctor was right and I was totally and completely wrong.

My personal recap of Drew's lesson is that women are actually the arbiters of how close a relationship is. If I am not bothered by no "title" in a relationship, neither is the guy. If I am cavalier about seeing other people while dating, so is he. If I am going to make work a priority over love, no man is going to yell, "Stop and choose us instead!"

But as of this moment I am legally bound to this job in the way most women my age are legally bound to a husband. I would be ostracized and sued if I tried to quit now, and the rest of my career might suffer. But as I realize I am probably going to lose this lover, I finally stop all the chatter in my head about some aunt whom my someday-children might call Granny. I am snapped back to the reality of focusing on a man and partnership that are both gratifying, passionate, and uplifting. Because if nothing else, space is about to come between us. So I'm making a fast plan to concede all the other space I can, right now.

WHEN SEUNG RINGS the doorbell of my house this night, I walk through my front yard and step outside the gate to meet him instead of buzzing him in. I step onto the sidewalk in my bare feet and baby-doll PJs (that I bought today to look accidental, but that I knew were cute as hell, to make me seem worth the mess I was about to cause). Here, on a very busy street in the middle of Hollywood, I tell Seung, face-to-face, that I am going back to my job in New York City in twenty-one days. A low-riding Mustang drives by us and yells, "Tap that!" at me. Mission accomplished on the wardrobe.

Seung looks at me solemnly, waiting to hear what that means for us. I feel almost as if I've stepped outside my body and I'm watching the following sentence come out of my mouth: "While I'm gone I would like you to have these"—and I hand Seung Chung a set of keys to my house.

I tell him that all of my adult life has revolved around work, but I am considering making some changes to that. However, they aren't going to happen as fast as I would like. In the meantime, I ask if he would be interested in moving in with me—while I'm not here—to give himself a chance to make my home feel like his home *and* practice cohabiting every other weekend, when I will fly back to L.A. to be home with him.

Seung looks a little nervous. Neither one of us has ever really lived with someone. And more than just the commitment this implies to each other, there is an even bigger commitment that would immediately be invoked, because as adults living in a big city, Seung would be giving up a rent-controlled apartment. Nothing proves love in Los Angeles like giving up rental real estate you have invested time in. On top of which, Seung rents a three-bedroom on the beach, with a six-hundred-square-foot party deck facing the ocean. I call it the *"MTV Real World* Asian Beach House," as his roommates are Chinese and Korean. Letting it go would put the nail in the coffin of his single life.

Thirty seconds have gone by in total silence, and I see panic in Seung's face. Which is just about to open a Pandora's box of fears in me that have nothing to do with apartments, but perhaps mommies or daddies or mean old aunts and . . . he clears his throat. As if he knows where I just went in my head and he does not want me to open up this receptacle of fear, because once that "I hate your family" energy is released, I'm not sure it can ever be put back.

Seung's big heart is clearly aware that this offer is way out of my normal comfort zone, but I'm seeing it is also so far out of his. He can't actually produce any words at all. But, white as a ghost, Seung takes the set of keys from my hand and unlocks the gate to my house. He then silently takes my hand and gestures for me to step inside with him and begin the rest of our lives together.

✻ I'M UTTERLY EXHAUSTED, AS WE LIE IN *OUR* BED for the first time in *our* home, twelve days after our first (of many subsequent) discussions about living together. Seung and I were both so nervous today as he merged his belongings with mine. There was a lot of gentle maneuvering when otherwise I'm sure I would have screamed about his two thousand T-shirts. And his jovial critique of my need to fill in every inch of floor space might have been more of a "Come on!" But today there was a lot of laughter and holding on to each other, as we silently prayed that each of us was ready for this. Tonight, well after midnight, everything has found its place. At least until tomorrow when I get up and start moving furniture one centimeter at a time until it feels like the home I always dreamed of. I'm rubbing my knees together in excitement under the covers as I say for the one hundredth time, "I can't believe we live together!" To which Seung takes my face in his hands to say, "Shhh. My mother might hear you."

We laugh because he's kidding, but he's also not. Seung is not telling his parents we live together, because it's outside of the K-playbook. Chastity is implied in Lessons Four and Five of being a good Korean that I got from the girls-gone-wild I know. Sleeping in the same bed on a daily basis does not allow for the illusion that we are saving ourselves for marriage. Specifically, that I'm not. I suppose I could be insulted by Seung's refrain, but I find it kind of debonair. He called his mom in Korea today—from the back yard. Hoping, I suppose, that being outside might aid him in omitting the fact that he lives inside with me. During this call, I couldn't resist standing in front of the windows of the newly arranged office, rocking back and forth in mock sexual positions within Seung's sight line. Seung very maturely walked behind the trash cans, almost into the bushes, to hide from my gyrations. Which is exactly what I find hot about this. He is trying to protect me from judgment. As I'm trying to formulate exactly what seems chivalrous about this, I'm just realizing that Seung may even be protecting his parents from me. From my nervous energy about being judged. (Which might explain why I'm gyrating while he is on the phone with his mother?) Wow. That's, like, doubly hot of him. If that is the case, then perhaps I should have enough faith in my man to discuss my fears about the bitchy comments from the aunts and the overuse of the Grandma title. Isn't that the point? To confide in my partner and let myself, and my relationship, grow with him? Not to just collect two thousand T-shirts and too much furniture together?

Staring into the possibility of my future with this man, I choose to try. I suggest we each say three things we hope for in the near future as live-in lovers. Seung starts by saying he looks forward to waking up with me every morning. I say I want to know the sound of his car pulling into the driveway so well that it becomes the sound of my day being complete because he is home. Mine is too wordy but the sentiment wins. Seung is raising an eyebrow to up his game for the next pithy love notion, when I start spilling my filthy fears onto the brand-new comforter. Como, Kuhn Ama, Grandma, Grandpa, Lisa and Dave's example of being pious, and my inability to keep my mouth shut when feeling attacked, and something about losing my house keys and being dependent on him to let me in. Every fear I can think of I spit out. To which Seung asks, "Who are Lisa and Dave?"

I feel like I'm living a scene from *I Love Lucy* where Lucy has some 'splainin' to do. I begin catching Seung up on my diligence, on how to best deal with his family, and he is smiling all the way. I have to stop and ask him why. He says he finds my earnestness flattering and sometimes even he can't believe "you're dating the Korean guy." I remind him that my dating the Korean guy "ups" my street credit. I was never taught to stay away from "Oriental people," as my parents called them, but only because they weren't even on their radar.

Which is by no means a compliment. Sometimes I take pride in the fact that Seung is on my radar. Seung is very handsome and educated and well traveled and I have no right to claim that I'm evolved because I find him attractive, but from where I started, I kind of am. From this safe place we just reinforced for each other, Seung throws out the next question.

"What makes you think I want you to be a mute about your needs?"

I'm backpedaling fast now because I think I have misrepresented Lisa, whom I don't see as speechless or weak. I see her as subtle and smart and . . .

"I love your big mouth because it houses that big smile *and* that sharp tongue. I don't want you to squash either of them," says the man I now share my bed with. "And if someone insults you, use the amazing gift you have in communicating your feelings so well. Even if it starts an argument. Diane, if my family insults you, they insult me. You stand up for whatever you want to and I will stand with you."

I want to fold into him. I want to kiss him passionately and thank him and believe that together we can see past the racially slurred trees and focus on the accepting forest and all will be well. But I don't. I have had enough lovers before this day, when I have decided to live with one. These lovers have each taught me something that I needed to know in order to make this relationship work, and I am hoping that Seung is not just another lesson that I need to experience in order to facilitate some other union. I am hoping he is *the* union for the rest of my days. And in order to make that a reality I have to let some of the romantic tides I like to be swept into pass me by. I have to dig my feet in and remember what I have learned about people's constitutions. That is, that people have an internal set of givens and that no matter how hard women try, we cannot change a man's nature. I know Seung has a deeply ingrained reflex to do the right thing by his elders. I'm not going to pretend that my fighting with them is ever going to be okay.

Instead I tell Seung that I don't want to argue with his family. Which is true. I tell him that I would rather find some strategy to appease them without canceling out who I am. Seung nods in agreement and adds that maybe the one couple that I spoke with isn't enough. And then I see the lightbulb go off in his head. He tells me to call Sonu.

Sonu is one of Seung's fraternity brothers. He is married to Jennifer. Sonu is from India and Jennifer is a plain old WASP, but neither plain nor old. There are two colors and two religions between them, and Seung remembers that there were some hurdles to overcome when they got together. However, the specific reason he wants me to call them is this.

"Sonu is so confrontational, he makes you look like a wallflower. I'm sure he didn't miss a single opportunity to fight any argument when he and Jennifer got together. He will tell you exactly how to fight your way into a happy marriage."

Seung is telling me to fight. He's actually telling me where to get lessons in fighting. He's trying to embolden my constitution as I'm trying to protect his. And this, more than all the adoration he has paid me over the last five months or the half of the rent that he ponied up this week or the countless *I love you*'s he has splurged on me today, makes me feel it is not the furniture being in the right place that will make this house our home. It is the pillow talk before bed—which, I once heard my mother tell her girlfriend, "is the most intimate thing you can do with a man." Today I see what she meant. And finally, I fold into him.

Perchance to sleep, perchance to dream another dream together.

CHAPTER 4

EVANGELICAL WHITE

CHICK LOVES HINDU

INDIAN MAN

IN MARYLAND

"She was honest with me. She said it was
going to be a problem, but I just didn't see
it as one. I had no frame of reference for
people who won't use logic or reason."
—SONU SINGH

S ONU AND JENNIFER actually attended the same high school.
Sonu (pronounced so-new) graduated just before Jennifer
began her freshman year, but Jennifer did see Sonu once. She remembers a poster hanging in their school for the then hit TV show *Miami
Vice*. Stuck on top of Don Johnson's face was a cutout photo of Sonu's
face. I ask Jennifer what she thought at the time, and she can't answer
fast enough: "What a wack job."

They ran into each other four years later in person. Jennifer was a
freshman again, at Virginia Tech now, and Sonu was "still" a senior there.
Sonu stopped in a local bar and Jennifer was bartending. They soon realized they were both *townies* who grew up in this small college town.

I've been to this town—Blacksburg, Virginia—because Seung went to college there, too. And I have stayed at Jennifer and Sonu's home with Seung. And I know their children. I also know that my husband greatly admires Sonu's family because when he was in college the Singhs were the first immigrants Seung ever met who allowed their kids to be American. To have pizza and beer while watching football with the family. To talk about girls they liked and parties they attended. Seung has a lot of time and love invested in these people. Which is leaving me somewhat paralyzed to speak on each of my first calls to Jennifer and then Sonu. I'm afraid to say or ask something that might embarrass them and/or something embarrassing about Seung's family. So mostly, I am just listening tonight. But as with Lisa, this is a story this couple knows well.

Back at the bar, Jennifer and Sonu made a plan to hang out over this weekend when they first met—their Thanksgiving break from school, while all their college buddies were back home. They went to a football game, a movie, had dinner, and Sonu just kept coming back to the bar. Jennifer believed he came because she was giving him a discount on beer. I find this hard to believe.

First, the beer was only fifty cents. Second, Jennifer is a nearly six-foot blonde who sang opera in college and designs her own jewelry now. Her personality is as shiny and jewel-filled as her pieces. Fifteen years later I'm not at all afraid to ask if she still thinks Sonu came for the twenty-five-cent savings. "Yes. I still think it was the beer."

I also ask Sonu and he can't answer fast enough. "There was this hot woman and I'd ask her to give me ten cents or half off on my beer—and she'd oblige me. It was a can't-lose scenario."

By Jennifer's birthday, three months after the inaugural beer clearance, she was saying "I love you" and Sonu was telling her he thought this was forever. Jennifer turned nineteen, and Sonu was twenty-two. They had no issue that Sonu was born in India and immigrated to America with his parents as a child and that Jennifer is white. But for Jennifer's family, who raised her as an evangelical Christian, faith was not negotiable.

From the time she was small, Jennifer's parents, the Jaasmas, told her a person of any race was fine for marriage as long as he was a follower of Christ. And she disagreed with them right from the start but didn't actually know any non-Christians until college. When Jennifer met Sonu she fell in love and was not concerned about her parentally prescribed boundaries.

Hmmm. So this couple's familial issue is like a side dish of race and an entrée of religious prejudice. But understanding how Jennifer and Sonu dealt with her parents—a mother and a father condemning a person their child loves, sight unseen, because he won't call their God his personal savior—sounds exactly the same as racism hiding behind the piety of religion. Which feels like an even harder mountain to climb. So, rather than looking at the racism in faith, I'd like to continue to understand the faith of exclusionism. This idea of: "You must be one of us or you are not worthy." Which feels as black-and-white as judging people for being black or white. So I'm thinking, if I can understand how this couple defended their love, even against the seemingly benevolent church, who can't I withstand?

"I just never fit in," Jennifer says about her parents. "I always felt like I was born into the wrong family." Jennifer is choosing her words carefully so as not to condemn her parents or perhaps oversimplify their plight. It seems she still has the strength to stand up for people she loves—even if their opinion is obviously different from hers. Even at nineteen, Jennifer never hid Sonu from her mom or dad. When she visited or talked on the phone with her family, Sonu came up regularly. "There was no big reveal. My parents just didn't see us as serious. Until I applied to the University of Arkansas."

Jennifer said she was thinking of transferring after her first year at "VahTech" because the music program at U of A was better. Sonu had just graduated and was also about to open a business in Arkansas—which Jennifer readily admitted was not a coincidence. Now the Jaasmas wanted to discuss Sonu, as their daughter's motivation to move across the country awakened them. So they asked Sonu to their house.

Conversations between Sonu and the Jaasmas lacked Southern hospitality right from the start. Jennifer's parents usually started off a talk with Sonu by saying that they followed the word of the Bible literally. Sonu would immediately ask if they handled snakes. The Jaasmas would then clarify that they believed in every word of Jesus literally. Sonu might then ask if they had the ability to speak in tongues. He remembers Jennifer's mother getting very frustrated, very quickly. Mr. Jaasma was calmer and a bit more reasonable, "but still did not listen to reason." Sonu once asked Jennifer's father if he believed in dinosaurs. Mr. Jaasma did. Sonu asked why, if there is no mention of dinosaurs in the Bible. Mr. Jaasma conceded that some things are unexplainable but their beliefs and Jennifer's are the same and very explainable, for this life and the afterlife.

The Jaasmas felt Jennifer had made her own choice to follow Jesus because they witnessed her choose this religion when she was baptized. They felt Jennifer's soul was at stake and that it was their duty, both as her parents and as good Christians, to defend it. But

Sonu had some defending of his own to do. He asked direct questions like, "Do you truly think Jennifer made that baptism decision herself, seeing as she was four years old?" Jennifer was witness to all of these debates. What was uncomfortable for her almost became a sport for her incredibly well-versed boyfriend. As long as Jennifer maintained that she wanted to spend her life with Sonu, there was no obstacle her parents could throw at him that he would let between them. However, Jennifer says she knew all along that there would be no changing anyone's mind. She just had to let them duke it out.

Her parents must have wanted to pull their daughter's hair out for bringing home a cocksure twenty-two-year-old who had the audacity to question their entire lives before he had even started his. Perhaps this is why the Jaasmas decided to take their next step: to call Sonu's parents. The Jaasmas asked Sonu's family to meet with them privately.

Sonu's family, the Singhs, practice Hinduism but, adds Sonu, "My parents didn't choose our social groups around ethnicity or religion." Both the Singhs have PhDs and are both professors at Virginia Tech also. (Ironically, Mr. Singh and Mr. Jaasma are both engineering professors at this university, but neither man, having different specialties, had ever met the other.) The Singh family did not hope or even passively suggest that their children should marry Hindus, Indian people, or people of Indian descent. But the Singh family's openness was of no consequence to Jennifer's family. The Jaasmas were sure, before having ever met the Singhs, they were going to hell.

The Jaasmas asked the Singhs to meet at a Hardee's. "Which is the Southern equivalent of McDonald's," Sonu explains to me, a Northerner. At Hardee's, the Jaasmas made no attempt to convert the Singh family to Christianity. They did not explain their feelings about their daughter's afterlife. Rather, they chose to tell Sonu's parents everything they felt was wrong with Jennifer as a person. They told the Singhs all of Jennifer's faults and every misstep she had made in life so far. They shared intimate, personal, embarrassing details of Jennifer's history—including details about the two boyfriends Jennifer had before college. The Jaasmas held this vomitous confessional in the hopes that the Singh family would find such fault in their adult child, Jennifer, that they would then force their adult child, Sonu, to dump her.

Jennifer and Sonu both felt that if any parent should have had a problem with the other's culture, the Singhs now had a right to. But the Singhs left this meeting finding only Jennifer's parents unfathomable. They were truly mortified for Jennifer and left the entire conversation that transpired at Hardee's in the trash there, where it belonged.

In the sadness that followed for all after this hurtful failure, Jennifer's parents made a last-ditch effort to save their daughter by conspiring with Jennifer's grandmother. With serious pressure from Jennifer's mother, Grandma followed up the Hardee's conversation by ringing the doorbell at Sonu's parents' home. She gave a similar speech to dissuade the Singhs from liking Jennifer, revealing more supposed inadequacies at their doorstep.

This event must have dug a ravine of pain for Jennifer. As she tells me this, her words are falling out of her mouth with incredible speed. But she is proud to add that her grandmother quickly apologized and, as Jennifer says, "was down with the brown." Jennifer feels her grandmother did what she could for her own daughter—at her vehement request—but then refused to leave her grandchild alone without any familial support. Grandma enjoyed a special place in Jennifer's life for many of the coming years.

Jennifer was not making any such turn with her parents. The Jaasmas' plan backfired more than they could have imagined. Feeling closer to Sonu and his family, Jennifer severed all ties to her own. She had minimal contact with them—perhaps once a year and only when absolutely necessary. This was not going to be anything like the civilized three-week hiatus that Lisa's family took. The Jaasmas would not see their daughter again for almost a decade.

UNCLE! I'M SAYING IT! Right here! I am sufficiently schooled in the possibility of how much could go wrong if you push or chastise a narrow-minded parent. I think I probably also have to make some phone calls and apologize to people I know who have traversed such insular thinking with parents—whom I advised to dig in and stand up for themselves. I had no idea that Dr. Seuss's *Butter Battle Book* was a work of nonfiction.

There is so much that I failed to think of when I savored the idea of telling off the *unaccepting* relative. I didn't consider that xenophobic or devout parents might push back. I think I imagined that all mommies or daddies in these situations would yell *mercy* at the first sign of being cut off from their kid. It really never occurred to me that the "wrong" side would send up a war missile of their own, because most people seem to at least understand they can't blatantly advertise their prejudices. They might speak them plainly in front of their own children, but I didn't consider how entitled some feel in their beliefs and, dare I say, seeming superiority. Clearly that lesson in the Bible about deciphering who loves a child most—when King Solomon threatened to cut the baby in half because two people claimed it as their own—is not a universal test for a mother's unconditional love.

JENNIFER NEVER DID transfer to Arkansas. Sonu decided to go into a different kind of business in Maryland. Jennifer still chose to leave college and move in with him, though. She says there were no agonizing questions for her as she left school, her family, and the only town she had ever lived in at twenty years old. "I always felt that Sonu would take care of me. I was just going with him."

Sonu found them an apartment and began working. After a year as a singing waitress on *The Spirit of Baltimore,* Jennifer re-enrolled herself at the University of Maryland and picked up her degree where she had left off. By which point the Singh family had emotionally adopted Jennifer. She was included at all of their holidays and celebrated with them on her birthday. This remained the status quo for five years.

As Jennifer approached twenty-five, her mother started to have new feelings. Mrs. Jaasma contacted her daughter to tell her that she still feared for her immortal soul but was also worried that this life was looking grim. Meaning, if Jennifer intended to marry Sonu, her mom wanted them to do it soon so that they would at least stop living in sin.

"Sort of like, love the sinner, not the sin, you know?" Jennifer asks this to see if I'm following this backhanded endorsement. I am, but I'm also sort of astonished that she seems unaffected by this turnaround. I get that this was not a joyous rebirth with her loved ones, but it was a step, right?

It didn't matter. So many years had passed that Jennifer had learned to live without her family. When most twentysomethings are suffering from the quarter-life crisis of "Should I get a real job now?"

or "Is it time for an apartment with one less roommate?" Jennifer had already mourned the loss of her mother and father and brother and sister. Their acceptance no longer held any weight.

Sonu's mother was having the opposite conversation with her son and Jennifer. Mrs. Singh advised Sonu and Jennifer not to get married until Jennifer had finished her degree and had a job. Mrs. Singh felt too many bright and capable women were left with few options later in life when their children had grown (or if, even worse, their husbands left them) and they had no skills in the workforce. Not surprisingly, these kids took the advice of the parent who seemed to be observing the life Jennifer was actually living, rather than the prescribed one written two thousand years ago in Nazareth.

Jennifer graduated from U of M and set up her career over the course of a year, and at a seemingly random steak dinner, Sonu proposed. The couple next to them leaned over to say congratulations and give sage advice based on their thirty-five years together. At the time of this interview, neither Jennifer nor Sonu could remember what the hell those old people said.

Nor can Sonu or Jennifer remember how they even told the Jaasmas they were engaged. After their decision to marry, though, Jennifer's family gave a financial contribution for the wedding reception and had no further participation. The celebrations to come were events the Singhs and the soon-to-be Mrs. Jennifer Singh planned together.

BUT FOR INDIAN PEOPLE, a wedding is about bringing two families together. Kusum, Sonu's mother, was having a hard time not including Jennifer's mother, Diana. After all these years, Kusum was holding out hope for a meeting of hearts over minds and to start anew. Kusum called Diana and invited her for tea. Diana accepted, if they could meet at the Jaasma home. When Kusum arrived after a day of teaching, Diana was knee-deep in the garden and covered in dirt. Diana was taken aback that Kusum was "so dressed up." Diana spoke directly about how simple her family was and that this "show" from Sonu's mother was not something she was looking for. Kusum remembers an attempt to explain that she had just come from work, but it mattered little. Both mothers' insecurity flags were flying high as they headed inside. Seated at the kitchen table, Diana opened the conversation by asking Kusum if she was a Muslim.

It was so off-putting that the Jaasmas still had no interest in Sonu or nonreligious beliefs or the life these children were embarking on. All Kusum saw were four parents who lived in the same town, with the same jobs, with the same number of children, who should have had so much joy to share as two of their kids joined forces. Perhaps Diana was just rude, but maybe Kusum's heavy heart caused her to dismiss the fact that devout followers of any faith rarely read material published outside their safety zone or converse with people leading a secular life. Either way, when Kusum returned home, her husband told her it was time to let all expectations go.

Hold, please! Can I say this whole *love story* is making me shit my pants at the thought of Seung's "not really fluent in English" parents meeting my "incredibly loud, drinking and smoking, barely been out of New York ever" parents? I'm not exactly sure these ethnocentric-advisory chats are a good idea anymore! I think they are making me more nervous than informed. So let me see if I can get these kind people to cut to the gore and get the hell of knowing how this turns out out of the way.

I pointedly ask Sonu if his parents ever privately worried about him marrying Jennifer—specifically because Jennifer might become a zealot later in life—and asked him not to. Sonu answered without hesitation. "My parents knew Jennifer. They knew she was different from her family. They saw that she was willing to take a stand and they knew this stand was meaningful to her because they saw what it cost her. After the run-in with Jennifer's mom, they really just wanted to plan a great party with us."

Tell me about that, then.

HINDU WEDDINGS ARE famous for their size and spectacle. Our couple spent two years raising their savings and working out enormous details to fully embrace both their backgrounds and entertain the five hundred invited guests. These guests received authentic invitations made in India, printed in gold ink, in both English and Hindi. Programs for the day explained the elements and rituals in both the Hindu and small Christian ceremony that would take place. A *pundit* (Indian holy person) who also happened to be on staff at Virginia Tech, working in veterinary science by day, but on the weekends performed weddings in both Hindu and Christian vows—would stand up for them.

Jennifer was excited to participate in all the Hindu rituals. She even allowed her future mother-in-law to pick out her wedding dress in India—which she did not see until the day of the event! But Jennifer still wanted a white dress for herself, for the wedding she had always imagined as a girl. She feared she wouldn't "feel married" if she wore only the Hindu attire. This was complicated, since white is the color of mourning in India. But who could deny Jennifer the one image she hoped to retain from her upbringing? She found a white beaded halter top and matching skirt in an Indian grocery store in Maryland. And for her stunning, statuesque figure, it was perfect.

Jennifer and Sonu preformed seven rituals with both their families standing by them, the most dramatic of which was lighting a sacred fire—during a 102-degree June day. Jennifer and Sonu, as well as their best man, circled this fire seven times to represent their seven vows. Their best man was not Indian and had no idea that this ritual was meant only for the bride and groom. To this day, Jennifer and Sonu joke that they are also married to a man named Paul Rossiter.

The new Mr. and Mrs. Sonu and Jennifer Singh threw a small brunch at their town house the morning after their wedding, which is also part of Indian tradition. In a moment of uncharacteristic vulnerability, Jennifer's mother burst into tears. She said to Sonu that she felt like she wasn't even a part of this event. Sonu spit back, "Because you weren't." Sonu had held Jennifer's hand when she longed for her mother to be a part of her big day over the past two years. These unnecessary pains Sonu witnessed spurred him on to tell his new mother-in-law exactly how he foresaw her future.

He warned the Jaasmas that day that if they continued to act in such a narrow-minded way, things would only get worse for them. "This is our home and you're not a part of it and someday it will be filled with children." He told Diana that she and Mr. Jaasma were becoming less valuable to Jennifer with every passing year. "You're going to miss all of it if you don't make a change." With this, Sonu closed the discussion with his new mother-in-law and moved on. By this period in their romance, Jennifer and Sonu were totally equipped to still enjoy the rest of their first day of marriage.

But the biggest surprise came after the honeymoon, when Jennifer Singh realized she was not actually married. The Indian pundit who ministered their wedding was not registered with the state of Virginia as anything other than a veterinarian. Therefore, Sonu and Jennifer went to city hall and had a third, private, civil, legally binding ceremony. Jennifer is wistful as she tells me this. Perhaps there was a gift in being made to have a tiny affair. It was still based on the love shared between two people, without any addressing of race or religion or family influence. The image I have of them standing at City Hall, alone, in blue jeans, is far and away my personal favorite.

SONU FEELS LIKE THE Batman of interracial dating to me. He fights injustice wherever he sees it. Honestly, though, he has more courage than I do. I'm living vicariously through him but sadly aware now that I don't have the stomach to put up the iron boundary that he did. Seung was right, though, because I do feel empowered after talking with Sonu. Now I'm even thinking that pretending every person doesn't have some degree of prejudice is naive. And I shouldn't sit too high on my horse, because at this moment I seem more evolved. Because there are people in my psyche that I prejudge and shy away from. Namely, actresses and preschool teachers. I know I shouldn't, but I do fear and judge them shamelessly.

But after talking with Sonu and Jennifer, I do feel more secure in my right to stand up for myself and my instinct that there must be a balance between respect for an elder and my own self-worth. I just don't know where my balance lies yet with Seung's family, and it's particularly hard to imagine with people I don't yet know.

Sonu didn't find this awareness overnight either, though. Even before Jennifer, he had some history of being the "Indian/brown/red/dark/one of them" guy.

Sonu grew up in Chicago until the third grade. As urban a city as Chicago is, its Midwestern location might explain why Sonu was the only nonwhite student in his school. But Sonu says he never felt out of place. Today's educational literature does confirm that skin color and what holiday you celebrate on school break seem to have no importance to boys until roughly fourth grade. For girls, the safety zone closes in earlier, at around second grade. Sonu moved to the southernmost tip of Virginia in fourth grade, and that is where the differentness began. There were a few black children in his class but no other variation of the white majority. He remembers classmates telling him stories about American Indians, trying to befriend him. No one seemed to know there was a country called India where Sonu's parents were from and he was born.

He says middle school was more challenging "for the odd brown man out," but quickly adds that by high school he could fit in any group. "I could hang with the nerds or the skate rats, and I was a jock. I didn't think I could possibly have had any more fun than high school till I got to college." I believe Sonu because his confidence is palpable. Because his childhood was not entirely defined by his race—even though he was the only person of his color in all his school settings—Sonu never even realized there might be issues having mixed-race children until they were born.

Jennifer and Sonu got pregnant on their first wedding anniversary. Jennifer wanted to name their daughter something unique, as Jennifer was the most popular name of the year twenty-seven years before. When their daughter arrived they called her Matisse.

In the early days of Matisse's life, Jennifer's mom frequented their home, as did Sonu's. Both gave advice and both went home. There was no fabulous awakening between Jennifer and her mother. There were no particularly loving moments that helped heal any of the actions from the past. All new mothers have questions and overwhelming feelings and a need to make urgent calls to someone they trust. Even though Diana was present, Jennifer still did not have the opportunity to reach out to her. But as she had been for years, Kusum was always there.

"She is a very 'huggy' person. She always has been. And I just couldn't be," says Jennifer. She has a lot of anxiety about her relationship with her mother-in-law. Despite Kusum's dedicated interest in Jennifer as her own person, Jennifer still does not feel that close to her. Jennifer identifies the feeling that prohibits their closeness as "guilt," and she still feels it today. Simply put, Jennifer finds it hard to share things with Sonu's mother because she feels guilty not sharing them with her own. She says with sadness that she has always kept Kusum at an arm's length. I can't help but think of other words to describe why Jennifer might be hesitant to bond with another mother. Words like *fear* and *loss* and *judgment* and *abandonment* stick in my mouth as I bite my tongue and just let Jennifer talk. She continues to bravely share her experience, not looking for any assurances from me, as much as my heart wants to give them to her.

One afternoon when the Jaasmas were visiting Matisse, Jennifer's father asked Sonu if he worked from home. Sonu's business had over one hundred employees by this time, who, needless to say, did not work out of his house. Sonu was home because he knew his wife needed his help with her parents. The Jaasmas' perpetual lack of interest in their daughter's life never fails to shock Sonu. He took this opportunity to lay down boundaries, as he realized they were all playing house but had nothing familial between them.

"I have always been decent, barring this one conversation about religion."

With his wife present, Sonu forbid the Jaasmas to ever speak to his child about religion if they wanted to continue to see her. He also told the Jaasmas that they shouldn't bother comparing how his parents would be involved in Matisse's life. "We have faith and trust in my parents. That is not something we feel with you." Jennifer's mother got upset, but her husband stepped in. Mr. Jaasma told his son-in-law that he understood. The conversation has never needed to come up again.

Four years after Matisse came to them, Sonu and Jennifer welcomed Seychelle Singh. "I found her name on a map," says Jennifer with candor. When Seychelle was born, Jennifer and Sonu had a plan ready for their family of four.

"In our home we celebrate Divali (an Indian holiday) and Christmas (with no Bible references) and Martin Luther King Day." Matisse has been to India already and there are plans for another trip to include Seychelle. The family plans to move somewhere more diverse when Seychelle turns five. They would like their kids to have a better idea of the world than just what their horse ranch presents. They are considering Singapore as their first option.

"We see our children as American and are raising them as such" was the quote both Jennifer and Sonu independently gave me. To address "what they are," Sonu tells his girls, "The good news is that Dad was born in India and Mom was born in America and they have the best of both!"

IN THE LATE SUMMER of 2007, Jennifer's mother asked both her daughter and Sonu to come to the Jaasma home. Jennifer's father's health was declining and his memory was leaving him. On the Jaasma family's front deck, Diana spoke for both her and her husband as she apologized. She apologized for seventeen years of bad choices. She apologized for everything they had ever done. Everything that was ever said. Diana admitted that they had grown to hate their actions and the way they treated both Jennifer and Sonu. They stopped short of saying they approved of the union, because they just don't. But everyone felt that what Sonu said the morning after the wedding had come true—and the Jaasmas finally wanted to change that.

At the end of this story, as it has transpired so far, Jennifer wants to be respectful to her parents. She feels there are extremists of all kinds and that there is no arguing logic with them. Today, Jennifer does not want to regret her own actions if she doesn't try to form a relationship again. So she is continuing to show up and rebuild with her family, all these years later, before her dad has no words left to speak to her when he is finally willing to.

Jennifer's life, ironically, seems to me to be a perfect example of being a good Christian. She shows love and empathy toward everyone. I also can't help but wonder if Jennifer's actions are a true example of what it means to live without prejudice. Acceptance, in any situation, is the eventual goal, right? Her family loved Jennifer when she was in their good graces, and I do see evidence that they still loved her even when they failed to be kind to her. But Jennifer's actions show love without judgment during all her family's actions. She distances herself from them when they hurt her, but she crosses back to them every time she is invited, without expectation. I wonder if Jennifer's kindness is more of what I need to be feeling when dealing with people whom I feel judge me. That is, if I'm not too prejudiced to extend a kindness to someone who I feel has already hurt me first.

Sonu feels that Jennifer is fantastic at being the bigger person. He thinks this change of heart came because the Jaasmas finally see what a minimal relationship they have with their granddaughters, as well as their "dynamic, whole-life-successful daughter." Sonu adds, "I'm supportive [of the reuniting] but . . . I still think they're nuts."

"I wish you could see these snowflakes coming down. They're enormous." It's January and even the South is feeling the winter. Jennifer is standing in her kitchen talking on the phone with me. Her now seven- and four-year-old daughters rush in from the cold. She offers them hot chocolate. I only want to ask Jennifer one last question so she can get back to her family and her real life, where seemingly peaceful philosophies don't ignite like lightning when they meet at her dining room table anymore. Where there is more laughter than heartache in their home and in their story than I have room to comment on here. I ask Jennifer what she hopes for in the future with her mother.

"Gosh, I never even thought about it. I haven't gotten that far. I'm just taking it day by day. I don't think I want to set a goal and then possibly fail at it. I guess if I can improve the relationship incrementally, every year, I'd be okay with that."

CHAPTER 5

MEETING

THE PARENTS

"Kimchi very spicy in our house.
You pour water on, if too much for you."
—YOUNG JA CHUNG

ALL THE VETTING is done. Seung is flying to D.C. and I am meeting him there in one hour—to meet his parents.

I am on a train coming from New York, where I am finishing my job—which I just *quit!* I play a firefighter on the TV show I'm vacating. The part is backbreaking and smoke-filled and not something I could do if I were to get pregnant in the next few years. So, I have asked to be written out. This is in direct contrast to everything I have been programmed to do as a workaholic child of the 1970s and '80s. No less, I'm quitting this job to move back to Los Angeles and be with Seung. Leaving a job to further a relationship with a man—excuse me, I just threw up a little in my own mouth—makes me feel like the victim in a Hallmark TV movie.

On top of which, actually quitting a TV show is like leaving a cult. After I talked to my producers about my decision to leave, at length, I then began the arduous task of telling fellow actors and crew members. Their reactions made me wonder if I had left part of my mind on the A-train. Most people on a set are actually kind of miserable during shooting because the hours are abhorrent if you are looking to maintain a life or relationship. But the work is so hard to get that many of us forget what we were looking for when we began in the business and now, we just want to keep a job. Maybe it's because my mortgage is small (and it costs me almost as much to keep a second home in N.Y. to do this role as I make doing it) that I have none of those fears. My fears, rather, are all based on the love/guy/marriage/babies fairytale. Perhaps I just made a huge mistake on both fronts and only my gut (which is continuously churning) is aware of it so far.

However, amidst the adverse reactions, I have one friend on set who keeps reminding me to keep my head out of the swirl of fear and ego that might be driving other people's advice. This colleague keeps saying that I didn't make the decision to leave this job from fear, but rather from a place of love, and that no bad could come of that. Uh-huh. I listen to her, but also google her name late at night to make sure she isn't part of some love cult. If I can just find some evidence that she is crazy, then I can jump back on the codependent bandwagon, which is much more populated than the express train to marriage and family that I am nervously trying to board.

All these fears aside, I told Seung I was quitting this job to be with him and he immediately asked if I would come meet his mother and father this weekend, who both happen to be in America at the same time. Seung and I have been together nine months, and I am less than one hour away from the final frontier in Chung family introductions at their home.

Even with all the advice I've gotten from other mixed-race couples, I still have no game plan for today. No one else's path seems to fit mine. I'm not a "wing it" kind of person, but hey, it only took me thirty years to even want to be married. After which I spent four years voraciously looking in all the wrong places for a life partner, and now I've invested three-quarters of another year trying to figure out what to do if I'm the "wrong" race for the right guy. So I only have a lifetime of evolution and years of therapy at stake if I blow this, right? (All of which is a circuitous way of saying—I'm very nervous.)

I like parents, though. I have many, many (many) shortcomings, but my mother raised me to do well at *how do you do's*. Of course, Korean culture has rules of etiquette that Westerners could never guess. You can insult someone while handing them a gift if you're not careful. But remember all the traveling I talked about when hitting on Seung at the engagement party? It has benefits beyond picking up guys at bars. I've been around the world enough to know the following about entering an Asian household:

I know to accept anything that is passed in my direction with two hands—both being crucial, as it shows humility and thanks. I will make sure both of my feet are always on the ground when sitting, just in case the Chungs are Buddhist. (Seung thinks he's Catholic, but all the holidays they celebrate are Buddhist by my account.) I have brand-new socks for every day of the weekend, as I'm sure their home is shoeless. I have a pashmina that matches every outfit in my bag, to tie around my waist—preventing a whale's tail of pretty underwear from breaching out of my jeans—if I am asked to sit on the floor. I have a gift of tea for Seung's parents: traditional and yet not alcoholic, since I fear my ancestral background might imply I am one if I waltzed in toting the other traditional gift of alcohol.

Yeah, I got this. And I shouldn't forget that I have met almost every aunt and uncle of importance. Although no one is particularly warm, friendly, or even nice to me, Seung says I'm doing great. Of course, Seung is not telling me the whole story.

While I thought we were fighting this good fight together, Seung has been working a simultaneous and private campaign of his own throughout our relationship. First, with his mother. He started telling her about me, the way most sons tell their mom about a person they care for, with little tidbits that he found endearing. But the information Seung is choosing to share is all leading his mother along a very calculated path—actually making her chase a very specific carrot. Because at this point in his life, Seung believes he has one card to play that, if used right, could trump all the other quotas he is meant to meet. Take a big breath and read this romantic statement:

Seung believes his mother is more worried that he is not married to anyone at thirty-five years old than she is about what race a possible bride might be. Ten years after Momma Chung's comfort zone expired, grandchildren trump race. Meaning, as long as Seung brings home a uterus that can carry this woman's grandchild, and do it soon, she will get on board. Now, this uterus does not have complete carte blanche—a) it must have at least gone to college, b) it should not have been utilized on any other children before Seung's, c) nor should it be too big or too small in size, for breeding purposes—but that's about it. If you bring these three things to the table, along with fervor to make a baby, you just might find yourself in the rose circle with Mom Chung cheering you on. Isn't love grand?

In Seung's first talk with his mother about me, he told her some of my more impressive traits but said he was worried because "Diane really wants to have children and I'm not sure I'm ready." Which was and is true, but not something either of us spends a lot of time on. Saying this unspoken thought to his mother, though, was like firing the starting gun at the eight-hundred-meter dash.

To further this cause, there were gifts. At Seung's mother's and sister's birthdays and again at Christmas, I went shopping with him. Before my debut, Seung had always bought his family lavish gift certificates. When I began suggesting actual items, which were less expensive but seemingly fancier, it was a win for all. And because these women also have uteruses, as well as estrogen running through them, they quickly figured out it was me who was picking their pressies.

Seung's mother talked incessantly about the dresses, hats, purses, gloves, photos, frames, coats, et al. . . . while on the phone with her husband in Korea. Which apparently caused a few run-ins between husband and wife—as well as full-on "Don't you dare" conversations regarding her support for this union. But it seems this is what motherhood, in a patriarchal society, is all about.

Seung's mother was doing her job as an advocate of her son by trying to absorb and exhaust most of her husband's anger, in order to move Seung closer to his goal with me. If she could take on the bulk of her husband's volume and rhetoric, she hoped it might soften both the men she loves for their coming battle. Like most mothers, she loves her son in a mighty way, but as a Korean mother in this family, she is also culturally disposed to throw herself under the bus if necessary, in order for Seung to carry on the family bloodline.

All that was left was for Dad and son to discuss me face-to-face—which, I didn't realize, had also already happened before my trip today.

SEUNG SAW HIS FATHER in Oregon four weeks ago, when his whole family met because Seung's sister underwent surgery there. The moment the only daughter of this family was put under anesthesia, Seung's father turned his head from the gurney she was lying on and said to Seung, "Who is this person buying your mother all these gifts?"

That sentence can be imagined a whole host of ways. (Even though it's hard to imagine at all when your baby girl is semiconscious on a hospital bed.) But don't fool yourself into thinking there was any leading or inviting tone like: "So, Seung Yong . . . " at the top of it, or any rib-poking, elbow-bumping, pat-on-the-shoulder "Huh, son?" at the end. Rather, it was asked in the tone of most questions between an elder Korean man and a junior Korean man—like an accusation from a superior officer that might come with a harsh punishment if answered incorrectly. Which Seung says is "just tonal to the language." While I think Seung "just" has a generous spirit.

Seung had already prepared an entirely different plan of attack for his father. He told his dad next to nothing, so nothing could be used against him. To this first question, alongside his drug-induced sister, Seung evenly said, "Diane." To which Seung's father repeated my name, in a convoluted distortion of vowel sounds. Seung said my name again for pronunciation and so did his dad. They did this until the older male got frustrated and said, "Well, who is she?"

"The person who picked out Mom's gifts." And with that, Seung left the room.

Seung still wouldn't pitch me to his father. And it drove his dad absolutely crazy. Mostly, I believe, because Seung's father knew his son was too old to be blatantly told "no white people/black people/ brown people/Japanese people/Middle Eastern people, or simply put—Koreans Only," so without a discussion of me, there was no way to bring this up. Seung, as we know, had been told this expressly in his youth, throughout high school and college, and even up to a few years ago when Seung actually lived in Korea and fell in love. Seung told his father during that time he just might marry one particular Korean national and live in Seoul with her. His parents were thrilled and their mission was almost accomplished. Except Tiny Tot, thankfully, called the no-hitter.

Tiny Tot, as I like to call her because I have seen her picture and truly wondered if I could fit her whole person inside my pants pocket (the front pocket, of skinny jeans), broke up with Seung long before their relationship got too serious. This seventy-inch, ninety-pound, black-haired Tinkerbell ended their summer romance because she wanted a man more ingrained in Seoul's society. (The upper echelon of Seoul's singles scene might be some of the hippest cats in the world. They come from a small circle of families who are all super-educated and super-loaded, whose kids get super-sauced most nights of the week at one exclusive event after another. Frankly, they make New Yorkers look suburban.) Wanting this in a man may sound pretentious of Tiny Tot and we might even assume that her brain is appropriately sized to the rest of her body, but, in fact, what she wanted was a Korean! Which Seung is only in heritage—despite his parents' best attempts and his numerous Seoul-based cousins who introduced him to the right scene. Seung tried, but he is a Yankee.

The only person who had the gumption to call this, though, was Tiny Tot. And I am eternally thankful for her.

Some form of this seems to be the recurring problem for all those born in the "zero generation." Seung was born in Seoul and came to America at three years old. Which means he is technically an immigrant, but how much culture did he really absorb by age three in Korea? All aspects of the Korean myth that he knows and loves were told to him by his parents, against the background of Washington, D.C., which he considers his home. The biggest hurdle for Seung, as a member of this immigrant-versus-national anomaly, is that his parents were fully formed adults when they came to America. In their hearts they probably had very little interest in giving up their way of life, but even if they did, they had no knowledge of American culture to give to their kids. And so each generation within this family began their journey on a very different path in their new American life.

Seung's parents would begin their American experience within the confines of a Korean subculture—with whichever relative had the most means to support them. After the parents found jobs for themselves and schools for the kids, they would eventually move to their own apartment but never leave that Korean community where they shared friends and language. They squeezed out the most Korean existence possible in the United States to make up for the deficits that immigration put upon them—loneliness, isolation, and the need to begin at the bottom of society. Thus Seung's home life became a romanticized/bastardized version of the culture they left behind.

Meanwhile Seung's own life—school, friends, language, literature, television, music, movies, and eventually cars, girls, drugs, sports, colleges, vacations, everything—was fully American and separate from his mom and dad. Seung had a hard time as a child: growing up in the projects, in a predominately black school, on free lunch programs and other subsistence from the government until his parents learned enough English to get them closer to the vocations they studied in college. By which time Seung had learned to survive in any circle. He fit in with ease amongst white kids or black—and never knew any Asians other than his relatives and parents' friends, but he flourished in their company, too. By high school, his family's passion for education kept Seung at the top of his honors classes. Yet sneaking around to do the things most of us try at sixteen and seventeen was also a breeze because his father was back in Korea then and Mom worked all the time to keep them afloat. Seung soared through college and graduate school, starting his career twice—once in D.C. and then again in L.A. He is just now, finally, at the crossroads he has been avoiding his entire adulthood.

With his life fully set up, Seung must now decide which life he will repeat: choosing between the life inside the house he grew up in and everything outside that door that he also grew up in. I don't think Seung has ever directly addressed this quandary. Rather, I think he has waited to see what will come his way. He fell "in like" and in love many times, with women of all colors, but when our union began, Seung says he knew within the first two weeks he would marry me. So as strict as the cultural limitations impressed upon him were, he had tried and failed the Korean way. And his father had witnessed it. Which now Seung hoped would have influence on the conversation he was about to have. After thirty-five years of wondering how this talk might go, in the end Seung only got to say two words.

After Dad saw his daughter survive her surgery, he finally cornered his son. The Chung women were hooting with laughter looking at pictures of Seung's life in Los Angeles—all of which prominently featured me—and Dad finally had a tangible excuse to address my race. Holding my photograph in his hand, Seung's dad asked a lot of questions in an angry tone. Seung did not take the bait. When his father was finally incensed, he yelled, "What is she?" at Seung.

Keep in mind the parents and children in this family don't share a large variation of words in the same language to have a nuanced dialogue about anything. Seung literally didn't understand what his father was asking him. His father said, "What is she?" louder or faster until Seung burst out laughing and said, "She is a girl, Dad!"

Dad did not laugh. Seung stopped laughing and respectfully said he didn't understand the question. "She" is Caucasian, obviously, so what else did he want to know? Seung's dad asked if I was Polish or of some other European descent. Seung explained that I am Irish and Italian and then raised his shoulders, sort of saying, what's the difference?

I fantasize that Seung raised "a shoulder" at his father—taunting him, almost daring him to say the thing that was really bothering him. That everyone in the family knew was a problem but everyone was now trying not to say. But having read the rules of this family and every family like them who almost lost their language, customs, holidays, and beliefs within these parents' lifetime, I know this was not the case. No matter how much Seung loves me, he would never goad his father because he understands where this fear (dressed as dislike of other races) comes from. Yet, in his own way, raising a shoulder at his father was still out of line because what Seung was actually implying was, "If you have a problem with her race, you should figure out how to say those words, because I'm not going to say them for you, in any language."

To which Seung's father said in English: "You can't love one of them."

Seung shook his head yes, locked eyes with his father, and said, "I know."

After these two words, Seung never let his father's gaze go. Which was not as much a challenge, as an outsider might imagine, as it was an apology. An apology from a son who was wholly aware that he was about to fail his father's greatest wish. But that he was going to do so nonetheless.

* I'M STANDING AT THE DOOR OF THEIR D.C. home. Seung's mother lives here most of the year, as does Seung's sister. Seung's father has just flown in from Korea and so has Seung from Los Angeles. They are all waiting for me on the other side. Several weeks have passed since the father and son face-off alongside the hospital bed, and as the door opens, I am peacefully unaware.

I bow when I see them all for the first time. As I stand with my head lowered beneath their hearts, it is Seung's sister who laughs at me for being "a better Asian" than she is. She reaches out and shakes my hand, pulling me upright and into the house—where she says in a hushed tone that I should not sweat the Korean "mish-i-gosh."

Is this a whisper in my ear—in Yiddish? I love this little huddle! I'm so excited that Eun Yi (pronounced ew-knee) is on my team that I have forgotten to let go of her hand. Yet even now, as I'm realizing it's time to let go, I can't stop myself. I'm frozen, waiting for her to slap me on the ass and say, "Go deep!" Eventually, Eun Yi takes both my hands in hers and pries herself free. I'll just walk shoelessly across the living room now and hope Eun Yi forgets that this ever happened.

Minus one for the "white" team.

For all the hurdles I have jumped through with Seung's extended family, Seung's mom and dad are warm and lovely when they greet me. And lovely with their son. Ama (exact translation is Mommy, but both Seung and Eun Yi call her this so we will also) is kissing her grown son, who I now realize arrived only a moment before me. Apa (that would be Daddy, and yeah, we're all rolling with that, too) gives Seung a bear hug. That's more affection than I usually get out of my parents, and I'm their only daughter. From his parental embrace, Seung is translating to me as his parents speak to him. They are telling him he looks like a bum because his hair is too long. (*Kuh-gee* is the Korean word for "bum." I cannot wait to whip this word out later on Seung.) His parents are offering me food and drinks now, as I'm being led to the best seat on the couch in the fancy seating area. They are clearly excited—and, dare I say, nervous also—to meet me. You know, in all the hoopla I kind of forgot that Seung's parents are human, too.

As the afternoon unfolds, many things become clear. Seung's mom speaks English, but it's choppy and I'm never confident that I understand what she's saying or that she is getting what I'm saying to her. So we're both avoiding direct conversation and doing a lot of smiling and speaking softly to Seung, and he speaks on both our behalf. Seung's dad doesn't speak in English. Seung speaks to both his parents in Korean with a sprinkling of English when he is stuck for a word. Eun Yi, on the other hand, speaks only English, so both parents must understand enough to get by with her, and they answer her in Korean—and everybody gets what they get.

This may be a factor in why there are so many more moments of "quiet" here than there are at my house. Ah, shit, let's be honest: Seung's family home is the picture of serenity compared with the cacophony at my mom's. And it's kind of great. Seung's sister is much softer and kinder than my siblings. I don't feel like she is interviewing me or judging whether I'm good enough, but she is doing an inventory of all my stuff. Bag, shoes, earrings, shirt. She likes it all, wants to know from where it came and what I paid. We seem to be recovering nicely from the doorway hand squeeze. That is, until Eun Yi asks me in front of her whole family, "So what's it like to kiss Daniel Sunjata?"

Oh God. Daniel Sunjata is an actor on my current job. I have a love story with him where we do much more than kiss. We have steamy, very close to naked, cable-style love scenes. Eun Yi is bringing this up in front of her mommy? And, oh yes, her daddy! And her freaking brother. Daniel is one of the prettier people on planet Earth, so it's not like I don't field this question five times a day. This living room is just the last place I want to discuss it in. Literally. When my eyes nearly bulge out of my head, it seems to inspire Eun Yi to follow up with, "Don't worry, they won't understand this conversation."

Uh-huh. But what if they do understand? Any part of it?

It doesn't matter. After all this work, I'm not going down over how some actor kisses. I burst out laughing. I'm hoping this inappropriate response should make the parents think they don't understand Eun Yi even if they do. I then say in a completely jovial tone, "I'm still not talking about this in front of your parents. So laugh back, right now, and I'll give you all the details later when your parents are sleeping." With this incongruent sentence, I stare Eun Yi down. Even she looks confused until . . . she laughs. She then turns to look at her brother. Seung shakes his head at his sister and then turns to me and says, "Nice exit." More to come later, as we figure Sister out. I'm currently being invited by Ama to sit for dinner.

Seung's dad is so expressive, and clearly funny, that I kind of get an idea of what he's talking about even before Seung translates for me. He is a charismatic entertainer—which was never what I imagined. I find myself laughing right along with everyone else just from his delivery. Seung's parents are actually fun—which is an adjective I also never considered I might use for them. Just as I pick up my chopsticks to begin eating, Seung's mother leans in and whispers something about the meal being made without beef because Seung said I do not eat meat. I think she is justifying why they didn't utilize the most expensive food for my arrival. I feel very flattered. Ama then whispers to me again: "And the kimchi very spicy in our house. You pour water on, if too much for you."

Ama smiles and nods to me many times, like she is doing little bows. I'm so flattered I want to jump across the table and hug her. But I'm not actually positive this is what she is saying and I don't trust myself after failing to let go of Eun Yi's hand earlier. I also think Ama would actually wilt if I touched her at this early stage in our relationship. So instead, I give Seung a prideful yet diminutive smile.

I kind of feel like I'm in a war movie, playing the role of the good-girl-American love interest. Seung swallows a laugh when I give him this look. I raise an eyebrow back, sort of saying, *What? I'm totally the good-girl love interest!* And I believe I am (although

I also laugh out loud when I'm alone in the bathroom, as this whole day is a tad surreal). Whoever I am while sitting at this table doesn't matter as much as the fact that I'm at this table. And no one is yelling or storming off about my being here. Seung shrugs at my role-play and continues talking in Korean with his family. Which, by the way, is hot.

Seung is doing so many sexy things at this table. He is sort of the master of ceremonies: translating, honoring, and entertaining everyone. He is handling the pressure fantastically. He is currently telling his father about my trip to Malaysia, which I guess I told him about the night I hit on him at our friends' engagement party. He is relaying details that I have no recollection of telling him, but no one else knows them, so it must have been me. As Seung finishes an impressive tale about my being the first American some devout Muslims on a teeny island had ever met, he winks at me. I think I love him a little bit more today than even yesterday when he asked me to come meet his Ama and Apa.

After dinner I am invited to sit on a couch next to Seung. We sit across from his mother and father, and sister Eun Yi pulls up a chair, making the five of us into a triangle. Seung's mother and father are not only eager to talk with me, but seem to be very much in love with each other forty years into their marriage. They are holding hands while talking. Seung then takes my hand. Apa asks me a question, via his wife. We talk this way for a while, about movies I think. The scene is so idyllic, I'm not even really paying attention to the conversation. I'm enthralled with how welcome I feel and how happy I am that I didn't give up before I even got started. I'm making a mental note to myself, that this is Seung's family and that the ancillary people who come with them shouldn't weigh me down. Seung's parents are caring, funny people. It is yet another bonus that comes with him. That and his disco dancing.

Dessert has been served and mostly eaten, so now I am ceremoniously getting up to take the finished tea service back to the kitchen. There is no way Ama is letting me in her kitchen, no matter how much she likes me, but this "cleanup test" is the one that finally puts me over the edge. With big smiles and heavy hands, Ama and Eun Yi push me back onto the couch, implying, *We're not kidding—you just sit there next to him. That's your job in this house.* As I settle back into the sofa, even I know . . . I'm in.

THE FORMALITY OF SEUNG'S parents' house makes me lustful. Like a kid in high school pretending to be asexual and studious at my boyfriend's house when his parents are around. The second the parents aren't around, though, I just want to make out with Seung endlessly. Seung is laughing as I'm attacking him in the downstairs bathroom before we go out for a "family walk." He is laughing hysterically as he says that he should have brought me home sooner.

I am still groping him when I hear him say something about my being the first person he has ever introduced to both his parents. That can't be right. I know he has dated a lot. One of his female friends from college told me that Seung kissed every friend she had at school. Wait a minute, that *is* what Seung is saying—I am the first girl he's ever brought home to meet his father.

This is not flattering. This is frightening. For a host of reasons I will get to, but right now I have to stop this session and become the sexless, high school girlfriend love interest again . . . and head out the front door for the walk. But there will be a whole other kind of digging and groping going on tonight.

After everyone retires to their rooms and I am safely tucked away in Seung's—as he has been banished to the couch—I can't even count to six before Seung sneaks into my bed. I pull him to the floor to talk and am totally confused when he lands on top of me. Oh no, Mr. Seung Yong Chung. We have some serious bridge-building to do between the Korean way and the American/Irish/Italian/white/whatever-the-hell-I-am way. Tonight will be about the extraction of details regarding why young ladies were not welcome here.

Part of it, I understood, was because many of Seung's love interests weren't Asian, but even those who were didn't meet with Dad. It turns out that love is just not something you share with Dad and in some Asian families even Mom—until you are ready for marriage. This might be one of the saddest details I've heard yet in this family's culture over the entire nine-month dog-and-pony show I have just completed, so I'm grilling my man on what he wants to keep from his family traditions and what he recognizes to be antiquated and maybe even dangerous for children today.

My mother was far and away the strictest of all the mothers I knew growing up, but I still went to her with my hopes and disillusionments. She met every idiot I ever liked. How easy would it be for a child to slip into a bad situation if no parent was monitoring where his or her heart was wandering? Contrarily, I'm not so enamored with my own experience to ignore the fact that most Korean American adults I know have had amazing success at work and in maintaining their marriages—compared with other Americans my age. But still, this is not a cultural tradition I am willing to take on.

I'm asking Seung, in multiple ways, like a border guard trying to confuse him and get to the truth within his psyche, if he is sure he doesn't want to keep such formal boundaries with his children. Seung promises that he has no intention of making formality more important than intimacy. Or males more important than females, or work more important than time spent together in our family. Eventually I start to believe him and I go back to the voracious make-out, right under a life-size photo of Seung playing football in tenth grade. Feeling reassured of the love we share—as two Americans who grew up in the twentieth century and want all that it has promised us—I have no interest in making it easy for my man to leave his junior high marching band jacket I've just put on over my otherwise naked body. Seung warns me that payback is coming: when he meets Momma and Poppa Farr.

CHAPTER 6.

MEXICAN AMERICAN
LOVES PALESTINIAN
ENGLISHMAN
IN ILLINOIS

"Oh, believe me, we know
what you are up against."
—DAVID ZUAITER

S EUNG COMES TO wake me Sunday morning and says we are leaving. The weekend has gone swimmingly but I'm packing now, not knowing if something horrible transpired over the japchae breakfast I missed. Within twenty minutes we are en route to the train station for me to head back to New York. On the car ride to the station there is silence between Seung and me. I study his face, looking for a clue as to what has gone so wrong. At the station, Seung tells me he's going to take the train with me, to introduce me to some friends of his for dinner, and then head back to D.C. tonight for one final conversation with his parents before leaving for L.A. tomorrow.

One final conversation about me or one final conversation for the rest of his life? I am just as confused as I was the very first time this to-love-a-Korean-or-non-Korean story line came up. Only this time I have something at stake, too. I have Seung's happiness, which, I realize as I stand in the train station and begin shaking from nerves, is completely tied to my happiness now.

"Is everything okay with your parents? I thought it was going well," I ask tentatively.

Seung grabs my hand. "Oh, it's terrific. It's going so well I thought we would celebrate with some friends who have an awesome love story to share with you, and then I'll head back to my parents to have the big conversation with my father about us."

I smack him. It's only on the arm, but it's a full-on smack. Then I start to cry. Seung's two sentences are the best argument to support Katharine Hepburn's idea that men and women should just live next door to each other and visit because we are so intrinsically different from one another. Seung scared the crap out of me, when his real intent was to celebrate our success. He was so thrilled by our integration with his parents that he was willing to take a long and expensive round-trip train from D.C. to New York just to have dinner with me and show me how successful we just might become via his friends.

But since Seung did not say *any of this*—for a moment, I thought I had lost. I thought I had been deemed *unacceptable* to love. Which, of course, sans the humor in this head game I'm engaged in, is enough to make any girl cry. But I know I am also spilling over with emotion, because there was a moment in this mess of a morning where it crossed my mind that if I really love Seung, I should just let him go. That I should just send him off to K-town, where he doesn't have to choose between his family and me. I thought about the other mixed-race couples I've talked to and how they might be the only people who would understand that I have all this guilt if Seung chooses me because there are people he loves who wish I would just go away. And although I don't acknowledge it, I'm sorry for that.

And on top of all this, I can't be mad or even show how close I felt to losing Seung in this bizarre beauty contest because his last sentence really does imply that he is about to tell his parents that I'm *the one*—right? Clearly all the other shit we've been through would point to this, but that's not how I imagined my man would find his way to asking for my hand. What I pictured is this part—where the guy tells his parents that he loves me most and then he tells my parents and then he hands me the magic box, which holds the mystical ring, which I wear forever, and we live happily ever after. That's what he's talking about now, right? Yeah, I may be crying over that, too.

✳ I LIKED SEUNG'S FRIEND SUZANNE IMMEDIATELY

when she entered my New York apartment, as she was carrying a larger bouquet of flowers than any man had ever brought me. David was equally charming but empty-handed, so Suzanne was my clear favorite. We were still in the hallway of my Nolita (this is a New York acronym for "north of Little Italy") rental when Suzanne said, "You got past the parents!" and hugged me feverishly. I looked over her shoulder at Seung as if to say, *Oh, they know everything?* Suzanne's husband, David, clearly understood my thoughts and said, "Oh, believe me, we know what you are up against. I imagine you have been so worried about meeting Mum and Dad that you probably haven't even looked at this big Mongolian foreigner to ask yourself, *Is this really who I even want to be with?* I'm turning my whole body toward Seung now, actually wondering if I had enough time to just consider him before the racial playoffs took over, when David jumps back in. "Don't think about it now. We have some samples from your mother's homeland to help you decide." With that, David opens his backpack and shows me four bottles of red.

Now I am wondering if Warren Beatty pays this husband and his wife to travel around America and convince people to live up to the mantra in *Bullworth:* that we should all just keep bonking until there is no more color difference left in this country. And if they aren't the spokespeople for this platform, seriously—who the hell are they?

Here's what I learned about this couple and their parents over the first bottle of chianti they sprung on me. This does not need to be committed to memory to understand the remainder of their tale or mine; it is just so utterly amazing that I'm sharing it.

Suzanne's father was raised in Mexico. He was fourteen when his father died, and he joined the Mexican military to survive. While in it, he went to college and then to medical school. He was then awarded a scholarship to Harvard University. While finishing his residency at a hospital in Boston, he met his wife, who was a nurse there. They fell in love and were married, and for their honeymoon they drove from Massachusetts to Mexico City, where they moved to practice medicine.

Suzanne's mother, a Caucasian, educated, American woman, moved into the home of her husband's family in Mexico, where no one spoke English and she didn't speak Spanish. Lacking all the comforts of her American life—family, friends, language, and freedom—Suzanne's mom spent a lot of time crying in the corner of her mother-in-law's home.

David's father was raised in Palestine. He was educated in Egypt and went on to medical school in England at the Royal College of Surgeons. While finishing his residency at a hospital in London, he met his wife, who was a nurse there. They fell in love and were married and immediately flew to Palestine to practice medicine.

David's mother, a Caucasian, educated, British woman, moved into the home of her husband's family in Palestine, where no one spoke English and she didn't speak Arabic. Her new husband promised they would leave if she hated the Middle East, but David's mom said nothing while she quietly cried in the corner of her mother-in-law's home for all the same reasons Suzanne's mother did. "She cried every day, for a long time," recalls David, who then adds, "but she's still living in Palestine thirty years later, so something is working for her."

WHAT ARE THE ODDS that the children of these two marriages would find each other and fall in love near the Great Lakes of Illinois— just after David and Seung finish graduate school together? And that David and Suzanne would then marry, have two kids, and call Seung *this* morning for advice about moving their family to a job in New York or L.A., since Seung has lived in both? And that five hours later these three old friends would be at my dining room table in downtown New York, presenting me the opportunity to discuss any hurdle they encountered when forming their union and family—which I am completely blowing because all I am thinking during this incredible story is:

Is Palestine an actual place?

I've traveled almost everywhere. Including Israel. I saw the border to the occupied territories. Is that Palestine on the other side? Am I just a victim of the American press or is Palestine an actual country now? And if it is, was it also an actual country thirty years ago when David was growing up?

I'm too afraid to ask. Here I am, neck-deep in the greatest cultural debate of my life, wondering if a really specific culture I see in the headlines every day has a homeland. What I need to do is seize this moment by faking it. Yes, I should just pretend to understand the entire Middle East conflict, and after my new Palestinian friend leaves I'll google his country. I would estimate I can learn the location, see how much infrastructure exists, and determine for how long—in three websites or fewer.

Looking at David gives me no clues to these unanswered questions. I'm not sure what I'd expect a Palestinian to look like, but David's looks catch me off guard regardless. He has fine, black hair with very fair skin and mostly European features. I would say he looks Egyptian-light. And while I'm making up words here, he speaks English-light. Meaning, he mostly uses American terms but has a lilt that is recognizably British. Combining his looks and sounds, I would never have guessed David is an Arab or an Englishman. But wait, let me not be a further victim of American propaganda—are Palestinians Arabs? Google is not going to answer this, so let me invite Suzanne into the kitchen.

While Suzanne and I open a (second) bottle of wine, I 'fess up and ask her to help me understand what it means that her husband is a thirtysomething man from Palestine. Her two-minute debriefing at my counter gives me a totally different insight than my personal travels through Egypt, Israel, Qatar, and the United Arab Emirates.

Palestinian people have never lacked culture or tradition, but they have been fighting over what they consider their land—in modern history—since 1967. In the United States we do refer to Palestine as the "occupied territories" on both sides of Israel. All Palestinians are not Arabs, though. Arabs come from Arabia—which technically is the peninsula at the junction of Africa and Asia. (The countries that constitute the Arabian Peninsula are Kuwait, Oman, Qatar, Saudi Arabia, the United Arab Emirates, Yemen, and Bahrain—which is actually an island nation off the coast.) They are Arabs. Geographically, parts of the Syrian Desert can be considered part of Arabia (which includes Israel and Palestine, as well as Iraq, Lebanon, Jordan, and Syria), but for these people, being an Arab has more to do with sentiment. So it's not safe to assume that any of these folks consider themselves Arab. Kind of like Texans in America don't consider themselves from the South—they are just Texans. And now that I see how much info I'm missing on a piece of the world, maybe I should get a weekly subscription to a British paper.

Or maybe I could come up with more reasons to keep Suzanne at my kitchen sink and have her fill me in. Looking at Suzanne, it would be impossible to guess her ethnicity, either. I understand, geographically, what it means to be half-Mexican and half-American, but Suzanne does not possess one North American Indian feature. Suzanne could pass for Danish as easily as Roman as easily as Argentinean. But I've run out of time to ask her more questions in private before she might wonder if I'm hitting on her . . . so back we go.

David is gregarious and not afraid to make inappropriate jokes, yet somehow he still seems perfectly polite. Which Seung says is because of his British education. David and Suzanne raise an eyebrow. I wonder why (inside my head) and Suzanne answers (outside my head), "It came with a price." I'm still wondering if these people really are paid spokespersons for interracial family planning. So now I'm asking intimate questions because I want some proof/answers/history/*dish*.

BORN IN PALESTINE, as the second child in a family of three, David began his education in Israel—at a nursery school run by Catholic nuns, of all people. He then attended a Palestinian school for a short while, but his mom or dad continually had to pick him up when situations erupted. "Older boys would stone passing cars in the occupied territory and all hell would break loose," elaborates David. Not one single day went by when David's school wasn't shut down at some point. For this reason, David was then sent away to an upper-crust English boarding school at eight years old.

On David's first day in England, he was separated from his parents to watch a movie in the library. "The movie was about Snoopy, and he never forgot it," replays Suzanne—as her husband has suddenly gone mute. "When the film finished, David's parents were gone." David wouldn't see his mother or father again for a long time. Nor was he allowed to write them. There are pictures from this period in David's life, of a little boy in his uniform standing proudly and alone at a train platform in a foreign country. This image breaks all four of our hearts at my dining room table tonight. Suzanne takes David's hand as she retells this for the grown man she loves, who she says still looks back to make sure that those who love him are not going to sneak out a back door when he leaves the room.

I look over to Seung, recalling the conversation I had with him last night—about how important it is to encourage children to talk to their parents. I can see on his face that this isolation feels all too familiar to Seung. In the summers, Seung and his sister were sent to Korea alone to live with their grandparents. And although he loved them dearly, all children seem to fare better when they can turn to a mommy or daddy with their most intimate fears and questions. And although his mother was always there for him at home, his father lived outside of the country most of his teen years. And when it came to his mother, Seung didn't always have enough words in common to discuss what he was feeling about typical childhood growing pains. So, even though both these boys had families that loved them dearly, feeling alone as children is something they can both relate to. I take Seung's hand and refrain from stating my case again.

David remained in England for all of his childhood until he was accepted into George Washington's International Program in Washington, D.C., and moved to the United States. He and Seung did their graduate studies together there, and America would become David's permanent home. He was living in Chicago after finishing his degree when he met Suzanne.

Suzanne's family moved from Mexico to Chicago when she was twelve. Suzanne spoke English at home with her mother and has always been a natural in social situations, so her move from one country to another was not as jarring as David's. After finishing college, Suzanne was working and living at home with her parents, as is the tradition in her family's culture. She was twenty-five years old and David was twenty-seven when she met him on a blind date.

"A friend of Suzanne's was dating a friend of mine," David explains. "My friend thought we would get along based on our humor. On the day of our setup, our friends broke up."

David called Suzanne to politely cancel, and she suggested they go out anyway. Suzanne confesses, "I never liked thin guys. And he was thin. And I had never dated a Middle Eastern person but David is so . . . English and funny and felt familiar. And he just kept coming around."

As David's name came up continuously, Suzanne's mom asked for "stats." Suzanne was confused and, moreover, shocked when her mother shrieked, "Muslim?" Like most Americans pre-9/11, Suzanne was totally unaware of how Middle Easterners, Palestinians, and Muslims are often perceived by the Western world. She had no idea how much prejudice preceded the seemingly kind and educated group of people she met in David's family. "But then my parents met David and they were very relieved," says Suzanne. She asked her father what he thought of her boyfriend after their first meeting. Dad told Suzanne something in Spanish that loosely translates to, "He was the only one wearing shoes." Meaning, he was the only contender he'd ever met for her.

Seung and I have to look at each other again and giggle. He is leaving in one hour to head back to D.C., presumably to have this exact conversation with his father. I wasn't wearing any shoes all weekend, but I hope the Chungs will see me as a contender, too. I can't wait to hear what they have to say—if I will be able to wrestle a word out of my boyfriend tomorrow night—but right now I'm trying to leave the dance floor open for Suzanne and David. I have a feeling Seung invited them here to warn me or at least manage my expectations of what his family might say, so I turn back to them in earnest.

SUZANNE IS COMFORTABLE in her own skin as she tells us her tale (and most of David's) but admits that people have always chided her that she's not "really" Mexican. She is light-skinned and well-off, and for her the most offending insult is when Latino people judge her. Suzanne speaks fluent Spanish and was raised in Mexico for twice the number of years she was reared in the States, yet most Mexicans consider her a *gringa*. Within the Latin community, Suzanne says, people judge one another by shade. Light-skinned Mexicans have an assumed sophistication because they are obviously not laborers and are probably of European descent. Just like many light-skinned Cubans assume a sophistication over their darker-skinned countrymen, as do many Puerto Ricans, Dominicans, etc. Which seems like a random thing to judge someone by, to Suzanne. Yet she softly supposes to us, with a hint of embarrassment, that her parents might have had more of an issue if she fell in love with a dark-skinned Mexican person, rather than a light-skinned Middle Eastern man.

I know in my own family's cultures, northern Italians call southerners *la gente de mura,* which translates to "dirt people," because they are darker in skin tone. In Ireland, the origins of the expression "black Irish" are debatable, but the subtext where I grew up was always the same. implying that dark haired Irish people are genetically mixed with Africans. David joins in to say his family's experience with *shade* is the same within the Middle Eastern culture. David is light-skinned but his father is darker. And his father diligently avoids the sun. For all his incredible achievements, Suzanne found it shocking to watch such an honored man jump between food stalls, desperate to stay out of the sun, in a city where he is the director of an entire hospital.

So, shade—within its own race, and to an outside race for sure— seems to conjure up a judgment about value. So much so that lightness or darkness seems inexplicably tied to the perception of *worth*. I think I was supposed to use the word *class* just then, but it's not just class or money or caste that shade inappropriately categorizes people into. It actually implies more or less value. And it happens all around the world—in our Latino, Middle Eastern, and European cultures represented here tonight in my apartment but also in the Southeast Asian, Persian, Arab, and African cultures we've all personally encountered. So why is darkness deemed "less than"? And if it's from something ancient, when major religions were first established or slavery was openly practiced, why does it still permeate today's culture?

As mind-boggling as this is, I should get back to the only two people I've met who don't have a race, culture, homeland, religion, or familial language in common—but no issues because their shades are equally matched.

"None of our parents had a problem with the other's race," David is saying. His family flew from North Africa to Chicago just to meet Suzanne. They immediately liked her "better than they like me," says David. Suzanne learned to cook Palestinian dishes so well that David's grandmother often says, "It's like she is Palestinian!"

THIS IS THE FAMILY relationship every mixed-race couple I've ever met wishes they started off with. My heart usually breaks at this point of getting to know other multiracial love stories, as I bear witness to the years people have wasted trying to persuade their family to just look at the person they have fallen in love with, rather than fear the person they are imagining. Could it really just come down to color?

I must be oversimplifying. This couple also had the Big Three going for them outside of their lightness/darkness skin match. Both sets of these parents dated (and in this case married) someone outside their own culture, and both sets of parents are highly educated and also well traveled. Any two of these ingredients would make the acceptance of another race, religion, or culture possible, but all three make perfection. In my experience with Seung's family, shade has nothing to do with our union. I believe what Seung's parents are really fighting for is culture, even though they call it race. I wonder if it feels less offensive to consider the mixed-couple "issue" a shade and culture problem—rather than putting it all under the combustible heading of *race.*

David's father took this whole discussion to the next level in a private conversation he had with his son. He told David he wasn't bothered by what race or religion his children married. He asked only that they choose a partner whose parents approve of their union. "My father feels that life always has something tugging on you that can pull your marriage down—money, stress, kids, work, something. With the addition of one parent who doesn't approve, your marriage will never survive."

WITH ALL FOUR PARENTS on board, Suzanne and David got engaged nine months into their courtship and set a date. They then very quickly surmised how to do everything they wanted—while making minor edits to the perception of things that might cause alarm or insult to an elder relative's feelings.

For instance: Their wedding was held in a church (even though Suzanne and her family do not practice Catholicism and David really wasn't even clear on who Jesus is compared with God) because that was the setting Suzanne had always pictured. So she found a Presbyterian order that would allow them a church service without any classes, converting, or proselytizing. As a couple they then printed two sets of invitations—one with the location of the church and one without for David's relatives in Palestine who might have taken this to mean David was disavowing his faith.

Maybe this seems hypocritical, but I find it thoughtful. It reminds me of my initial thoughts about Seung and me, before the war games began. I did not find it a burden to adjust my behavior to respect whatever Seung's relatives needed to see—because I didn't see it coming up all that much. Now that I'm listening to Suzanne talk, I'm thrilled to see it's true. Having also completed one tour of duty on the front lines of "biracial family feud," I also understand that I am allowed to holler back when my territory feels too encroached upon, allowing Seung and me to find our balance.

During their church ceremony, Suzanne's brother did a reading from the Bible and David's friend quoted Arabic poetry. "Our priest added an American Indian tone to the end of the ceremony, which everyone loved," says Suzanne. David adjusts, "Everyone who saw it—as it was removed from the 'Palestinian cut' of the video." A mariachi band came up full force as guests left the church and headed into the reception. During dinner Suzanne's father and uncle sang Mexican opera, which was followed by a Middle Eastern belly dancer. An American big band played for the duration of the reception.

Now I just want *to be* Suzanne and David. I look at Seung and either this story or the third bottle of wine has completely erased my poker face. Before I can say a word, he says, "I have to go. My parents are all that matters in my family and they like you as much as I do, so now I have to tell them my plans. But your new BFF is going to stay here with you tonight so you don't worry. Is that okay?"

Seung Chung arranged a babysitter for me because he knew I

would be nervous? Can we just sneak into the bathroom again for another make-out session before he leaves? I'm overflowing with love and hope and . . . wine. I kiss my lover passionately, completely forgetting that his friends are sitting across from us.

Seung gets up to go and David goes with him. (Their kids are back home in Chicago, but David still needs that advice about which city to take a job in, so he will head back to the hotel after walking Seung to Penn Station. Suzanne is having a slumber party with me.) We wave to the men as they leave, and Suzanne doesn't miss a beat.

"What's the scariest thing you want to know about being in a mixed-race marriage that you have been afraid to ask anyone?"

Wow. First, I ask if she will get me some water, to stall, so I don't blow this opportunity. When Suzanne returns with hydration, I tell her I have two questions and I want to take them one at a time.

"Have your kids ever been teased in school for being Muslim or Palestinian?"

I'm not just gossiping about Suzanne's family. Over the last nine months I have recalled every "Oriental" joke I ever heard in my childhood. I have dug up every slope, slanty, flat-faced, gook, chink comment—who smelled weird because of their weird food that they weirdly ate with sticks, all while wearing their pants too high, with thick glasses (because they can't see through slit eyes), who ruined the curve on test scores for everyone else because they were such geeks. Who all grow up and move to California and can't drive because they also can't see through said slit eyes. I also quietly mulled over all the lyrics about Chinese dirty knees, turning Japanese, and the TV shows, movies, and news reports featuring Long Duck Dong, stick-wielding Singaporeans, Laotian children without teeth or limbs, geisha girls, Thai hookers, Cambodian killers, Vietnamese hustlers, and expressions like "Jap-ing" someone out. I tried every one of these slurs on for size because I thought I should brace myself not only for how much this could hurt the man I love and our possible kids, but for what hell it might feel like to be the mother of someone who is teased for being a minority, when I myself am not one.

Suzanne also has the same cocktail of unique things in her off-spring that I might. Which is an ethnic last name, specific to a cultural group that may be presumed guilty until proved otherwise, depending on world politics. (Yes, clearly, I have spent some time thinking about this. But it's a closer reality than you might think. Suzanne's bag is filled with a decade of hatred against Muslims and two decades of American judgment against Palestinians—in this country alone. And I live in abject fear of the United States going to war with anyone in Asia within my children's lifetime, particularly Korea or China, and my husband or offspring being thrown into an internment camp. And as preposterous as this may sound to you, just consider—Guantánamo Bay.)

Suzanne says her kids have not been teased. But she has taken some minor precautions. When she and David found themselves preg-nant not long into marriage, they both thought to give their son an Arabic middle name to honor David's father. But David's father said, "Please don't." Grandfather said he has always felt the pressure that a man from Palestine lives with when traveling the world. Every airport check constitutes secondary conversations about "what holidays do you celebrate at home?" David's father had faith that his grandchil-dren would enjoy plenty of Palestinian culture and didn't feel they needed a label in a passport to prove their heritage.

Suzanne and David named their son Alexander James Zuaiter,

which is a wonderful mix of Egyptian, Muslim, and Christian names—none of which is specific enough to flag him. And not just flag him at the airport. When the coach is yelling at a soccer field or a girl is sending a Valentine's Day card or when Alexander himself is applying to college—none of these names is so specific that he can be "preconceived" as anything. However, when Alexander's sister came four years later, Suzanne and David were feeling more confident in their original idea. Sophia Iman Zuaiter was given her name to honor her grandfather's life (in Arabic, *iman* means "faith") and because Suzanne and David both thought it was beautiful. And so do I.

Today Alexander and Sophia are seven and four years old, respectively, and I wonder if this is too young to know if their cultural background will yield teasing. But I've got another doozy of a question anyway.

"Do your in-laws favor your son over your daughter?"

"Not really" is Suzanne's answer.

We nod at each other. Suzanne is thinking something and so am I. Who knows if they are the same thing, but I am just going to sit here for a minute and hope she will elaborate. Because for the first time tonight, I'm not sure I believe Suzanne.

"My husband's grandmother will ask me when I visit the Middle East: 'When are you having more children, Suzanne? When are you having more boys? You need to have ten more boys like Alexander." To add insult to injury, this woman's daughter-in-law is translating these whopper sentences from one woman to another. Suzanne is not having more children, but that is not a cultural argument she feels the need to have with an octogenarian. But saying that sons are more important than daughters is an idea that Suzanne can't quite let lie.

So she softly asks David's grandmother if all her daughters know she feels this way about sons. Grandmother says, "Of course!"

Because in Palestinian culture, daughters have to be married off. This still, today, requires monetary gifts at the time of a wedding. Daughters also have multiple opportunities to shame an entire family throughout any point in their lives. Nor are daughters privy to inheritances or owning land. They do not generally bring in income. If they can't produce a child, they can be shunned and possibly left and their family has to take them back. But most important, sons bring a woman power and good social standing. Sadly, this thinking is prevalent in many cultures outside America. Including Korea, for different reasons but yielding the same result. Suzanne doesn't feel it is her job to credit her daughter or any other with all they bring to the world—to an old woman she loves regardless of these views. She does feel comfortable schooling me, though.

"Diane, you're imagining downsides of marriage and motherhood by what you can conjure up on paper. The things that will be tough on you are not those kinds of 'issues.' What will be hard are the small ones that take you by surprise."

For Suzanne it was the inexplicable desire to baptize her son immediately after his birth. Her parents had warned her and David to talk about what religion they would raise a child in before getting married—but neither Suzanne nor David really had any interest in organized religion, so they didn't listen. And this need to baptize was not something Suzanne imagined or worried that she might feel. She was just as surprised as David. She was more than surprised, though, when her husband told her, "You can't do it."

Under Muslim law, inheritance is subject to living life as a good

Muslim. Meaning, if David's father were to pass away and he wanted to leave his home or his books or even a pair of shoes to his son or grandson, any inheritance he wishes to give can be contested by any member of his entire extended family. Inheritance can be revoked if any family member could prove that Alexander was not being raised as a Muslim. If, for instance, Alexander had been baptized. If that were the case, the Palestinian state could override a deceased grandfather's wishes.

Having never had any outside constraints put upon her relationship, Suzanne found this mandate grossly unfair. Given the horrendous weight the Catholic Church has put on baptism—that all babies go to purgatory regardless of sin without this sacrament (until early 2007, when the current pope revoked this notion)—the stakes were really high for her. As we are having this conversation seven years later, it is still through gritted teeth that Suzanne says they never baptized their son or daughter.

With an impending move to a bigger city, to one coast or the other for David's work, Suzanne would like to find an institution her children can visit once a week to develop a relationship with a higher power. She is not sure if that will be "Saturday school" for Muslim teachings or Sunday school for Christian ones, but she is open to either. At home their family celebrates Christmas and Easter, as well as Thanksgiving, Halloween, and every American holiday in between them. To honor Palestinian culture, Suzanne and David offer food and music, as well as trips to the actual old city almost every other year. "We do not celebrate Islamic holidays, but we don't celebrate other holidays all that much either because we try to revere our family members all throughout the year." Suzanne and David's children speak fluent Spanish with Mom and a cross between the Queen's English and American with Dad.

All of which, Suzanne then tells me, really doesn't matter. She says softly, trying not to offend me now, that I can't plan who my family will be before they exist any more than someone can plan who they or their children will fall in love with. She then puts her glass down and leans in closely to me.

"The work you have done to support Seung is kind and thoughtful and earnest but you have to let it go now—and just be who you and he are supposed to be as a couple. The rest of the world will have to adjust to you now, not the other way around anymore."

To which I am honestly left speechless. With no words, I pour the last few ounces of our fourth bottle of wine for Suzanne and myself and raise my glass to her. When she meets mine with hers, Suzanne says, "To love."

CHAPTER 7

GETTING AROUND MINE

"Oh, Diane! He has the
most beautiful hair!"
—PATRICIA FARR

T HE PEOPLE IN my family are rough. And unforgiving. They expect men to act like men, and their definition of "manly behavior" is narrow. I'm talking narrow enough to fit in a garden hose. I was pretty sure Seung was going to fail at his first meeting with my family because polite is not something in my brothers' playlist of acceptable guy behavior. And although Seung is multifaceted, his family's entire culture is based on respect. There is no disassociating this from him or, from what I can see, the rest of his people. Koreans are so polite they don't even assassinate Kim Jong Il, and he is starving most of the population in North Korea. How long do you think a short, bald, fat guy wearing a green onesie and Jackie O sunglasses would last as the leader of Italy? Or the mayor of Brooklyn? If either of those were the case, his ass would be buried in Grant Park already.

Therefore, I know Seung won't be able to just shut off his instinct to make a first meeting with the men of my family entirely about my father's comfort. I'm just hoping to inspire him to tone down the earnest, gentle, nice-guy side of himself and allow a bit of the cigar-smoking, scotch-drinking, hot rod–driving, eager-to-gamble guy's guy (that I like so much) to come out. Because my familial line of men respects a man you can't ignore. They expect a new alpha entering our herd to make a statement. And if you don't make one—they will make you into one.

So ten months deep into our relationship, two weeks after our D.C./N.Y. weekend, I still hadn't gotten many details out of Seung about his final conversation with his father, but I was coming home to L.A. for the weekend. I hoped in our quiet time together I might unlock the vault of Chung family discourses. Mind you, my time would be limited because my dad and two brothers were also flying in from Florida, New York, and Costa Rica, respectively. I bought tickets to a Cirque du Soleil type of event at UCLA—specifically because I thought it would be the perfect way for my men to meet Seung for the first time. Perfect in that it would take up half the night and Seung couldn't do any talking. Yes, that's right, Seung—the guy who I was just so impressed with for speaking two languages—is the one I wanted to shut up. So much so that I bought $450 worth of modern-dance tickets.

Armed with my conversation-proof show, I also warned Seung. I told him three times before my dad and my brothers flew in (because I figured five times would make him nervous but three times might prove that I wasn't kidding): "Whatever you do, do not be polite to them. They will eat you alive."

Seung is cool, so I know the men in my family will get it eventually; I just hope they might like him right from the start. So to that end, here we are in a black-box theater, watching other men throw women around in a slightly erotic and slightly skilled way. But it's not feeling right. It's actually feeling like a colossal mistake.

Before this performance tonight, I went to a rehearsal of this show to make sure it was acceptable for my familial frat. It's unfortunate that I watched a private showing of this troupe with the man who represents the company, who was selling me on them for two hours. He has a huge financial stake in the show and I am on television. Perhaps he thought I might bring some famous friends to see it. All this went right over my head at the time. Nor did I care that this man is not heterosexual. I didn't think sexual orientation mattered at that time. Now, with all the very, very heterosexual men in my family here, I'm thinking it does.

Because my brothers are seeing nothing but a bunch of guys in tights running on their toes. My poor father has just landed on the West Coast and is asleep in his chair. Seung and I are still newly in love, only three hundred days into our courtship, and will do anything just to be next to each other—and even he seems bored. But I know for sure this was an error in judgment as we're walking to the lobby during intermission and my brothers are telling inappropriate jokes about the dancers' "helmets"—loudly—and random strangers are applauding them. I'm bagging the second act and heading for a diner off campus.

At the diner, Frick and Frack—as my grandmother likes to call my brothers when they act moronic—are idling high with jokes aimed at me, the city of Los Angeles, and men in body stockings. This is the moment of truth for Seung. These are his choices: (a) make fun of the show even though I suggested it, planned it, was excited about it, and paid for it; (b) make fun of me with my brothers, even though they might turn on him for it; (c) defend me even though they are my family; or (d) ignore them and say nothing.

I think, maybe, Seung has found an even better option, as he is speaking to my dad about anything else that he is deeming neutral. My anxiety level is coming down, until I see that Frick and Frack have caught on. I know my kid brothers. They see this mature posture as a sign of fear. And now they are moving in for the kill.

We haven't even ordered when my siblings begin making inside jokes that they are going to order "dog" for an entrée because my father once infamously asked a Korean if she enjoyed that native delicacy. My father didn't know this would be insulting. My brothers do. I am actually feeling a little dizzy as I bury myself in my menu, trying to think of some way to throw Seung a paddle. My ears are ringing, so I can't be sure, but I think Seung might be laughing. As I steal a glance over at him, I see he *is* laughing. Yes, Seung! Get in there!

As if on cue, my youngest brother's pint of Guinness arrives. Seung asks my father, almost behind my brother's back, if he knows why God created beer. When my father shakes his head no, Seung whispers, "So the Irish wouldn't take over the world." To which my other brother visibly sits up at attention. How sad that I am encouraging my very respectful boyfriend to make prejudiced jokes right back at my family, but if this was a game of blackjack, Seung has just doubled down. He is now following up the Irish joke by ordering four shots of an aged scotch that none of my family members can possibly stomach, and insisting that any man who fails to drink this, in one take, will have to pick up the bill tonight. My father is laying down his arms, or, more precisely, raising his hand, saying, "I'm out—I'll pay." Before the waitress pulls out of Dodge, Seung takes my brother's dis on my dad (and Korean people) to the next level by ordering "Poodle Parmesan." The whole table bursts into shocked laughter, myself included. Each of us kids subsequently orders a dog entrée, while my father apologizes profusely to the flummoxed food server.

And a brother-in-law is born.

When dinner is done, I end up alone with my brother who is closest to me in age while waiting for the valet to bring Seung's car. While staring off into the abyss of the underground parking lot, my brother says, "Remember growing up we called every Asian person 'Chinese'?" I turn my face to see more of his, to be sure I correctly understand wherever he is heading with this question. I am pleasantly surprised to hear him say, "We were so stupid." Maybe the occasional prejudiced joke amongst family members has some medicinal purposes after all. My brother, having said all he needed to, then steps off the curb and walks into the darkness of the car park, moving my family one giant step closer to the twenty-first century.

Seung not only is "in" but has somehow made my people look at how we grew up. Yup, that's just another Seung Chung bonus, right up there along with his 1967 Lincoln Continental—turquoise blue with suicide doors—which is pulling up now. I get in and wave good-bye to the rest of my family as they step into their shitty rental and Seung laughs out loud at all of them. My father gives me a thumbs-up. I'm not sure if he is commenting on Seung or shutting up Frick and Frack, but the approval feels good all the same. Seung shuts my door and together we sail off into the Hollywood Hills.

I have only one more hand to play at this blackjack table, before Seung and I can get on with the rest of our lives. But, of course, she can be a m-o-t-h-e-r.

ON THE DAY MY MOM finally gets to meet Seung, she is panicked. Unlike Seung's mother, mine is fully aware that we are living together. She is so afraid that if I've made another Mr. Wrong choice, I may never recover from a second marriage-miss. My mother would never accept the word of anyone else in my family that Seung is okay, because the apple didn't fall far from the tree. If I am wise, she is older and therefore wiser and if I am a type A/overachiever she is a type A/control maven. As if the stakes weren't high enough for her, my brother thought it would be fun to set my mother up today.

My brother called at 4:00 PM, before my mom's 7:00 PM introductory meal with Seung tonight, and said, "Ello Mizzus Fah. Dis is Sing Chunnnng" in the thickest Korean accent you've ever heard. And what did my mother say?

"Oh! Hello, Sing! Sooo nice to hear from you!" My mother said this loudly and slowly because not only did she believe that Seung did not have a full command of the English language, she also thought he was deaf. My brother went on to pretend that Seung and I were at Kennedy airport and had no money for a taxi, so "You get in car and pick Diane and Seung Yong up? Now!" My mother was already searching for her keys, when her degenerate son finally burst out laughing on the phone.

As if I wouldn't have mentioned it if Seung didn't speak English fluently? It matters none that her own naiveté caused her to fall for this—Momma was now at DEFCON 1.

Seung and I are actually flying together to New York and are unaware of the tizzy my brother has caused. I am about to finish my last week of work in this city, and Seung is going to spend it with me. While here, we will take the weekend out by the beach where I grew up so Seung can meet my mom and her boyfriend, as well as see my youngest brother again, and both of us will meet his girlfriend for the first time. And we have more than enough money for cab fare, thank you very much.

We have more love than we did even one month ago also, because I have taken Suzanne's advice to heart. I have checked the family baggage and am trying to live my life with Seung as unencumberedly as possible. I think he feels my lightness and finally, today, decides to open up to me about his conversation with his father last month.

When Seung got off the train in D.C., he was shocked to find his father waiting for him at the station. As they walked to their car, Seung's father intercepted whatever Seung had planned to say by asking if *acaponey* would come to a wedding if Seung and I were to marry. Seung wasn't sure if *acaponey* was a Korean word or a bad version of an English one. He asked his father to repeat the word a few times before finally asking what an *acaponey* was. To which his father said, "Not what, who?" Seung, thoroughly confused, then asked, "Who is *acaponey?*" To which Seung's father said slowly, "A Capone-y?"

"Your father asked if Al Capone would attend my wedding if we were to get married?" I ask. Seung smiles and nods his head. "Was he kidding?"

He was. Papa Chung had no other questions or demands or threats or promises for Seung. Father let his son go. And was making Italian jokes at him to boot.

I, on the other hand, am not sold. "They had no fears? No rules? Nothing?"

"Well, they had one," Seung finally coughs up. In a gentle tone Seung explains that his mother said she was worried because I am an actress. Before I can say, "What . . . an actress . . . is this just an excuse to . . . " I hold my tongue for one brief second and think of Lisa. I decide to just nod in understanding and wait for an explanation—careful not to say something that could seem mean. This pause does allow Seung to find his way.

However, he can't even meet my eye as he says that his parents see magazines and gossip shows that actresses are always on the cover of or the lead story in—because they are getting a divorce. His parents have seen me on TV here and in Korea, and in magazines—both alone and with their son, too. They said to Seung that they hoped I "am different" and that his heart will be safe.

I not only find this to be a valid concern, but have worried about it as well. Seung is a good guy. If one of us was going to blow our union, even I would bet money the fault would be mine. Primarily because my job is a breeding ground for adultery, but also because I am the live wire in our twosome. Seung's mother's fear is based in fact and I imagine her lying in bed wondering if I am going to work over her kindhearted kid with my fabulous jet-set life, only to leave him in the dust when I run away with a soulless TV star. My heart is already in my throat, but watching Seung's strange smile and an inability to meet my eye has me confused. As I'm trying to suss him out, Seung mutters, "They are pretty provincial, huh?"

I have dated very few actors, but my mother was particularly obnoxious to all of them because she wanted them to know she was completely unimpressed with their "terrific-ness." My mother had the same fear that Seung's did, only my mother attacked because of it and Seung's mother humbly and bravely addressed the status variable.

I lean into Seung and whisper, "You know, your mom is a very smart lady. If I ever found myself close to a situation I should not be in as a married woman . . . I will now be thinking of her. I don't think she's provincial. I think she is brave, Seung Yong, and her point is well taken." Seung finally looks me in the face to check that I am being sincere. I then bite his ear to put that thought out of both of our heads forever and prove that I have no intention of being a good girl with him.

MY BROTHER WE ARE SEEING in New York has just moved in with his girlfriend, who was raised as a Hassidic Jew. Her family has just disowned her because of their union. And my mother, who was married to my dad for thirty years, has recently moved in with her first boyfriend since tenth grade—whom we jokingly call a "retired gangster" because he is so Sicilian. And of course I am bringing The Giant Korean. Where the hell can we six share an introductory meal?

At a Brazilian restaurant in midtown Manhattan, my mother gets plowed drunk over ceviche and steak. She is so nervous as she diligently questions Seung through our first course that she blows through three martinis in rapid succession. By the second course she stops asking and starts listening, before her ability to analyze Seung becomes impaired. And by the time I order dessert, and she her fourth drink, Mom was clearly thrilled with Seung and full-up on vodka.

She is actually downright jubilant about Seung. My mother is laughing so loudly at everything Seung says and does that my brother and I start calling her Mrs. Chung. Seung, having no idea how to respond to this, just smiles. To save him, I warn my mother that I am going to sit on her boyfriend's lap if she doesn't leave mine alone. I let this show of gigantic acceptance for Seung go on a little longer because frankly, he deserves adoration. Until the waiter clears the last dinner plate and my mom has a clear path to him. She immediately leans over and touched Seung's head. "Oh, Diane, he has the most beautiful hair!"

I ignore her hand and go right for Mommy's cup of vodka, taking it away.

"No touching the boyfriend, Mom." When my mother comes closer to me, in an attempt to recapture her drink, I "Irish whisper" that we should give Seung a little break now because this really has been a lot of English for him tonight. Momma Farr earnestly shakes her head yes and smiles longingly at Seung. She then kisses me on the cheek, full of happiness. And the cultural war games are over.

At least with our immediate families.

And unbeknownst to me, Seung Chung has just cashed out a portion of his life savings and purchased an engagement ring. Please remain seated as we venture into deeper water now, as the waves of desperation to prevent change may otherwise knock you down.

CHAPTER 8.

A RINGER ON

MY FINGER

"Your wedding is so inconvenient
for everyone but you."
—TAE CHUNG

S EUNG AND I have a little ski house together in Mammoth. We
bought it right at the end of a ski season when the market was at
its absolute most expensive. What we owe to the bank for it now is more
than its total worth. But three major events—that will be among the
most defining of my life—will take place in the three tiny rooms that
comprise this vacation home, making it worth every penny.

Now, at thirty-six, I have been working nonstop for fifteen years,
but still I don't have quite enough money to buy a second home myself.
I was very close to buying a party house in the ski town with friends,
but I'm thinking my days of a share in a crash pad are numbered. I
casually ask Seung, seven months into our relationship, if he has any
interest in purchasing a second home as an investment because I'm
considering . . .

"Yes!" is Seung's immediate answer. "Buy it! I'm in!"

"Really? Don't you need to see it?"

"Nope."

I love this man. He has so much faith in me, he is willing to go halfsies with me sight unseen—on a house. And it feels so poetic that we would buy something together here, on a mountain where we have so much history already. Seung and I spent our first New Year's together here, and I taught him how to snowboard over the course of that week. The altitude also caused us to fart in front of each other for the first time, and he saw me throw a full-tilt fit when I got stuck in four feet of powder and could not dig myself out. And he still loved me after both incidents.

I bring my dad, who is visiting at the time, with me to sign the papers for this condominium. On the long drive up to Mammoth, my father asks how much I know about Seung's finances. Not much, other than the amount of money I saw written on his down payment check for the place, I say. Cautiously, my father then asks how I would handle it if Seung suddenly couldn't make his half of the mortgage. I have to smile at my daddy. Not because I have such blind faith in my boyfriend, but because I am nothing if not a pragmatist. Buying real estate with anyone is a terrific avenue to fight with them. Buying real estate with someone you've know for less than a year—whom you are sleeping with—warrants writing *Dum Dum* on your forehead if you don't have an escape plan in place.

Before this drive to the deed signing, Seung and I have already filed side agreements with our attorneys about how we would disassemble our co-ownership of the condo if we were to disassemble as lovers. And this piece of paper, which was drawn up without fighting or funky feelings, feels just as romantic to me as everything else about this endeavor.

SO HERE WE ARE NOW in our little vacation getaway, just a week before the one-year anniversary of our first kiss in Mexico—and my life is so different because of what I share with Seung. I have left New York entirely and have a new TV job, eighteen minutes from our L.A. home. Two days after quitting *Rescue Me,* I was offered a job on *Numb3rs* in Los Angeles. I play an FBI agent on the show, but it's mostly behind a desk, as I am the resident psychologist. Which all means I can have babies while under this contract. And I get to actually live with The Giant Korean in both Los Angeles and our weekend getaway, where we have retreated today. I am laughing hysterically at Seung, who is right now pinned between the two-ton, possibly two-hundred-year-old pullout couch and the nearly completed green wall we are painting.

The furniture in the ski house is not only left over from the 1970s and rustic (read: *shitty*), but also mountain and bear themed (super shitty)! We are painting one wall in every room to try to make a kitschy theme of this mess. But right now we are laughing so hard because we are trying to move the ancient sofa and it's proving stronger than both of us put together. As Seung falls on top of me into the couch and an impromptu make-out session begins, life feels so perfect that I just have to stop it.

I pull back to look at Seung and confess that my life is not always as melodic as a top-forty music video where I stop what I'm doing to just laugh and kiss and smell the roses. As he starts unbuttoning my blouse, I feel the need to warn my man that my true nature is to paint every room in this condo and replace all the furniture in the same day, with no regard for food, going to the bathroom, or enjoying sex, especially if there's a half-painted wall and a couch in the wrong place. Seung tells me this is why we make a perfect yin and yang: because he would sit on this behemoth settee and watch football until the entire season ends before finally noticing the walls or the furniture for the first time. But together he makes me work less and I make him do everything I say—and isn't that what coupledom is all about?

I would have thought Seung's summation of why we make a great pair was in the interest of getting the rest of my clothing off, but instead he asks me if I want a tea from Starbucks. Amazed that he could be so "girlie" by wanting to take our chat to the next level rather than take me into the bedroom, I say yes, I'd love one. And off he goes, to hunt and gather tea with sugar for us while I finish painting the living room and "wallpaper" the kitchen with gift wrap and thumbtacks. I am so thrilled that I have the place to myself at this moment—to be as myopic as I like about completing a task—that I never even give his spontaneous departure a second thought.

I WAS UNAWARE THAT SEUNG bought an engagement ring when we'd been dating for just nine months. In hindsight now, though, I can guess the exact day because when he came home from this purchase he was a complete mess. Seung was so worried that he would never make enough money to have children and send them to a decent school in Los Angeles, not to mention afford mortgages and college tuitions and still have any time left for me. Thank God I took the time to sit him down and remind him that we had at least nineteen years to worry about college, and a whole month before the next mortgage payment was due on the Mammoth house, and thirty-five years of work left to fund everything we wanted to do in life. The fact that he was so shaken up should tell you that he bought an amazingly beautiful ring that was completely out of his price range.

And Seung has been carrying this not-so-little gem around in his pocket ever since! After eleven weeks of his life savings rattling around in his pants, bringing us to today—just one week away from our one-year anniversary as a couple—the stone must have finally burned a hole in said pocket. Because on the way to Starbucks to get our tea, Seung pulls over on the side of a mountain to place a call to my father.

Of course, I'll hear about all this later, but after a round of casual greetings, Seung cordially asks my dad permission to marry me. And then the phone cuts out. Both my father and Seung frantically call each other back, only to get the other's voice mail—three times. When Seung finally gets my father back on the phone, my dad reassures him that he did not hang up because of Seung's request. After putting Seung at ease about how my family feels about him, my father then decides this would be an appropriate time to warn Seung about how my family feels about me.

My dad solemnly asks Seung if he has "taken a long drive" with me yet. My sweet boyfriend would never even consider that my father would use this opportunity to make jokes at my expense, and so he begins earnestly selling my father on how much driving and flying we have done together (since I also tend to act like a jackass if I am late for a plane). My father is leading the witness as he seriously asks Seung if he is sure he still wants to marry me given these behaviors.

Does this annoy anyone as much as it does me? Especially considering I don't really live in a culture where anyone needs to ask my father permission for anything in my life. This is just a warm and fuzzy courtesy call, not a time for my father to vent about my less attractive behaviors. Would you have any more empathy for me if I told you that this was not the first time my father received this kind of call from a suitor—and he made the same jokes that time, too?

WHEN NIGHT FALLS, SEUNG IS getting ready to shower before we go to our favorite local restaurant, and I refuse to bathe. I have paint in my hair, up my arms, and all over my clothes, but I'm fine to just change my gear so I can continue to rearrange and hang pictures until the last possible moment. When Seung tries to cajole me into at least scrubbing off the spots of green and blue that cover my body, I instead pull out a pair of full-length gloves from my ski collection. The gloves cover me from my fingertips to my biceps. There is literally no possible way to get a ring on my finger.

Cutting his losses before I break out a chastity belt, Seung takes his shower and then steps out of the bathroom in a full suit. And I begin to wonder what the hell is wrong with him. We like to call Mammoth Mountain "just good enough." The snow is terrific, but that's about it. The service at everything, anywhere near the mountain, is the pits. It's so bad that sometimes we wonder if the locals are growing acres and acres of weed beneath the slopes in gigantic igloos, because that would explain why everyone is in such a fog. As well as why things take ten times longer than they should and fail to materialize no matter what you are promised or prepay for. We've found that consciously imagining that every hospitality employee is stoned keeps us from finding them as frustrating. Now, the farther you get from the chairlifts, the better things get, and the restaurant we are headed to is one of our favorites in all the world. But still, no one inside will be wearing a suit, unless they had a court appearance earlier in the day.

Seung tries to brush off his wardrobe choice by telling me that the bag he has up here in Mammoth is the one he took to a wedding we went to last weekend. And I believe this because Seung never packs until the last second. I am standing on a chair, drilling into drywall above the faux fireplace, when I see Seung heading out the door. I yell to him while balancing screws between my lips, asking where he is going. He says he's going to return the touch-up paint to the front desk of the lodge. So many of the owners of these condos come to Mammoth just for weekend getaways that the building has a little concierge service in the lobby for us. But now I'm thinking Seung is really sleep deprived, because it's eight at night and the desk is closed. Seung quickly tells me "it's fine" as he dives out the door. And why am I not suspicious? Because I really want to keep hanging this picture. So much so that I leave my bicep-length gloves on to get it up as fast as possible.

Thank God the screws are out of my mouth and into the wall when Seung walks back in, or I might have swallowed them. He has a bottle of champagne in one hand and a ring box in the other. And it still doesn't sink in. When I see he has tears streaming down his face, I am just concerned, and moreover confused, but when I look down from his chin and notice he is now wearing a silk tie, I drop my drill and gasp.

Still standing on the chair, I put both my hands into my mouth like a nervous child and say, "What are you doing? What are you doing?" over and over again. Of course, the wool from the damn gloves makes me feel like I am eating dog hair, so I promptly begin to gag. Seung is so choked up from emotion that he can't speak and I am coughing, and maybe even drooling a little, and at thirty-five and thirty-six years old, we are a general mess in the middle of the room with all the bear-motif furniture piled in around us.

From the bended-knee position, Seung says many beautiful things that I barely hear as he opens the ring box. And then I can't hear anything else at all.

I AM THE ONLY ONE LEFT of my high school and college friends who is not married. Only two in my circle of friends in Los Angeles are betrothed, but I am older than the rest. I have spent many years wondering and privately worrying if anyone will ever pick me as their partner. Yes, I have a lot of things going for me and I'm very cavalier, but inside I am still just a girl who's always wanted to be asked to the dance of the rest of my life as much as anyone else.

I actually wanted this so much that I stopped going to wedding ceremonies for a few years, as they induced panic in me. I also stopped practicing yoga because I would find myself looking down the line of mats in the downward dog position and see nothing but bejeweled ring fingers. There was no relaxing for me while my hand lay on the floor, spread and empty. I'm not even a fan of jewelry, but what an engagement ring had grown to represent for me had nothing to do with a diamond or its size. It meant that a person was willing to promise their heart and take all their hopes and fully invest them, with their savings, into someone they felt was worthy. It had begun to feel painful and embarrassing that I was not that person to anyone. Particularly as my window to have children would soon begin to close.

Another ring, one of desperation, had begun to form around my heart, and with each passing season it grew a little thicker. But here I am before the man I love, who is extending that question, that offer, and the other ring—the one that can encircle my heart so much for the better and act like the kryptonite I need to purge my desperate fears.

I get down on the floor beside Seung and hug him and we both cry. I breathe a strong "yes" to his request, right into his ear because I want to be sure he hears me. I am not a girl who is easily surprised and I don't particularly like it when I am, because I'd rather give a person the response they are hoping for when they make a big effort. When I'm really caught off guard I can't be as effervescent as the person deserves. I cannot even think about making a fuss for Seung and all he has done to make this moment happen because I am frozen still, just staring at this beautiful jewel inside a silky box. Other than giving the one-word answer I am required to speak for my part in this ritual, I am completely checked out. And I can't get back inside this moment with my *fiancé* because I'm stuck staring inside the box. I am actually afraid to even take the ring out because my mother once told me it was bad luck to try on another person's wedding ring. Even with Seung's proposal in evidence, it still seems implausible that this beautiful thing is for me.

Then, of course, I am nervous and my palms are sweating and I can't get the fucking gloves off. And Seung is so nervous he strolls over to the kitchen, opens the champagne for himself, and begins drinking it directly out of the bottle. In the fog of all this, I eventually reach in, take the ring out, and put it on my own finger—after which Seung and I walk to the couch like zombies and both just sit and stare at my hand. And now I wish I had listened to Seung when he was still my boyfriend and suggested I shower to get the paint flecks off my fingers.

IT'S A QUIET NIGHT, just for two, at our favorite restaurant, and then we are back on the couch to stare at my left hand some more. I ask Seung if he planned this, this way, and he says his only strategy was to do something simple and indicative of our lives together because he knew all the other events this decision would manifest would include the masses. Seung wanted our engagement to be just about us. Which in no way should imply that this is calm or easy for either of us.

My heart never stops racing and my head never stays in the present all night. We suck down that bottle of champagne he proposed with and then another and yet we are both still sober. There are so many people to tell and so many decisions to make and so much shit to do that I can barely breathe. I am a list-oriented person, and this decision begins what seems to be the biggest list of my life. Not just the actual physical wedding, but our whole lives forever after. And, of course, because there are all the expectations of others—the usual expectations of a wedding and the very particular ones of our families. So along with this beautiful sparkler on my finger, I can also feel an anvil making a new home on my chest.

We decide to take a break from looking at my bejeweled ring finger to call each of our four parents individually. Everyone is thrilled, except Seung's father, who doesn't pick up and so we just leave a message. We never hear back from Apa, but considering it's the middle of the night when we call Korea, it does not seem cause for alarm. We also call every person who will eventually become our wedding party. After they also jump for joy, we go back to staring at my hand until we fall asleep. Or rather, until Seung falls asleep and I lie there freaking out.

With Seung passed out next to me, all those years that I hoped for a partner, rather than just a lover, disappear in an instant and now all I can see are the challenges that getting married presents. The many challenges that I could fail at. My inner (fearful) child begins chipping away at the happiness I felt just a few hours ago and creates a space for me to hide in for the long term. A place where I would remain alone for eternity, but intact from disillusionment and the fear of change or the disappointment of others. A place whose entryway is etched deeply with five letters that I could easily get lost in forever— as this is a place called *doubt*.

Really, *doubt* should be a four-letter word, because it is a foul thing. And it causes subpar behavior. I value fear as an emotion, as it instructs you when it's necessary to run, hide, or hustle. But doubt makes you consider running, hiding, yelling, manipulating, testing, suspecting, and other unattractive verbs for no actual cause. And doubt has just taken me over and I seem to have no control as it permeates my whole being.

When Seung wakes in the morning I am sitting over him waiting. He gives me a big smile and I tell him this ring is way too big. That we need to leave Mammoth now and go to the jeweler *today* to have more prongs put on it so I don't lose the stone in the middle. Gee, what in the world could that be a parallel fear of?

Seung talks me into eating some food before getting on the road. I decide to make breakfast for him—for the very first time in our entire relationship—because now that I've been engaged for half a day, I feel the need to channel June Cleaver. During breakfast, I inform Seung that I will need final say over which of his relatives are invited to the ceremony. When Seung looks at me, wondering what evil spirit has suddenly taken over my body, I raise an eyebrow at him, inviting a challenge. My man is too smart to fall for this bait, but the mood in our relaxing-weekend-getaway-space is decidedly tense now.

While we are packing to get out of Dodge, I sit down on the bed and casually mention that when we have our children, Seung can pick any name he wants for them . . . from a list of names I then hand him. Seung bursts out laughing. He is thinking this is too absurd to be true. When could I have possibly formulated such a list? Um, maybe over the eight hours you were sleeping and I was becoming Bridezilla? All I needed was a pen and paper . . . and both of those things came with the furnished condo. So, here are your children's names.

Seung, obviously, is a patient man (given all of the other behavior I have already mentioned about myself, even previous to today). So rather than being angry with me, he is just plain old bummed out. He can't quite formulate why, but I can see the shine in his eyes from yesterday is gone. But by the time we are driving away from this special weekend and I am asking Seung if he would be willing to let us both date other people in our marriage, he loses his mind. As he begins slamming his hands on the steering wheel and asking me what kind of game I have been playing with him for the past year, even I realize that I have left myself.

If you look closely at the first three mandates, you can see where my self-doubts were born: a fear of losing him, a fear of his relatives judging me, and a fear of coparenting children. When these three missiles failed to start a fight, I believe I threw out the open-marriage request like an atomic bomb. I was not consciously aware that I was looking for a brawl or that my doubt had put me into a state of panic, but seeing Seung's despair immediately awakens me to the fact that I am trying to kill our union. Seung has too much at stake to recognize the fear behind any of my terrible behavior. Instead, he just begins to circle the drain with me. We fight and I cry for many hours on the way home from Mammoth this day. And although I argue with him to defend myself, I am already aware that I am the problem.

NOW, WITH SOME DISTANCE from that terrible day (the one I completely ruined not even twelve hours after the magical one Seung arranged for me), I can say that most of my marital fears had to do with what I brought to the relationship with Seung. I'm not at all sure that the short obstacle course of my "not being Korean," which we had just traversed, was even a small part of my emotional demise. I know that I could use these events, though—like so many people do when they pull the race card—to convince myself and anyone who would listen that those obstacles were evidence that this marriage was not meant to be. However, I was so lucky to have very long-term friends who could see past my well-spun story and tell me I was just afraid and I was handling it badly. Which forced me to run, not walk, to therapy before I did irreparable harm to my terrific relationship.

The therapist of course wants no part of my discussion about cultures clashing and how dangerous that is for me in a possible marriage to Seung. He wants to begin with my last engagement. Which seems like 150 years ago now. But the first thing I realize as he makes me recount every detail of my last brush with marriage is that none of my former boyfriends over the last decade came from the same culture as I did, including my former fiancé. Most of my previous partners do not even speak English at home. So who am I kidding that maybe I have an intrinsic fear that a marriage to someone of a different race or culture could not work? Finding something in common in a culture that's different from mine is exactly what I'm attracted to.

In fact, the only fear that both the therapist and I can even find in me—despite relentless searching for one due to race—is my own fear of failing. Which has nothing to do with my last engagement. Although that man was also born outside of the continental United States, he was a very good friend of mine whom I decided I liked in a romantic way. When he asked me to marry him, after only six weeks of dating, I believe it was his attempt to show me how important I was to him. When another six weeks passed and he realized he couldn't live up to all the promises of marriage, he was man enough to admit it immediately. Which, two and a half years later, makes me simply admire him.

My fear of failure, on the other hand, is entirely about who I am as a person. That is, an overachieving, workaholic, recovering beauty queen who wants to excel at things in the way a heroin addict wants to get a needle into their arm. And for better (in so many ways) but also worse while standing here on the precipice of a marriage, I have fallen in love with a man who has the same internal drive to achieve, win, and please that I do. Not only is he, like me, an oldest child, people-pleasing, overly organized Virgo by birthright, but he is also Asian. Which could be a generalization, but from my experience, it

As a single girl, my day was never complete without a little dancing on the furniture.

RIGHT
In turnout gear on the set of *Resuce Me* in uptown Manhattan.

BELOW
On the couch, talking about something silly no doubt, on *Last Call with Carson Daly*.

© MICHAEL SIMON

© MICHAEL SIMON

© AIKEN WEISS

ABOVE
In between takes on the set of *Numb3rs*.

RIGHT
Happy actress, just hanging out in boys briefs, for *Esquire* magazine.

© LAURA KATE JONES

LEFT
Seung Yong Chung, and
the camel he rode in on,
when we were dating and
visiting Morroco.

BELOW
Seung and I just after
we moved in together,
and just days before we
got engaged.

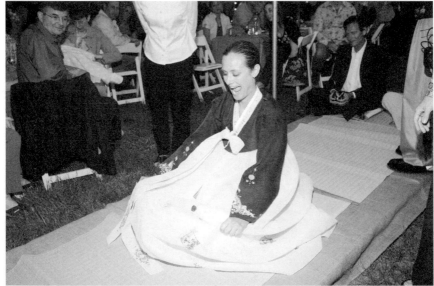

THIS PAGE
Seung's father, then mother, then me and Seung, outside the ballroom in Seoul, Korea—bowing to every single guest as they enter
our reception; Seung and I on the dais during the reception, wearing our heirloom hats.

FACING PAGE
Seung and I enter our Friday Night Korean Wedding Ceremony.
Seung carries me on his back as one of the rituals; I catch jujubees
with my dress for another. Seung and I seated center, surrounded
by our guests, listening to toasts under our homemade marquis
of lights.

THIS PAGE

Five Buddhist monks entering the ceremony site, Seung and I walking into our wedding reception; Diane Farr as a happy wife.

FACING PAGE

The wedding party heads to the ceremony, held in Mammoth Lakes, CA; "Just Married" in our Gondola en route to the reception; and our "other" first dance, after being pronounced husband and wife.

ABOVE
First comes love, then comes marriage, then comes three kids within sixteen months. Beckett (three years) clapping hands, Coco (two years) sits on mom's lap and Sawyer (two years) has a hand on Daddy's (or Apa, as they call him in Korean) chest.

BELOW
Lisa and Dave, as well as Jennifer and Sonu, on their wedding days.

is like tripling the desire to do right and do well, firstly for Mom and Dad, and then for everyone else after them.

So for Seung and me, merely figuring out where Mommy and Daddy's needs end and ours begin is hard. This takes much deciphering by both of us, together and individually, and then weekly when I ask him to please join me in therapy. Although this inability to find the line—of what I need versus what is expected of me at my wedding—is not uncommon in couples of the same race or varying ones, neither Seung nor I can completely remove ourself from thinking about how our wedding and our marriage will affect his family—specifically because of race. And not even because of any actions or postures his parents are currently taking but, again, because of who we are as people.

In actuality, Seung's parents say nothing about their needs for our wedding. It even takes seven days until Seung gets his father on the phone after that first voice mail from Mammoth. Although this was unsettling to both of us initially, when Apa does call it's immediately obvious that Seung had called a wrong number in Korea! His father has no clue that anything transpired between us, and when Seung tells him our news, his father is filled with excitement. I am suspicious during the call, and immediately after, and . . . for most of our engagement, waiting for the other shoe to drop, but Seung's parents continue to pleasantly surprise me just as they have from the first day I met them.

SEUNG AND I ARE BOTH sure we want to get married over the course of a weekend, rather than just having a ceremony and reception in one day. At least two-thirds of our guests will need to fly to our big day—and that seems just too big a trip for just one day of celebrating. Plus, we got together as a couple at a destination wedding in Mexico and saw how bonded the entire group became. Seung and I are hoping that three days of activities and time together in a new place might do the same for our families—all of whom will be meeting for the first time at the rehearsal dinner in Mammoth.

Seung's top priority for our nuptials is having as much of his family present as possible and mine is to put every single person in one hotel where there is absolutely no need (or possibility, if I can find a way) for anyone to drive drunk.

We discuss the possibility of a New York, D.C., or Los Angeles wedding, but the costs of a wedding in these cities seem prohibitive to both our main wishes for this day. Super early in our dating process we also decided not to take a trip to Seoul as a couple because, as Seung said at the time, "If we get married we will go to Korea then." So now we also briefly consider having our entire wedding in Korea. But because we fear we wouldn't get to enjoy the country because we would be so busy looking after friends and family, this plan dies a quick death, too. After which it seems like all of the places we call home are cut as contenders for the big day. Until the answer finally comes to us and it feels so obvious.

We will get married in Mammoth. In summer, when the snow is melted and the Tioga Pass is open, Mammoth is twenty minutes from Yosemite National Park. Despite the season, I have skied almost every Fourth of July there for the past ten years, so I know a late June wedding would allow friends to ski by day and attend wedding events by night, as well as fly-fish, hike, and horseback/motorcycle/snowmobile ride around the Sierra mountains and lakes. The best of both summer and winter seasons will be available to all. Plus, the plethora of national parks, as well as central and Northern California vacation options before or after our event, make us feel like a summer wedding on the mountain would be perfect for us and our guests.

UNFORTUNATELY, THERE IS NO air service into Mammoth. But if I could find a way to bring all the guests up to the mountain together, it would make my dream of a drive-free wedding a reality. So perhaps I could bus *everyone* to the mountain from Los Angeles? Five hours away! And then put every guest in the same lodge and have them walk to our events?

Yeah, not so much. After some initial inquiries, there is not one restaurant or venue in Mammoth that can hold even one hundred people for a meal. And we aren't serving just one meal—we are planning on three: a Friday night rehearsal dinner, a Saturday night ceremony (then reception with dinner, followed by dancing), and a Sunday morning brunch. And keep in mind that this is the town where the entire hospitality industry seems to be sky-high on marijuana, so I can't really assume they might step up their game for our wedding. Which leaves Seung and me with one massive option if we are actually going to commit to getting married here . . . including not only busing in all the guests, but also bringing in all the food and staff for it, and building every event under marquis tents in open fields around the mountain.

Now, let's face it, this kind of plan puts me on par with Julius Caesar where ambition is concerned. I only vaguely understood at the time that this kind of undertaking means worrying about things that no bride should ever have to think about. Like transporting porta-potties into a national forest, as well as six hundred chopsticks. Lest we forget secure parking in a mountain town for fifty-person tour buses and learning how to maintain a wedding cake in high altitude, as well as the life expectancy of fresh flowers in thin air. And emergency medical services for pregnant and elderly guests at ten thousand feet, bear whistles, alternative shoes for women in the grass, blankets in case of a cold spell, gondola transportation around snowy areas, lighting that can be installed the day of and moved to various locations over the course of a weekend. Oh, and shlepping generators, a wooden dance floor, a DJ, and his equipment into a field, and so many more incredibly daunting things that has nothing to do with what I am *supposed* to be worrying about.

And I mean really worrying about, like my recently divorced parents being in the same room together for the first time, and which of our religions to embrace for the ceremony and the rest of our lives, as well as how to include the Koreans and their language in some way so they might even understand what is happening as their son/nephew/cousin gets married. And how I will get from this tiny town on the side of a volcanic hill all the way to Asia the next day.

Cue my mother, who steps in to forbid me from having my wedding in Mammoth! She insists that adding that much pressure onto Seung's and my relationship is just me trying to sabotage our union. Which is probably true, but she might as well have signed a deposit check for the rental tents with that warning, because all I hear is: "You can't handle this." And that is all the inspiration I need to get started.

That's a literal "I," by the way. American wedding coordinators seem like babysitters for rich women and their mothers to me, who give everyone the same thing for every wedding, only packaged slightly differently according to assumed income. There is no way I am getting caught up in that mess. And in just my first five phone calls, it is immediately clear that using the word *wedding* when asking for a quote automatically doubles or triples the price of anything, from napkins to trash removal! So I decide then and there to arrange all of this myself, in between takes on my TV show, starting by telling vendors that I am running a conference in the Sierras.

AT ALL THE LOCATIONS we visited, the largest event held in Mammoth or the surrounding towns was for 150 people. Seung and I settle on pushing the envelope to two hundred guests. We agree that more will go wrong than right, but Seung's first priority will be met and so will mine.

We decide to risk working with the stoners who run the actual ski facilities for just one of our events, albeit the big one—the wedding ceremony. Considering it will only be thirty minutes long and requires no food or drink, we think maybe they can handle it. If they get it right, we'll become husband and wife at the midpoint of the mountain on an outdoor patio, fully walled in by glass. Our guests will have a 365-degree view of the entire mountain range, covered in snow, while basking in eighty-degree weather on our platform. The "catering manager" (and I use that term like "Santa Claus," because that's about how realistic a manager she was) is required only to turn the gondola on when my guests arrive, have 150 chairs available for my siblings and wedding party to set up the morning of the event, and have someone ready to push PLAY two times for music. Seems plausible even for a stoner pretending to know how to run an event, right?

Probably not for a bride who is obsessive about paint in a three-room condominium, though! Can you imagine how meticulous I'm going to be about a wedding I've waited until I was thirty-six years old to plan? So, to keep the control freak within me from freaking, I ask the best producer I know if I can pay her rate for the weekend to "produce" my wedding. She will be the director of the day, whom I will give a notebook to—detailing every fifteen minutes of all events from Friday to Sunday—along with a staff of production assistants from my television show, FBI-grade walkie-talkies that they can use to communicate with each other, four party buses and union drivers, all at her disposal to corral my guests. I'm also giving this producer all of my incredibly capable Irish relatives, who are the very definition of hardworking. She will have ten people available to her, alongside the five assistants, before every event to set up anything they need. Yes, controlling people are annoying—unless they're really, really organized. Or at least that's what I'm telling myself.

No sweat! says the bride-to-be.

And really, I thought we could handle this. I know how to party and Seung knows how to wrangle. And unlike what we saw in both our parents' marriages, we have an active interest in learning how to communicate with each other. So after our first fight about wedding logistics, I go out and buy two clown masks. From that point forward, anytime we discuss the wedding, we each have to wear a big red nose, huge ears, and a comb-over toupee. This never allows us to take ourselves too seriously when planning what is really just going to be an epic party.

✳ ONE OF THE MORE IMPORTANT THINGS SEUNG

and I discuss, sans the clown getup, is religion. I had learned from Jennifer and Sonu, as well as Suzanne and David, that this discussion needed to happen.

Seung calls himself Catholic and I was raised as one, attending Mass every week. But Christianity was not a faith I wanted to pursue for my family, so I need to ask Seung how he would feel about a Buddhist wedding. His immediate reaction is to balk, saying without even thinking, "We have to have a Catholic mass because that's what our parents would want." And that statement is the exact reason why everyone should go to couples' counseling before getting hitched. Because Seung and I have recently learned in counseling that we must separate our parents' needs from our own. That is by no means saying we have to ignore our parents' wants and desires, but rather that they are not conjoined with ours.

When I remind Seung of this he restarts our talk, saying he personally didn't really have a preconceived idea for the ceremony. I ask Seung how many sacraments he has completed as a Catholic, to which Seung answers, "What's a sacrament?" and the Catholic option is off the table.

I have completed all the sacraments (milestones that Catholics require to consider someone a practicing member of their faith), but in order to be married in a Catholic church, or even off-site by a Catholic priest, many parishes require completion of these events, including classes and fees for Seung and then another series of classes called "pre-cana" for both of us. I don't have to get very far into this diatribe when Seung says, "Next option!"

From here, I go digging under our bed to take out Seung's family photo album (a.k.a. a shoe box) and unearth photos of his grandfather's funeral. This is something I've been thinking about for a long time, and now seems a good time to bring the discussion to light. Seung was in middle school when he and his father flew from the United States to Korea for his grandfather's burial. Seung had been very close to this man, as he and his sister had spent every summer alone with him and their grandmother during elementary school. So later, at his death, Seung also had a part to play.

As I sit with Seung now, I can point out the specific reasons why I have always felt his family is Buddhist. His grandfather's funeral was a Buddhist ceremony, which all of his relatives clearly knew how to participate in. There are also several other holidays pertaining to honoring deceased relatives that I know his family subscribes to. I understand that once living in America, Seung's mother frequented a church and that they celebrated Christmas at home—but I believe this was either something Ama found available in her native tongue or something she was embarking on as part of her own Americanization. No matter what the reason, these photos of Seung's grandfather's funeral procession, prayers, and burial make me certain that his family will not react in horror if we have Buddhist monks presiding over our union. Seung is coming around to my idea, but he brings up a valid point—that although I follow my own dharma, I don't attend a temple regularly, either.

So we jointly decide to find a Buddhist temple together—to join as a spiritual community for our family—and to ask five monks to come and bless our marriage. (Three monks perform a Buddhist funeral and four is not a number that sits well for ceremonies—so five would be the ideal number if we can find that many who are willing to travel.)

Seung likes all these ideas as long as we can still celebrate Christmas in the "American way" with our family. Which I want also, as well as Easter. I also add that one of my favorite things about attending a mostly Jewish high school was going to friends' houses for Shabbat. I loved sitting by candlelight and talking with families over dinner, and I tell Seung that I want to borrow this tradition for our family, too—thus birthing our hodgepodge of Buddhism, Christianity, and Judaism in our home. Although some might consider this a cultural mess, we also eat Korean and Italian food one-quarter as often as we eat sushi in our house—so I like to think of it as the American way.

Seung then jumps ahead and asks if I imagine the monks presiding over our wedding ceremony or just merely overseeing it with good vibes. I'm hoping for the latter, but this brings up another issue. I know it's possible to go on the Internet and make anyone a minister. At the wedding Seung and I got together at, the couple had their friend, who was a male dancer in real life, officiate their ceremony. My oldest and dearest friend, Barry, from elementary school, who lives around the corner from me again in L.A., is so smart and empathetic I know he would be terrific at this minister job. Seung has also adopted Barry like his own brother—so much so that they travel around the country once a year to watch each other's favorite college football teams. So I think Seung would be into this . . . but my fear is that some of Seung's relatives are actual ministers. These cousins are on Seung's mother's side and although we don't see them much, I really like them. If I fear insulting them and I've only met them twice, how on earth is Seung going to reconcile having a Jewish lawyer marry two Catholics in a Buddhist wedding ceremony, when three actual religious pundits are in the audience?

"Barry is a great idea!" says Seung.

"But what about your uncles who—"

"Barry is perfect. He knows us both well; he will get the importance of the job, and the levity. And you can write the ceremony with him. Actually, we can all make it together."

"Okay, but I'm just saying—"

"Done!" says Seung, who is so excited I have no recourse.

I try my last resort. "Don't you care that your parents won't understand one word of your wedding ceremony if the whole thing is in English?"

Seung's immediate answer is no. "Because they'll understand the Korean wedding ceremony," he tells me.

The what?

* WE ARE HEADING TO A DINNER WITH SEUNG'S relatives—the usual relatives (who are not usually warm toward me) and some new ones who are visiting from Korea. This visiting uncle of Seung's is the oldest male of all his father's brothers, making him and his wife the mac daddies. They and their two grown daughters all speak at least four languages at home. Their daughters are slightly older than Seung and I, and went to prep school with a former president's children. Both these women earned impressive undergraduate degrees at top American universities and then were recalled right back to Korea, to marry men their family deemed appropriate. All of which is making me want to sing "Baa Baa Black Sheep" because that's how I think I will be treated over dinner tonight.

Except that now I am marrying an eldest son. Which could

make things better or worse for me. Maybe I'll become the Cinderella of this zero-generation interracial wedding story tonight!

I'm also kind of interested in the father of this new branch of Chungs. This uncle had a stroke several years back, and his two highly educated daughters, who now have two children apiece with their appropriate husbands, took care of their father every day of his recovery. Korean culture holds family in the utmost esteem, but I can't imagine being a working woman, with small children at home, having the means to provide in-home care but instead choosing to drop everything to nurse my father back to health. I find the humility of the act awing. And admirable. As we drive to dinner, Seung is remembering his uncle as wicked smart and always elegant, as well as the best golfer in the family. Seung is actually nervous to see him because he imagines his inability to speak, in the aftermath of the stroke, a tremendous loss. "Like a library burning down," says my creative fiancé. So as much as I'm dragging my heels, I am also optimistically intrigued.

But I can only half-concentrate on the relatives I'm about to meet because Seung is also telling me about all the things we "will be doing" in our Korean ceremony. Which is something I've just learned about tonight. And yet it seems to be a given. A foreign and silent Asian ritual, performed in silk robes before all of our guests, is right up my alley, but the ceremony does not sound like a simple thing. Seung *thinks* there are, like, twenty rituals that comprise it—over two days—but also *thinks* we only have to do about five. *Five?* How long does each one take if twenty take two full days? This is what I want to ask, but it sounds a little pointed, so instead I open with, "What are the five rituals?"

Seung can think of one that has something to do with me giving gifts to his family and him bowing to mine. Then there are other bows to him and at some point he also has to carry me on his back. For the ceremony, there has to be tea and there has to be fruit. Then he thinks there are some other cakes and offerings present, specific foods that are made only for a wedding. Oh, and his relatives get to tell me what to do and I have to put my head to the floor before them.

Stop! So in the middle of our actual wedding ceremony—the one we're planning for midway up Mammoth Mountain that's supposed to last only thirty minutes—I have to do a wardrobe change and then serve food and tea and fully prostrate myself? And, oh wait, at some point my future in-laws throw food at me and I have to catch it. *With my mouth?* Like a dog?

Is there a hidden camera in this car? 'Cause this is a joke, right?

From what I am learning now, there is no video rolling on me and I am actually supposed to catch the food with my dress, not my mouth. Which doesn't sound all that much less degrading.

Breathe in, breathe out.

I'm just gonna let this lie for a minute because there will be cousins at this dinner who are fun and cool guys—and we're almost there. I will save all of my questions about this until dinner—especially since I have a feeling that Seung has only a minor grasp on this event I'm to star in, which has no script yet.

ONCE WE GET TO THE restaurant and to our private room, I can't help but laugh out loud. The Khun Ama (wife of the older brother of Seung's father, who lives locally) is in charge of this shindig and has set up a kids' table for Seung and his cousins. No one at the kids' table is under age twenty-eight, but still we are off in Siberia. For a brief moment I wonder if this table was set up to keep me away so the family could talk freely, but then I remember that the elders speak to each other in Korean whether I'm present or not. So the banishment can't have anything to do with me.

The super-fancy daughters of the visiting aunt and uncle are home in Korea with their families, so it's just me and the male cousins tonight. And I must say, for all my misgivings about the Chung aunts, their kids are kind, polite, and fun to hang out with, and they dote on one another the way you imagine cousins should. No matter what fault I find in Seung's relatives, there is no getting around the A+ they deserve on the outcome of their children. Children who are currently treating me like the princess bride.

All of the boys are so excited for Seung's wedding. When I begin probing for details on Korean weddings, I'm shocked that none of them knows a single thing. They are all unmarried males, yes, but not a single one of them can remember a single thing from any of the Korean weddings they've ever attended. When I ask them how this can be, the answer is that no one under age fifty has ever been to a Korean wedding.

So I'm required to plan and participate in a cultural milestone that your family never even included all of you in?

I want to ask this but I know the answer is yes and I know why. Because it's one thing for two Korean or Korean American people not to have a traditional Korean wedding, but it's much more important for Seung to participate in a Korean wedding now, since he is not marrying a Korean. And in truth, I kind of agree with this. This ceremony is an indication that we plan to include his family's culture in our family. So rather than ask any more questions of "the kids," I turn my head to the "grown-up" table, because these people are the other reason I am going to do this ceremony. Truth be told, I'm not really sure what the hell it is I'm wanting to do as a promise for my future and a statement to them. And whatever it is, I certainly don't want to do it wrong, because this table full of people before me—they will judge. They may even heckle me on the day if I get anything wrong. Really, they might.

These elders have all the information I need, but how will I get it from them? If I just flat-out ask, it would be like my saying, "Could you just give me a quick hit list of your wedding ceremony so Seung and I can do a dog-and-pony show at an otherwise American event and then get on with our very American life?"

Maybe not. Let me follow in the footsteps of Jennifer and not take my own insecurities and project them onto others. Instead, like her, I should give these family members the benefit of the doubt and see what comes. Because why would they, who have a vested interest in Seung's life, want to shoot me down when I'm trying to make an homage to their traditions? I'm about to take a big breath in, sit up straighter, and muster up the courage to address the aunt closest to me, when suddenly one of the uncles calls out my name.

Hearing him call me in his very strict tone immediately takes me to a flashback of Catholic school. My eyes widen in fear as I look to this man, who is the husband of the aunt who jabbed me about my parents' failed marriage. While waiting for his command, I realize this is the first time I've ever seen him in person. He is the Khun Apa (older brother of Seung's father), who lives in Asia most of the year, making as much money as possible for his family (from the rules we reviewed earlier). As does my future father-in-law in Korea, and so many of this generation. The room goes silent because an elder is about to speak to a wee one. I have to pinch my leg to snap myself out of my fear. The 1970s are over and no one is going to hit me with a ruler! I'm a grown woman and these people are not my parents. They are not even Seung's parents. What is this white-haired man going to do to me with his words across a crowded restaurant that could really harm me, anyway?

But the guest of honor, Seung's visiting aunt, has just cut Khun Apa off. The visiting aunt is saying in perfect, cordial English: "Diane, we saw you in a magazine on the plane on the way here."

Holy God, have I done any half-naked thing in *Maxim* in the past year? Or *Esquire?*

"It was a picture of you and Seung Yong in a tabloid, announcing your engagement and showing your ring."

Praise be to *somebody*. Everyone laughs and tells their story of having seen it and the cousins add how hard they laughed at Seung. Then there is a polite pause, and I get the feeling this is my turn to speak back. I share an innocuous story of my mother leaving me a voice mail that she saw Seung in a magazine and how excited she was, never even mentioning that the story was about me—just that it was so fun to see Seung. The cousins giggle, but when they realize the parents are not laughing they stop.

It takes me a moment to realize I have just called my fiancé "Sing," which is what everyone including his cousins and his sister call him— but not his elders. Either they didn't understand my story because they have no idea who I'm talking about or they are condemning the Americanization of his name. And this silence is so embarrassing that

I will never ever forget to say his name in the correct Korean pronunciation in front of his relatives for the rest of my life. Or as close as I can get to it, as it's a mouthful. Seung Yong Chung sounds something like *sung-young-chung*. Yes, they all do rhyme. Which not only invites teasing but it makes it really hard to say them all together. So hard, in fact, that when Seung was five years old the kids on his block in Maryland started to call him "Sing," and he has been deemed so ever since. Except, of course, at this table.

But I am also a performer and this is not the first bomb of a joke I've ever told, so I am perfectly equipped to smile and invite everyone to move on. I now tell the visiting aunt and uncle how excited I am to meet their daughters and that I hope to see them at our wedding. And now the whole table laughs. At what? I'm not really sure because then there is a quick discussion in Korean while everyone stares at me. And finally, Khun Apa, who originally ordered me to attention, speaks.

"Why are you getting married in Mammoth? It's so inconvenient for everyone but you."

This is the first mention of Seung's and my impending wedding. No one has actually congratulated either one of us. Nor inquired about our plans. Nor asked if my family is excited.

"It's actually not all that convenient for us, either," I offer.

I stop at that because it's clear no answer would bring a kind response. I continue to look my soon-to-be uncle in the eye with a smile. This goes on for quite some time, until his wife, perhaps not liking the silence at her dinner party, says, "Okay, children, go back to talking amongst yourselves." I turn back to the kiddie table—and that's that.

So, in fact, nothing is different now that we're engaged. Same self-centered focus from Seung's family and same rudeness in their delivery.

Did I mention that I'm not changing my last name?

* WE ARE WALKING BACK TO OUR CARS ACROSS a giant hotel lobby, when I find myself in stride next to the visiting aunt. She, like all the other Chung wives, is very beautiful. She also carries herself like old-fashioned royalty. I'm not sure if it's her amazing posture that makes me stare at her, or the fact that she honestly seems interested to talk to me. She asks me sweet questions about my postwedding trip to Korea and about Seung's sister and shares her hopes to introduce me to her children. I'm so flabbergasted by this show of warmth that I mark it in my head to ask Seung if she is "allowed" to be kinder because she is the wife of the eldest and has no need to jockey for power.

Maybe it's because of my girl-crush on this new aunt that I just blurt out to her—with the Khun Ama present and Chagun Ama (wife of the younger brother of Seung's father), who are now waiting for their cars—the question I've been dying to ask all night

"Thank you all for this lovely dinner. And I was so excited to see you all tonight because Seung has just told me that we will be having a Korean ceremony at our wedding. (They nod. They are with me.) And I'm very confused about it because there are so many parts. Is there anything that you could tell me about your ceremonies that would be particularly important to know?"

The new aunt just smiles, and the two I know laugh out loud.

Funny how there was no laughter at my one actual joke tonight, but everything else I say is hilarious. Well, before I condemn, let me see if maybe this is just a language barrier. I will ask for help on a smaller scale.

"Or perhaps you could tell me about the food? Specifically, the cakes? I understand there are particular desserts we should have present at the wedding ceremony?"

I'm losing them. They are giggling and talking amongst themselves in Korean. I turn to the new aunt, looking for a life raft because now I just feel like a fool. The tone she displayed earlier makes me feel cautiously optimistic again, that she will at least help me to save face while the others are treating me like an underclassman whom they are just too cool to speak to directly. "Is there a name or a phrase for the kind of cake I am meant to buy that you could share with me? I speak a few languages myself, and I could probably remember the words or at least tell them to Seung. Or maybe . . . "

The visiting aunt is just smiling at me now. She is no longer listening. As an actor, I have become very attuned to when my costars are listening and when they are just waiting to say their parts. And in this moment, I can see this aunt has her answer in her mouth already and is just waiting for the opportunity to set it free.

"You're not going to be able to just buy cake. This is a complicated ceremony. And very important to our culture. I'm afraid you won't be able to do it."

Then this woman—who was so kind just moments earlier—turns and walks off to her car with her sisters-in-law, leaving me kicked to the curb in a way I don't think I will ever forget.

I AM MANY THINGS, but a *competitor* is somewhere near the top of this list. And Seung's aunt's misinterpreting my need for information and using it to underestimate me gives me an incredible upper hand at this war (did I say war? I think I meant wedding, but you get my drift) on which I'm about to embark.

I'm smiling and waving as the relatives pull away because their condemnation is only a slap in my face if I let it end here. My hand is raised because I intend to swing it now also—when I knock my Korean ceremony out of the park. Not only will I be able to "do it," but it will no longer be a little skit in the midst of my actual wedding. I will throw a full-scale Korean event for my Friday night rehearsal dinner at my wedding weekend—and silence these narrow-minded people once and for all. And their ceremony will then be dwarfed by my bigger, better *American* ceremony the next day.

I am trying not to storm off into Seung's sports car, or slam the door, to give away how incensed I'm feeling, but Seung is racing out of the parking lot anyway because he can see my face is bright red. I refuse to discuss this with him because then that woman would win. Rather, I'm dialing my phone. Because I am now officially done hiding behind the anonymity and advice of strangers. Now I'm calling my people with whom I can be frank and candid, and maybe even show a little of my newfound *rage*. My first call is to my friend Natalia because I want a goddamned New Yorker in my corner who is going to tell me exactly how to beat these people at their own exclusionary game.

'Cause it's on.

CHAPTER 9.

NUBIAN FASHIONISTA

LOVES WHITE BROTHER

IN NEW YORK

"I always knew Jake and I would make it;
I just wasn't sure if his mother would.
I still think she might drop dead from a
heart attack on her way to our wedding."
—NATALIA

NATALIA AND JAKE are a lot like Seung and me. He's an
easygoing, understanding man who may be the only person
on Earth who can handle the intensity of his smart, capable, funny,
yet "deadly as a weapon with her words" woman. And, in truth, Natalia makes me look timid. So hang on . . .

When I met her, Natalia was being interviewed on the evening
news over a sparring match she'd just had with Princess Michael of
Kent, the Queen of England's cousin through marriage. A mutual
friend of both of ours introduced me to Natalia to witness the fireworks she was about to set off. I stood on a soundstage and watched
this fantastic force of a woman with my jaw on the floor—knowing I
wanted her as a friend of mine.

Over the course of this news conference I'd come to learn that Natalia had been eating with friends in a downtown New York eatery, Da Silvano, the day before. Her party of six was composed of all well-connected media people, including two on-air entertainment reporters, who had all been asked to form a board to save a fledgling African American magazine—because all six of them also happen to be black. "Even as a black woman, never do I find myself at a table of all black people, because New York is such a melting pot. But there we were—six of us. And yes, we were having a good time," she tells the newscaster currently interviewing her.

The patron next to Natalia and her friends was huffing and puffing at the noise from Natalia's table. She gave looks, she made audible sighs, and when the laughter at this table of six hit a fever pitch, the not-so-neighborly woman reached over, slammed her hand down on Natalia's table, and hollered, "EEEEnough already!" When the entire restaurant stopped to look at this demonstration, the woman told Natalia and friends that they had better quiet down. "All of you!"

"It was like the entire restaurant gasped in unison." This woman then asked the owner to move Natalia's party away from her. It's doubtful that Silvano even entertained moving six press-savvy regulars on the orders of an entitled, visiting snob. Even after another patron recognized her as Princess Michael of Kent, a member of the British royal family, and another added, "She gives the trophy at Wimbledon," moving the party of six still wasn't a consideration. Rather, the snobby princess was moved.

As she got up to move to her new table, however, the princess just had to add one more thing. Princess Michael wedged herself between two people at Natalia's table to say, "Back to the colonies with all of you!"

Oh yes, she did. In New York City, in this millennium, a member of the British royal family "banished" six Americans due to their skin color. The whole front room of the restaurant heard it, just before Natalia's whole table screamed as if someone had been murdered, while the restaurant staff stood by, frozen in horror, and other tables started yelling, "No, she did not!" But, again, oh yes, she did.

Natalia, seriously fearing she was going to have a heart attack, stepped outside to call her parents. Her mom could do little more than listen because it wasn't long before Natalia was talking herself back to the reality of who was wrong and what needed to be done to make this right. Mom gave Natalia permission to address the woman directly, so she wouldn't lie awake in bed for days going over and over the details of how the exchange could have or should have gone down.

Surrounded by friends and the waitstaff, Natalia approached the princess and asked what she meant when she told her and her colleagues to go back to the colonies. Princess Michael looked Natalia in the face and told her there were rules in the colonies. And that they were good rules. And that Natalia should think about that.

And God bless Natalia, because I would have smacked the bitch upside her head, but Natalia regally told this princess she was not in Kent anymore. That rather, "This is New York and it's the twenty-first century, and you are rude and your behavior is unacceptable." Natalia then leaned in close to say, "Now, you take a good look at my face because I want you to remember it when I make you regret this."

The story didn't just make the gossip column on Page Six; it was on the cover of the *New York Post* the next day. The day after that it ran in many newspapers of note in America and every news outlet in Britain, as well as news and print periodicals throughout Europe and all the way into China. By the time I met Natalia, she was giving interviews via satellite to British chat shows. Some of them even invited her back the following year to rehash this tale of a racist royal and a New Yorker who wanted to make sure that at least this behavior would never happen again.

Thattagirl, Natalia.

* LIKE ME, NATALIA WAS BORN IN BROOKLYN. BUT while I have woken up around the world and settled on L.A. as my new home, Natalia has stayed true to the fair city of New York. She has also grown into a perfect representation of all it can be. She is an artist of many sorts. When I first met her she was doing PR. Then she began designing clothes. Today she is also doing jewelry. Her timing is that of a comedian, but it's her candor that I need right now in the aftermath of this exchange with Seung's relatives.

Five years after meeting her at her own press conference, I beg Natalia to fit me in for a dinner while she is showing her jewels and dresses in L.A. this week. Because I need to talk to someone about this. Someone who will not be afraid of how angry I'm feeling. Natalia agrees, and on my way to meet her, I'm racing through the details of how she and Jake met so I can ask questions about exactly how she dealt with each season of sinful behavior over the past five years of her relationship with a man of another race.

She'd known his brother, Judah, really well when they were both working different angles in the nightclub scene. Natalia knew Jake's sister and his mother and all their friends also, but Jake was just a guy she'd said little more than "hi" and "bye" to. Until one day when Natalia and Jake got stuck outside the front door of some happening place and sparks flew. They talked all night long and decided to just walk home. In fact, they never stopped seeing each other ever again from that night onward.

Her first instinct after getting together with Jake was: "Don't tell anyone we're dating." This had nothing to do with Natalia's being black and Jake's being white, but rather, Natalia wasn't sure she wanted her private life on parade. Even though Jake wanted to share their romance with the world, she asked him to keep it on the DL until they hit the two-month mark. If they still wanted to be in a relationship at that point, then he could go "blabbing it to all the world."

You gotta love a girl who is not hung up on ceremony or pretense.

Natalia's birthday is just after New Year's and there was a dinner planned. She finally gave Jake permission to tell his brother and the rest of his siblings—five in total! Jake was relieved, but also confessed, "This could be a problem for my mother."

EVERYONE DRIVES IN L.A., but I'm riding in a cab to this dinner that I've begged Natalia to have with me, because I intend to drink profusely. I have to look out the back seat window now as I remember her first words in response to this statement by Jake, because they always make me cry. I'm trying to stop the tears before I arrive because I'd prefer that my friend not know that her first heart-to-heart with the man she loves causes me to weep every time I think of it.

"In what way could this be a problem for your mother?" Natalia asked him.

Not even understanding how or why this could be a problem makes me envision Natalia as a child. I see her at about four years old in a sandbox, trying to play with Jake, who says he's not allowed to be Natalia's friend. And when Natalia asks why, he must tell her, "Because you are black." Jake's family wouldn't necessarily forbid him from playing with Natalia, but yes, later on he would specifically not be allowed to love her. And my stomach drops. It drops both for the adult woman who had to open herself up to this conversation in a Greenwich Village apartment and for the four-year-old girl in the sandbox, whose own parents tried to fill her up with love and confidence and education and resilience. Parents who probably also told Natalia that she could be anything when she grew up. Only to discover on a random Wednesday evening, thirty years later, that she could be anything but accepted by this man's family.

I'm wiping tears for all that good stuff Natalia's parents gave her that could be eviscerated in one fell swoop by the admission of another—the admission of a boundary that this man does not believe in and never subscribed to, but to which he still must admit because it is part of his history. So as embarrassing as this discussion is to both these people, Jake and Natalia can never distance themselves from it because it came from the people who made Jake. And thus they both feel shame and embarrassment and hurt. And nothing will ever take this conversation, or those feelings, away entirely.

WHEN JAKE TOLD NATALIA that his mother might have a problem with his dating someone outside of his race, Natalia had to ask, "Really?" And then a moment later ask, "People really still have a problem with that?" And thus began a conversation regarding a former girlfriend of Jake's who wasn't the prescribed color, either. And his mother's cutting him off for seven years.

What bothers me most in this story is that Natalia was blindsided. Not so much by Jake, but by America. For a long time I even doubted Natalia's initial response to Jake because I honestly couldn't believe that any woman could grow up in this country and not imagine that dating outside of her race might pose a problem to others. Because we have a long history of antagonizing fellow Americans for race, religion, and culture. But most especially by color.

Still, I grew up in this country and never imagined that someone would not be allowed to date me because I am not of his race. And frankly, I found out how wrong I was the hard way—twice before even meeting Seung—and still I am consistently and completely shocked by the sentiments in his family.

IN MY OWN EXPERIENCE, there were two men I liked, nearly twenty years before even meeting Seung, who were not allowed to date me. I was off-limits to the first because of my color—or lack thereof. He was African American, and we were sophomores in college. It was clear that his family's interest in his dating within his race was even more definitive than my family's. The first time I met him, he nicknamed me Eve because I was the forbidden fruit where he grew up. The name felt sexy and cute, but I knew the sentiment beneath it was neither. However, it did not frighten me. Although I was taken by surprise by it, I actually found it poetic. His parents' xenophobia perfectly balanced my parents' xenophobia, perhaps even canceling each other out in the universe. But there is no denying that I was totally shocked when I ended up being on the "no way" list.

Of course, we tried anyway. The first morning I woke up in his dorm room, Matt (whom I, of course, called Adam) was running his finger across my bare shoulder. When my eyes met his he whispered, "Poor little girl, born without any color." I think you had to be there, because we both laughed heartily. Although neither of us agreed with the mandate taught to us at home, at nineteen years old it did prevent us from moving too far forward and our relationship was short-lived.

The following year, I transferred to a university in England and met an English man whom I "fancied." He came from a long line of public school boys in the north of his country. He did his best to soften the blow, but it was clear that he and his people weren't fond of Americans. I also found this shocking, yet never took it too personally because, frankly, it was absurd to me. America's really big! How could you not like *all* of us? I couldn't imagine what another culture might hold against America and Americans at this early age, but eighteen months in England and another six spread throughout Europe taught me everything even the Western world dislikes and presumes about Americans.

But at twenty years old, I still thought I could change people's views. I hung around this bloke and did my best to charm him. In the end it was clear that he liked me but it was not a feeling he was ever going to act upon. At the time I was mostly satisfied that I made an impression that Americans were not all "septic tank Yanks." Now I find the effort I made extreme and doubt I would ever again work so hard to try to change anyone's opinion of me or my countrymen. Which saddens me in its own way. But at least I got the chance to try, because when it comes to judging someone based on skin color, charm doesn't stand a chance.

I never imagined that a person in my social sphere, with my level of education, could be told, "White/black/American people are equal to us in all things—but still not acceptable in this house to date/to love/to marry." And yet, I am one generation away from that conversation! I was also told by my parents which races I was allowed to love. My parents didn't have rules about whom I could befriend or work with, just like Seung's didn't and just like Jake's didn't. But all three of us had at least one parent who openly taught us boundaries on love. Which, so sadly, must be the reason I doubted Natalia's shock.

But as Natalia walks toward me in the restaurant tonight, I look at her differently than I ever have. I see her shade and her features and wonder what about them, exactly, would deem them "unworthy" to someone like Jake's mother. The answers to this question are complex, ingrained, historical, ignorant, but still I indulge them. After recalling my own experiences, I am certain that all people who venture outside the small circle they grew up with must find themselves to be the "wrong choice" to someone at some point in their lives. And if you're a person who grew up in a household with parents who filled your cereal bowl with milk and love each morning to build your strength and confidence, you can be smacked upside the head yourself when you come to find it's your turn to be at the bottom of the barrel on someone else's race card.

I smile as Natalia reaches our table because I know she will work my anger over about what's transpired with Seung's family. I stand up and hug her, though, because I have just recently found out, truly, what it feels like to be ostracized for reasons that have nothing to do with me by the family of someone I love. And I'm so sorry for everything Natalia has had to go through, even though she takes it all in stride so beautifully.

Natalia and Jake have been engaged for two years and aren't yet married. Which makes me kind of nervous for her. In all our discussions about The Crow (as she likes to call her future mother-in-law, due to her pointed and screeching attitude), Natalia has always been adamant that she has nothing to do with the pace of her and Jake's relationship. But tonight, I gently ask if Natalia still feels that Salome (The Crow's actual name) has not changed or at least interrupted her wedding plans and life with Jake. I can't even get the whole sentence out before Natalia begins talking.

"Yes, she has," Natalia concedes. "This delay in my wedding is all because of her. And them. I know exactly what I want to do for my wedding, but I also know them. And the two don't mix. Jake wants to go to city hall and get married tomorrow and figure out the party later. But I'm really not willing to give up *my wedding* because of these people."

Did you just hear that alarm bell go off about my wedding? Or was that just in my own head?

Natalia says she wants a three-day excursion, for her and Jake to have a beach wedding on the island where they first vacationed together and said their first "I love you." (Sound familiar? You think you are so unique and then you realize you're just part of the zeitgeist.) But three days with Jake's family is not an option because of how many times Natalia has been burned.

AFTER JAKE FIRST WARNED Natalia about his mother's attitudes toward interracial dating, Natalia was sure that this behavior must have been caused in reaction to Jake's ex-girlfriend, who was also a black woman. "I thought, *Well, that is just ridiculous. I don't know how that other woman conducted herself, but I know how I do, so let's just see if I can fix this.*"

That sounds like a brave and noble choice, but it turned out to be a lose-lose scenario, not only for Natalia, but also for Jake, because prejudice has little to do with actual behavior.

"But Jake knew the deal," she says, recalling a story I'd heard before but am now lapping up in a whole new way in light of my own recent experiences. "That this had nothing to do with anyone but his mother and his family. But he didn't hide or shy away from the truth. He said, 'I'm only telling you this because I want to be honest. I want to stick by you and I hope you will stick by me.' But still, I just couldn't even imagine it."

Natalia was ready to take the high road and try her best with Jake's family, only to find she was immediately banned from joining. "Ignored, ostracized, uninvited, everything. The Crow gave the other siblings a mandate—to get rid of me."

Jake's family is also of a different religion than Natalia, and The Crow originally said this was the reason she was not welcome. But Jake's oldest brother married someone outside the religion, who's Asian, and The Crow took no issue with either of these differences. And one of his sisters married someone of the same faith, and The Crow is not a fan of him, either, so they are rarely invited to anything. Still, neither of these other partners was banned. Then there was the previous banishment of Jake's ex-girlfriend, and another brother's similar excommunication when he dated someone with dark skin. So it was pretty clear that the problem had little to do with faith.

Natalia did what she could to make things as symbiotic as possible despite this. "I said, 'They don't really know me yet, and I think this is disgusting and hideous, but you go see your family without me.'"

Natalia, like Sonu—my personal Batman of interracial dating—does not hold back. However, Natalia does not fight with Jake's family because it would only degrade her. Which I think also holds true for me. (Although I'm not afraid to rant endlessly tonight, or call my own wedding a "war" behind a dismissive relative's back.) But Natalia also completely speaks her mind to her man. This works so well for them because Jake understands that Natalia's feelings about this are big and need a place to land. Jake lets her go off when she needs to, and they make a plan of how to take each step forward together. Which seems so beautiful. It is perhaps the one great thing about this sad reality because they've formed a very solid unit together, right from the start, partially because of this condemnation.

Of course, this makes me worried about my own plan on how to move forward in my relationship. I originally thought that fighting with Seung or showing him my anger might be an amateur move, but having feelings about my relationship that I'm only sharing outside my relationship can't be good, either.

"You should be afraid of saying too little. This is not a pretty picture, and it's not favorable. But no matter how nice you are to each other, the ugliness is still there, so you can't be afraid of the ugliness," Natalia tells me. "You have to ask yourself how much you are willing to fight to be with this person because you have to fight each other sometimes to get there."

Jake went to two family occasions without Natalia and then became scarce. He did not feel it was okay to leave her out of his life.

Jake's family then felt they had the right to give their opinion to Jake about his not showing up for them. However, none of the siblings stood up to their mother on behalf of Jake or his relationship, or even the idea of alienating someone due to skin color. This was particularly hard for Natalia to take from her former friend Judah.

"He was my best friend for many years, and he did not say one word in my defense to his mother. Nor did he say one word on the subject itself. And it really made me wonder if we were ever really friends at all."

Silence then became the status quo between Jake and his large family for the better part of a year after these heated discussions. Natalia puts all her sound and fury away for a minute and says how difficult this is for Jake at times. Mainly because no child should ever be asked to choose between love and family. But if it's presented, Natalia says you shouldn't be afraid of the choice. "In the beginning, I said I didn't want to be the reason he didn't talk to his family. And I meant it. And after I fell in love, then I thought, *Damn right, I am the reason.* Because although I might be the reason, I am not the cause. She is the cause."

✳ MY GOD. I LISTEN TO THE HELL MY FRIEND HAS

been through, and aside from her pain I think of Jake's, too. Natalia reminds me that she and Jake have a mantra in their home: "Nothing easy is worth having." I look at Natalia's ability to explain her feelings and defend herself with envy. I want to stand up tall and puff up my chest and own this situation like she does. I really do. And even though it's my nature to do so, something about retaliation or fighting back does not feel right. Is this inability to nail down all the feelings that racism brings up the reason the race "conversation" is so stifled—particularly between parents and their children?

I know there was a turning point where Natalia was allowed into Jake's family's house. "How did you even begin to interact with Jake's mother? Was it something that Jake or perhaps his father did?"

Jake's father, a brilliant surgeon and the patriarch of this family, had been deceased for five years by the time Natalia's family invited Jake to his first holiday with them. Accepting an invitation to spend Thanksgiving outside of his own family caused an uproar that involved all of Jake's siblings, culminating in Jake's oldest brother, Jonathan, stepping in and taking a stand.

Brother Jonathan, who by then was a married man and had a child of his own, said, "No more" to his mother. This was at least partially due to his own experience years earlier when he dated a black woman and his mother would literally cross the street to avoid having to face them, but also because he had seen enough of the hurt Jake was facing. And now Judah had begun a relationship with a black woman and was telling their mother that she was Greek because that was more acceptable than black!

"People of all backgrounds come in all colors, but let me be clear here," says Natalia with her dander up. "This woman Judah is with is black. And knowing his mother has a problem with her kids dating anyone darker than a brown paper bag is why Judah lied. And he lied for *two years*."

Jonathan finally told his mother that if she didn't accept Jake and whoever was important in his life, he would not only stand with Jake, but also take his child with them to avoid teaching her the racism he was witnessing. He also pointed out that all the alienation their family was participating in was not hindering Jake's relationship. If anything, the shunning was making Jake and Natalia stronger, while the siblings were being torn apart. He advised that everyone give Natalia a chance before they lost their son and brother forever.

Why don't I remember this being as good as it sounds hearing it again now?

"Because The Crow finally let me in the damn house, and yeah, yeah, yeah, she tried her best to put on her happy face and be mannerly and decent. But it was clear she could have choked at any moment," says Natalia. From here until the spring of the following year, Jake's mother would invite Natalia to group events and act like she was not repulsed by her presence. Until, finally, Natalia got frustrated.

"I'm not an ex-con who's rebuilding a life. I'm accomplished and successful. Why is she 'trying'? And why are we giving her credit for it? I was damn tired of her behavior at this point and also over my own animosity with his family. They are the ones missing out on being friends with me. They have wasted the opportunity. I always knew Jake and I would make it—I just wasn't sure if his mother would. I still think she might drop dead from a heart attack on her way to our wedding."

Natalia did set new boundaries for herself and Jake in their future together from that point forward. She told Jake that if they have children, they will be black. "And I do not feel safe that your mother will not say awful things to them," she told him. "What happens if my child is with their grandmother and asks, 'Why is your skin different from mine?' How can I possibly trust her to say anything smart or reasonable when she has never displayed those things to her children or to me?"

To which Jake responded they could make any boundary with his mother that Natalia needed. Which is so wonderful. And romantic in its own way. But it also puts the pressure on Natalia, because if she closes his family out, then she is the bad guy. Yet if she continues to let them into her and Jake's life, they don't seem to be afraid to do or say all kinds of hurtful things to her.

"I hate it when people say, 'But you are not marrying his family.' 'Cause you are," she concludes.

Now I'm speechless. I'm no longer frightened about the hurdles of my interracial marriage in theory, but I'm frightened about the actual situation I am in right now. Natalia and I are both engaged women and our fiancés' families would love to send us on a wrong-race-girlfriend cruise through the Bermuda Triangle. Natalia fights all her battles in private and conducts herself admirably in the face of the people shunning her, yet she's treading water. There is no forward movement, and I am afraid "standing still" at this phase of her relationship, which is not being allowed to move forward by the constraints of her future mother-in-law, is going to exhaust her. So what is all the diplomatic behavior really yielding her?

Wait a minute! I know Natalia had a "come-to-Jesus talk" with her mother-in-law, in which she got to call her out on all her bad behavior. In fact, the last time we spoke she said she could finally feel at peace having children with Jake because of it. So I'm asking, really begging, Natalia to remind me how that went and if that changed things.

"It only changed things for me."

Two days after Jake proposed, Natalia got a call from someone saying, "Congratulations! Are you so excited?" Natalia said yes and asked who was calling. When the caller responded, "Your future mother-in-law, Salome," Natalia's jaw dropped.

Salome was calling to get Natalia's mother's phone number.

"Um, no. I don't think so," Natalia responded. "What's your schedule like next week?"

Natalia made a date with Jake's mother to flat-out tell her, "You have not done the right thing by me in three years. You do not get to try to befriend my mother. She knows who you are and is fiercely defensive of me and is well aware of how you have treated me. She is not going to be interested in talking to you."

But The Crow had her own plan. She invited Natalia to the house and had food and drinks waiting, and when Natalia arrived, she talked about herself for most of the afternoon.

When Natalia finally found an opening two hours later, she gave Salome a piece of her mind. She confessed her reason for coming and proceeded to tell her everything she intended to. And at first, Salome acted like that was just old news.

"As if I had been pledging their family for all these years and now we're gonna kiss and make up on hell night? Oh no, lady. You can't go from zero to sixty without addressing the past. Nor do these appetizers make up for all the previous meals I was barred from in this house."

Finally, Jake's mother said it can be a very difficult thing when your child is in a relationship with someone who is different—and Natalia jumped in to stop the next line of pretense. She asked if Salome was now going to speak to "different" like her other daughter-in-law, who is also of a different race and religion from her, or "different" like this—and Natalia put her finger to her own forearm, pointing to her skin.

Jake's mother said, "I guess I didn't handle myself in the best way."

So, five hours after she arrived, Natalia held fast that her future mother-in-law not call her parents and ignore all the years she failed to even get to know Natalia. She said if she had any real interest in her and her son's future with her, she could put the time in now.

All the laughter has left our table. And I'm not sure why. I hate to ask, but I really don't get why this feels so . . . empty suddenly.

"'I guess I didn't handle myself in the right way' was the most I ever got. That day felt really forced and it continues to feel really forced. There was no 'I'm sorry.' No real change of heart or in behavior. She did not have an epiphany before she called me to end the standoff, nor did she have one after I came clean. She would have gone right on pretending. But after a few days, the junk was still there. And two years later, I still haven't gotten what I need to have anything real with anyone in Jake's family. The difference is, they know where I'm at now. But nothing has changed."

But something is *different*. It seems to me that having said her piece, Natalia no longer has the right to fight about the inconsistencies she feels in Jake's family. She is no longer banned, but the way she's included isn't particularly welcoming, either. Now if she complains, she seems problematic or like she can't let go of the past. So the hurt is still there, but the right to take action has been removed. And finally I see why I am afraid to fight. Because absolutely nothing will change about why I am "not the right choice" for Seung, but if I were to call out any of his aunts or uncles on the obvious subtext when I am given lessons on "why I must understand how hard life has been for Korean people and how much I should value their culture or my marriage will fail" (literally I was told this at a dinner once), then I will have exposed myself to them. And nothing will change but I will still have to, silently, put up with the "subtext" forever after.

"You know, we hang politicians if they use the 'N-word' or don't openly condemn those who do. Racial profiling by law enforcement is judged and shamed and bad and all that. Yet if a parent tells a child that 'black people aren't good enough to love,' that is just overlooked. Let me say it out loud, so it is perfectly clear: That is *racism*. Even if you only say it in your own damn house."

Natalia is a thick-skinned girl. And so am I. And sometimes anger is the only way people like us know how to show hurt. "I could punch somebody, I get so mad sometimes. I don't deserve this. All I wish for with them is ease. I see relationships where the guy's family is decent and respectful to someone they wouldn't have necessarily picked for their son or brother, and I wonder why I don't at least deserve that. This weekend was the original date I set for my wedding, and I'm sitting here talking with you. I will marry him, but I hate them for all the dis-ease they have caused in me."

* OF COURSE, IT'S A BLESSING THAT NATALIA

didn't feel or confront this kind of prejudice until her thirties, because her terrific family had all that time to give her every resource to be the shining star she is, which in turn allows her to fight like hell for the man she loves. But perhaps even more important than Natalia's ability to articulate her feelings and fight when necessary to defend them is that even in the face of another's judgment Natalia still knows her own value. And maybe this is the gift that I should take away and model from her, rather than good ways to redress my anger.

Specifically, perhaps I should hold myself up to my highest standard, rather than fight with someone else on their playing field. After Natalia's brush with prejudice, when she was belittled by

Princess Michael, she told her off in hopes of not lying awake in bed for three days. Yet she lay awake for exactly that long nonetheless. And as much as Natalia and Jake have made a cocoon around their life together to keep them safe from his family, I see that Natalia is still victimized by their duplicitous actions, even after having her say. So firing back does not seem to win the long-term battle. In fact, it might only yield a quick fix that then leaves your arsenal exposed forever.

Not that I believe Natalia has disabled herself in any way. But even she says, "Sometimes this could cripple me, but I don't let it. The most important part of our relationship is 'us.' Yes, I get anxious and don't want to go before we do anything with his family, but when we are there, Jake and I hold hands and kiss and reinforce for each other that we are what's important. No one would ever know anything was ever wrong."

But that's only because Natalia is smart enough to be honest with her boyfriend and tell him she can only last about one hour in his family's company. She has to stifle herself so much that nothing gets in or out, so seventy minutes is literally Jake and Natalia's limit in his mother's house.

In my heart, I know that Natalia would love an apology from Judah, so they could be friends again. And a kind word from any of the other siblings addressing their or their mother's behavior toward Natalia and Jake would go a long way. And although I laugh at the well-crafted jokes that make us feel better about bad-mouthing The Crow, now I see nothing but pain behind them. And I wish I could hug my tough-ass friend and tell her to let it all go before these other people's shortcomings take hold of her and never let go. But I don't want to belittle Natalia and pretend that's easy, when I can't even do it myself. Especially when her situation feels much more hurtful than my own.

Natalia leaves me with these parting words:

"When I look at myself, Diane, I see very specific things: I see shoes, an outfit, and a cute face. And all of this has been such a blow to my ego because it never occurred to me that other people see something else when they look at me. That they see something entirely different. That some people look at me and see Aunt Jemima. Or the maid. Or the help. And it wasn't a pain-in-the-ass royal who taught me that. It was Jake's mother. The grandmother of my future children. She is the one who stabbed me in the heart."

CHAPTER 10.

THEY WILL NOT BE

JUDGED FOR ME

"What are you doing with a gun?"
—SEUNG CHUNG ON THE DAY WE
PICKED UP OUR WEDDING BANDS

'VE HIRED A COACH.

I know I need another tool to possibly find peace for myself, and it has to be something "proactive" that I can do instead of keeping score about who says what to me. The closest thing I have to a "plan" for combating the attitude I get from Seung's family looks exactly like Natalia's. That is, to always behave "appropriately" around damning family members, so as not to give them ammunition, but be as honest as I possibly can with my man and make a game plan together on how to handle each hurdle.

But I'm haunted by the idea of my friend Natalia playing all her cards right *for five years*—by facing every truth with Jake and never slinging mud in the pit his mother is fighting her in—and her still feeling hurt, angry, and vulnerable. Not to mention that she is not yet married and her wedding plans are stymied due to his family. This last part is particularly pressing to me because I have a date set and have not yet found middle ground for how to deal with Seung's relatives. And it's only six months away.

To try to "clear the brush" to find my path, I keep reminding myself of the following things every day: (1) The people I feel belittled by are not Seung's parents; (2) although these aunts and uncles are the ones I see and interact with most, this is only due to a common language and location; and (3) the aunts' and uncles' disapproval of me, or of Seung's marrying me, has to do with their wants for their own children—not me. This leaves me with one conclusion: The prejudice I feel from the older members of his family is not my burden to carry.

Only I *do* feel like it is my burden. Or at least I have some responsibility in it. I don't feel comfortable saying nothing while someone says, "Some races are not okay/worthy/acceptable for us to love." I fought my own mother on this and she came around a long time ago. However, I understand that I can't fight anyone else's mother, or aunts, on anything. But it doesn't stop me from wanting to change people's views.

I get that the best way to right the wrong of stereotypes is to continually rise above them. Which, of course, is a lot of damn work to do in hopes of changing something that is not supposed to be "my burden." I'm also stuck because I want to tell myself these people are not important—but they *are* important. They are my fiancé's relatives. Which brings me all the way back to the beginning of this circle: To care or not to care? To fight or not to fight? So I try to remember my three notes to self, until I get so annoyed one morning while trying to meditate on these thoughts.

I'm supposed to go wedding dress shopping with my mother

today. She's flown all the way to Los Angeles from New York City to partake in this ritual with me, and I'm wasting our time together venting about people who don't like me. Why the hell? And more important, if I'm going to spend time thinking about the other people involved in Seung's and my life and wedding, who do I want to think about?

My parents, who are thrilled that I am marrying Seung, and Seung's parents, who are thrilled that he is marrying and don't mind that it is me.

Hmm. I can't really say that they are thrilled about me, but they also don't really know me. I think they are hoping to know me. And they have completely let go of the fact that I'm not of their culture and will let Seung and me lead any kind of life we want. But I love their culture. I love the holidays, the food, the spirit, the dedication to education and travel, as well as the electronics and the luggage. I can't wait to see the country and celebrate all the rituals his culture has to offer—in our wedding and with our children. But, of course, Seung's parents don't know that. So maybe I need to find a way to further a relationship with them?

Thus, the coach.

* SEUNG AND I GO ON THESE DATES THAT I CALL

"famous Asian night." Los Angeles has one of the highest concentrations of Asian Americans anywhere in the country, and the largest group of Koreans anywhere in the world outside of Seoul. Of course, it has lots of artists, too. So naturally, Seung and I have become friends with many Asian actors and TV personalities. There are dinners we attend with this group of friends where one member of every couple is on television. And I am often the only dinner guest who is not Asian.

We both feel especially close to Karl Yune. Karl is of Korean descent but did not speak the Korean language growing up. For months before a world tour of perhaps the second-largest Asian American book turned film, *Memoirs of a Geisha,* Karl worked every day to learn Korean before going there to promote the film as an actor in it. We got to see his hard work in action when he spoke fluently to a waitress one night while we were all eating in a tiny K-town restaurant. Just a year earlier he could hardly order his own food. When Seung got up to take a call, I asked Karl for the number of his language coach. While typing her details into my phone, I asked if Karl thought she could teach me some things about the culture, especially things that would help me with my wedding and impending trip to Seoul. Karl said nothing but gave me his million-dollar smile. In a mock accent he told me, "You will make a gooood Korean wife, Di-han!"

I meet with Un-Nee (which translates to "big sister" and is what she has instructed me to call her) three times a week for two-hour sessions, unbeknownst to Seung, for three months before our wedding.

At our first meeting, I give her a typed page and a tape recorder. I have printed out a speech I would like to give to my future in-laws on the day of my wedding. I ask Un-Nee if she can translate it and record her voice saying the speech; I will learn the sounds and commit it to memory on my own time. Un-Nee agrees but feels her language and mine are so far apart that I might be better served by her teaching me some other Korean basics first so that the sounds might come more easily to me in my memorization process.

I smile at my new big sister, because I'm just now realizing that my proactive and positive choice of how to embrace Seung's parents will simultaneously knock the rest of the family on their asses when all their "very important cultural secrets" are exposed and executed—correctly.

THERE ARE SIXTEEN WAYS to say "aunt" and "uncle" in Korean and four different ways for me to address cousins, which are all very important in showing respect to family members. There are another four ways I should address women and men whom I am not related to. There are two different ways to say goodbye, determined by whose house I'm leaving. There are age- and gender-appropriate gifts that I must bring to each of Seung's relatives whom I will meet while in Korea. I have a separate bag already packed for my trip to Seoul— with everything I'm collecting here for every possible visit there. Once in country, there are two appropriate ways for me to accept anything that is handed to me (including a wedding gift), and there are three different ways to bow. And I know 'em all.

Across Asia, people bow instead of shaking hands. For people my age, the various bows have all lost their meaning in today's world, much like the meaning of a handshake to Americans my age. A handshake was about the removal of a sword from your right hand to offer friendship with it. And a bow was about lowering your head below another's heart to recognize and honor it.

In a casual meeting among two Asian people of similar status, they each do a head nod toward one another (although people under age fifty seem to do a handshake and a head nod, or just a handshake at times). In a more formal setting, the more senior person may do a small head nod, while the more junior person should bow their head below the other's heart. And the third bow is only really done during a wedding ceremony, or if I manage to get an audience with a king or queen while touring the Far East.

Un-Nee stands up and puts one foot behind the other and turns the back foot out. She bends both her knees until her back knee touches the floor, and then bends from the waist until her head touches the ground. Full prostration, Asian style, looks so graceful because you are erect when first lowering down, and then your entire upper body folds over so that you look like the Leaning Tower of Pisa during descent. I will do this bow in excess of thirty times over the course of my Korean wedding. Un-Nee tells me that Seung's female relatives will assist me. I have my doubts about this, but I keep them to myself.

Un-Nee is unsure of which rituals I should do for my Korean wedding because she is unmarried, but as I research or hear something about a particular step, she can tell me exactly what it is supposed to look like. And since I have never met an Asian person under age fifty in this country who has even seen this ceremony, I'm gonna pick which rituals to do and call it a day. And where am I learning the most about this ancient skit that my future relatives are not willing to help me with? The Internet.

Not just any old site on Korean culture. I finally piece together my entire Korean ceremony on IKEA'S website. Yeah. A Swedish teenager founded a store for affordable yet attractive furniture that can be built by anyone, as long as you have fifteen hours to spare. It has morphed into a worldwide phenomenon in home furnishings—and spawned the most articulate, thorough, and crucial provider of information for my nuptials.

A section of their website honors different homes around the world and links to a page on traditional weddings. I pick my five rituals from this site and use them exactly as a framework for the entire event.

The much harder thing for me, in fact, is figuring out where to tell Seung I am getting all this intel on his culture without revealing my private language and culture studies. My Korean big sister also gives me a ton of reading material, including a book by an American who immigrated to Seoul and has become a popular newscaster there. His book is like a *Korea for Dummies* on culture and language. I keep telling Seung I am learning so much from this man, when in fact his is the only book she gave me that I actually have not read.

But really, Seung and I are so swamped trying to work as hard as we always have, plan our three wedding events and the honeymoon, and talk to our parents almost daily that there is little time for talking to each other. On good days, we combine our wedding homework with a date. On bad days, we combine our wedding homework with a fight. Most days land exactly in between.

The day our wedding bands are finally ready is a particularly busy day for me at work. But we are both so excited to see the rings that I am sneaking out for a "lunch date" anyway. We found a jeweler in the Valley who would make both the rings we imagined and let us each put a secret message, engraved inside, for the other. We've decided to let each other read this message today because there are so many payoffs on a wedding day, but you really need some reminders that the event is supposed to be a celebration of your love during the planning phase.

But I am shooting eight scenes, all on the FBI "war room" set, which means pages and pages of exposition to read, remember, and recite on camera. I can usually do this easily—except when it comes to names. And on a crime show, there are always a lot of names. Each episode brings the bad guy, the bad guy's friend, the bad guy's friend turned informer, the bad guy's former friend who is the mislead for the bad guy, the victim, the victim's friend who speaks or vouches for them, the victim's nefarious friend who might also turn into a bad guy, and so on. I write these names down on things. On my folder or message sheet that I carry in the scene, or on my computer screen, or even on my hand if it works for the situation. And if only one hand "works" on camera, I write names on the other hand that will stay off camera. On this day, my left hand has five names written across it. It looks something like the cover of *Everything Is Illuminated* by the time lunch comes.

As soon as the bell on the soundstage rings, signaling the last shot till after lunch, I run to my car. I am racing to the jewelry store for the forty-eight-minute break, of which I will spend at least thirty minutes in traffic. My friends in hair and makeup will say that I don't need touch-ups until I'm on set, buying me eight to ten more minutes before the assistant director will knock on my trailer, telling me, "Back to work!" in the most polite way possible.

It isn't until I'm being buzzed through the second set of metal cage–like doors and looking up into a security camera that I realize I am still wearing not only my wardrobe but also my props—meaning I have a gun strapped to me.

As I step inside, through the last security precaution and into the private showing room, I have an urge to disclose my very real gun. But to just come clean and explain to the people behind the counter that it's not loaded, I would have to "pull the gun" here in the doorway of this room filled with diamonds. So instead, I begin panicking and talking incessantly.

Sitting down next to Seung, I'm chattering like a crazy person. He asks what's the matter and when I don't answer him or stop talking long enough to even inhale, he is probably worried that "ring day" is setting me back into my fears of marriage. Then he sees my hand, with five men's names written across it. I imagine that this feels like the paint spots all over again. And where is my beautiful engagement ring? Seung wonders. Pinned to the inside of my underwear, like it always is when I'm filming.

There was no way for me to get my hands into my pants and unlatch the safety pin securing my jewel near my jewel without exposing the fact that I am packing heat. But you know what, I'm here. And I have fifteen minutes before I have to turn around and head back to work, so I'm going for it and getting my engagement ring anyway. But as soon as Seung sees my shoulder harness, he, too, goes into panic mode, wondering through clenched teeth, "What are you doing with a g   "

"Hello! I'm on my lunch hour!"

But Seung's panic is different from mine. He is inherently honest where I am controlling. So while I'm trying to manage the situation, he comes clean. Of course, he doesn't foresee what will happen after he immediately turns to the jeweler and says, "She has a gun but it's . . . "

Yes, time stands still in that moment. And I begin talking louder than Seung, trying to bring the jeweler's attention to me, as well as all of the mounted cameras that are moving toward us because the owner just hit his silent panic button. First, I remove my fake FBI badge and lay it on the table. Then I take my fake FBI personal photo ID and lay that next to it, so when I then swing open my coat to remove my gun to lay it on the counter, perhaps no one will shoot me. Needless to say, by the time I am done explaining all of this again—to an actual policeman who is very annoyed by me but perhaps empathizes with the fact that I am trying to pick up my wedding band on my lunch hour, so he lets me off with just a warning—I barely have time to see my hidden message.

"Seung for Diane," as in "sing a song for Diane," is what he wrote in mine. I kiss Seung and whisper in his ear that I want him to sing for me when I get home tonight. I then leave him with both rings in his hand, to take back my props and race out the door to get back to work.

Once I get outside I turn back to look in the window, knowing Seung can finally breathe in and read his secret message. Etched in platinum I wrote, "K-Power forever." Which refers to a "gang" Seung joined as a child. When his family first came to America, they stayed with a relative. When they were (barely) on their feet they moved out of that house and got their first apartment. This one-bedroom that mother, father, Seung, and his sister would live in was not only small, but also quite dangerous for him, as it was in a low-income project that no other Korean people lived in.

Gang members only a few years his senior picked on him and sometimes physically attacked Seung, even in primary school. To find the strength to go to school in these early years, Seung told himself that he was in a gang called K-Power, for Koreans only. And that someday it would be filled with his people. It was only a few years until his parents could afford to move to another, bigger one-bedroom apartment, thankfully in another suburb in Virginia where he would not be accosted because of his race. Seung thrived in this safer environment, but still didn't know any Korean or Korean American classmates. He privately clung to the idea of his gang—of one, but a gang nonetheless. Soon after he asked me to marry him I asked if this meant I was a member of K-Power. Seung inducted me on the spot. Since then the couple that introduced us has been included as well. Neither of them is Korean, either, but we all want to run with Seung, which was what he was really yearning for anyway.

THE GUN EPISODE IS later topped in stupidity when we are almost arrested a second time, while planning the wedding. The Korean ceremony will take place during our Friday night rehearsal dinner, in the middle of a field alongside an abandoned farmhouse and a babbling brook, under a tent frame with only fairy lights hung around the metal frame (sounds so pretty, right?). Unfortunately, the terrain is so flat. In the center of twenty surrounding tables, the ceremonial rituals Seung and I will be doing with my parents and his will mostly be done on the ground. So in order to raise us up high enough in the grass that people can see the goings-on, I need a stage. I then have the same problem for the following day's American ceremony on the mountaintop deck. Barry has agreed to officiate for us, and we're still hunting for Buddhist monks who will do chanting and a blessing. But between all of them and a maid of honor and a best man, and two readers, we need two levels on the "altar" or there will be so many people standing during the ceremony that it might look like backstage at a U2 concert.

I decide the best way to make a stage that can be transported around and rebuilt over the weekend is to collect discarded shipping pallets. They are four-foot squares about eight inches off the ground that are used to ship tile or paint or other heavy industrial goods on trucks. They are generally discarded and sometimes very beat up after shipping, but if you're willing to scour an entire major metropolis for the best trash, they are like grown-up Legos.

We don't exactly steal the pallets from garbage piles behind retail stores in my area, but we don't exactly ask for them, either. Outside one particular Home Depot, whose dumpsters I begin to visit almost every night, Seung and I start fighting over wedding invitations. We are loading our fourth or fifth pallet for the night into my SUV (to add to the thirty in our garage to go underneath the buses) when both of our strong feelings prevent us from noticing the security guard who's obviously had enough of our nightly pilfering.

When I see the guard is fast approaching us, I tell Seung to get in the car and do so myself. Seung, of course, wants to address this man who is feverishly talking into a walkie-talkie. I get the car going and pull it alongside Seung and roll down his window. I then "ask" him to get in the car for a second time, but let's understand my tone is well beyond an "ask." When Seung ignores my loud voice, I try a soft one. I promise that if he gets in the car this second and lets me dust this rent-a-cop, I will never ask him to get another pallet with me for the rest of his life. Seung gets in and I race out of the Home Depot parking lot just as they are locking the gates to the driveway to keep me inside!

Seung and I do not laugh about this "getaway" for a long time. And we have a steadfast rule about not letting the sun go down on our anger. After this second incident with the law you would think I might have slowed myself down, or perhaps reconsidered a wedding planner. Because just as threatening as jail time should feel, I'm also an actress who is occasionally mentioned in gossip rags. Stealing what at best might be considered construction material, but in print would probably be called trash, is not a good look for me. But by now I have slipped into the zone that I warned Seung about just before we got engaged. The one in which I can become so myopic about getting a task done that I get swept inside of it and lose the meaning. I am aware that Seung has tried multiple avenues to get me out of "wedding-or-bust" mode, but it's not until he finally realizes why I am doing all this insane planning that he awakens me to my own fixation.

When I give Seung a list of things to call his parents about, to ask them if there's anything on it they would like me to do—including invite people I've heard them mention only once, serve a specific kind of liquor to their guests that is very expensive and I would have to import, and have six-foot flower arrangements that I have seen at Korean occasions but really have no idea how to find—Seung says, "No more."

He actually grabs me by the shoulders and asks why I'm running my decisions by his parents when I'm not even consulting my own. It takes more than one session of pillow talk with Seung for me to even realize and then articulate that I am trying to make his parents proud of me and thank them for their acceptance of me. Yes, I want my wedding to be all I can dream it to be, but I celebrate myself all the time. I've never felt that a marriage, or the party to usher it in, defines me. But the competitor in me who feels shunned by the extended family is trying to now use my wedding to put on a show on behalf of Ama and Apa. I worry incessantly about embarrassing them or making them look foolish for supporting me, thus driving me to the overcompensation lane of the bridal superhighway.

So now it's back to the therapist's office so I can further admit, even to myself, that I am also trying to prove to the other relatives the error of their ways. Which is not what this day is about. At all. When I get out early from shooting one day and finally throw this admission onto the kitchen counter, with the samples I am also carrying from a Korean grocer who was suggesting menu items I might serve, Seung calls a moratorium. No seeing his elder relations for one month and no wedding planning for the entire weekend. He also asks if I will join him for dinner with his cousin Charles and his girlfriend, Breanna, this Saturday night.

* CHARLES IS SEUNG'S COUSIN. BREANNA IS AN

actress I worked with years ago who was the catalyst for Seung's talking to me the second time he and I met at karaoke. They have been dating for almost five years, but I haven't seen Breanna in a long time because she does not attend many family events. Which may have to do with the fact that many Koreans and Korean Americans do not bring dates around their family until they are betrothed to marry them.

Or it might be because Breanna isn't Asian. She is a mix of just about everything else—black, white, and American Indian, to name a few. At first glance, though, she is a strikingly beautiful black woman. Although I have spent a lot of time with Breanna at work and on the evenings when the cousins get together, I rarely get to see her just with Charles. By his side at dinner tonight, she is demure, supportive, and a gentle influence. At least here, with

Charles's cousin Seung present, Breanna lets her man do most of the talking, and this charms me somehow.

The four of us talk about the fun parts of our wedding, and we ask Charles if he will introduce us to the guests at our Korean ceremony on the Friday night, and perhaps explain something about why this entire family is so gigantically tall. Charles agrees. Breanna kindly compliments our invites and says she already knows what she is wearing. Part of me wonders how this first group outing will fare, when Seung Yong marries a "white" woman and Charles brings a "black" woman (whom we both hope he will marry) as his guest with all the family present. Until two days later, when I hear that almost none of the relatives are coming.

Seung is busying himself with something in our bedroom and not facing me when he says all of the aunts and uncles who live in the Los Angeles area are not coming, nor are any of those who live in Korea. From what he can tell so far, every member of his father's family other than the Como (who lives in Hawaii, and, although I still don't believe it yet, sang my praises) is declining.

The Chungs are a large family, and like most, they have their own drama. Seung is clearly very upset about these mass declines, though, and he is trying his best not to wind me up further. Apparently this is a done deal. He says the siblings have been talking and trying to find a way to all meet on common ground despite some family rifts—but that it has failed. Of course, no one bothered to address us in this matter. But via his mom and dad, Seung is learning that none of the relatives he was so excited to share this big event with will be in attendance. Seung is saying this has only to do with their own issues and not the fact that I am Caucasian. But I am doubtful.

Regardless, I'm trying *so hard* to find that voice I had a year and a half ago when I first told Seung his family's support was not important to me. That all I cared about was him. That I would support him in any way he needed while he did his best to manage his people. But this sentiment seems to have left me. Or at least it's being held hostage because I can see these people have hurt Seung—my wonderfully kind man who complains about nothing.

Why is no one seeing the fact that this is not Seung's fifth birthday party? He is a grownup with his own feelings, and he loves these people despite everything I see them do. And what exactly is this about, anyway? Is there a rift between these grown siblings? Does that exclude their wives, then, too? The answer in everything I have seen so far in Korean culture is clearly yes, but I'm also well aware that these wives have their own relationships with the other relatives and their children—particularly Seung Yong. So how am I supposed to believe this doesn't have something to do with our marriage being biracial? Is there any way to take that out of the fray, along with the obvious domino effect that is already in motion when the other sons in this family bring their non-Asian dates?

WHEN SEUNG LEAVES for work in the morning, I take matters into my own hands and call his cousin Charles. Charles is a prolific businessman with an uncanny ability to make art and money come together without compromising each other. He has a mystical quality in his honoring of others' needs, whether that is advocating for his clients on a deal point or ceaselessly tending to his grandmother whom he shares very little language with.

When I first get him on the phone, Charles has the same shocked, hurt response that Seung does. These men are so respectful, though, there is no anger in their tone toward any of their parents but more bewilderment with a side of sadness. I flat-out ask if he will help me change not only this decision by the family, but also the future of how our whole generation will speak to and honor what being Korean American means for our children. I do not want to repeat this insular cycle that feels put upon me by the elder relatives. I specifically ask if Charles will rewrite "the myth of being Korean" with me for all of our future families.

Nearly ten years ago I taught a class in myth building. I had been teaching acting in a maximum-security men's prison to juveniles who were incarcerated for long-term sentences but who were not yet ready for the "big house." This, as fate would have it, was my "pay the rent" job while I was auditioning for acting roles around Los Angeles. After two years at this, I was asked to speak to unwed mothers in South-Central Los Angeles who were between the ages of fourteen and eighteen years old—as they were mostly the "baby mamas" of the incarcerated teens I had worked with. As part of the state-subsidized program that kept these teenage mothers in school, I taught a short seminar called Rewriting the Myth of Life, whose purpose was to try to inspire these young mothers to see what they wanted to teach their children versus the myth their parents taught them.

My classes began with my encouraging the girls to air out everything they did not believe that their parents said were "facts" or "rules." Like if you had a baby by your fifteenth birthday, you didn't get to have the big party or wear a white dress at your *quinceañera*. Or that it was okay to hit children if they were bad. Or that it was okay to throw children out on the street to find work and food by age ten or eleven. Then we would begin to think of what we would prefer to tell their children about what we, as a group, believed was right. By the end of the class, they wrote a collective "mother myth" of what they valued and decided as a group to tell their children about the culture of their home. This was empowering, not only for them but also for me. It was some of the proudest work I have ever done.

And now here I am asking an Ivy League–educated man to make a new myth with me so that we can inform our future families of why the Korean culture is beautiful without any of the boundaries or judgments that were inflicted on the "zero generation" in this family. And this includes people like Seung, who came as a child from Korea, and people like Charles, who were born here—even though both grew up in an entirely Korean house but have led a very American life outside of it.

I also ask Charles to call his mother and ask her to reconsider attending our wedding because if she will, I think the other relatives will also. I then ask Charles to tell his mother that Seung is greatly saddened by this action even though he would never say so. Charles is ready to oblige, but warns that there seem to be issues that, of course, have nothing to do with Seung. I ask him to try anyway, which, as I'm pushing him, I realize probably isn't the right way to handle this. Charles is earnest, like Seung and all the rest of these fine men I have met in Seung's generation of his family. My asking him to fix all of this is like asking a priest for absolution on a deathbed. I know he will work tirelessly at it. And I'm sort of asking Charles to question his mother. Suddenly aware of the can of worms I have just opened, I race off the phone and cancel my evening plans in order to confess this call to Seung. Mind you, I haven't retracted my request. I just want to get away from it now, confess to it, and really hope that it still gets done.

SEUNG HOLLERS AT ME. Which is only the second time I have ever heard him raise his voice. He takes his volume down immediately, but it looks as though his head might pop off.

He understands my intentions but he doesn't give a shit about them. I am wrong. I crossed a line. I inserted myself in matters of his parents that even Seung is not privy to. If he didn't have the right to question this mandate in his own family, then I certainly did not have a right to. And I am wrong to have asked Charles to get involved at all, on Seung's behalf or my own. Seung is not sure what part race is playing in these declines, but he doesn't care. A second relative, an uncle from New Jersey, accepted the invitation today, and Seung is thrilled to have one aunt and one uncle and almost every cousin flying in from as many as five states to attend. Seung stops short of telling me to never, ever manage his family again, but I get the point. The line in the sand has been drawn, and I am on the other side of it.

I have to look at myself and really wonder what my disappointment was about: Was it just that I wanted to fix Seung's hurt feelings, or was it a little bit about not wanting to let go of showing off all the Korean language and culture tricks I have spent months learning?

And I could just throw up in disgust with myself because I know there is no separating the two.

CHAPTER 11.

ISRAELI JEWESS LOVES

TRINIDADIAN HEATHEN

IN WASHINGTON

*"No one was walking me down the aisle because
I was giving myself to this man."*
—ELLIE GOLD

I AM ON A plane to Seattle because I'm so ashamed of my last action. I am embarrassed for both Seung and myself that I overstepped into his family matters by calling his cousin Charles and asking him to convince his family to attend our wedding. I am so embarrassed that I need to get away from my own house, my own wedding, and my own perspective. I need a safe place to confess my sins and create my own form of penance regarding how to move forward with Seung. Even though he is no longer mad at me, I am mad at me. I don't like my own desperate behavior, and I'm not entirely positive it won't happen again. So flying to see Ellie for counsel is a preventive measure.

I met Ellie Gold on a film set nearly ten years ago now. There isn't anything I don't feel comfortable confiding in her. Although I am as sure as ever that I want to marry Seung, I need some guidance from someone who's been at the intersection of love and race for quite some time, because I feel like I'm running in a Korean Habitrail. I'm going around and around, expending a ton of energy for no good reason. I'm not making fans of any of the family members who have shunned me, and now I'm even annoying those who love me. I recognize that it's my choice to get off this cyclical race to nowhere, and yet . . . here I go again. Running to Washington state to do more talking about his heritage and mine, his relatives and our mutual bad behavior now— and to hopefully figure how to stop making race such a consistent theme in my otherwise tranquil path to marriage. So although it may seem like I'm furthering the drama by flying to Seattle and hiding at Ellie's for the weekend, sequestering myself for fifty hours in a city that always seems to be weeping with rain, might just be the ticket for me to resolve my issues right now.

Ellie was the first of my peers I ever heard openly discuss her fears about entering into an interracial marriage. Her parents took issues with her choice in a partner, but their approval was not the only cause of Ellie's deliberations. It was many years ago that I sat across from Ellie, during the last days of her single-in-Seattle life, when I found myself speechless as she solemnly confessed to me, "If I marry him, there are only about four cities in America I'd feel comfortable living in, and that frightens me." This was a shocking statement in 2005—coming from a woman who knew more about the world and all its cultures than most any American I knew. And yet she was unsure if the world was actually ready for her and James.

They had met when they were both working for one of the biggest Internet companies in the world—when most of the planet didn't even know what a blog was yet. But Ellie and James were ahead of the curve in many ways. Both writers, he a journalist and she a novelist, they were both trading in their backgrounds to try "journaling on pop culture" for the masses. James had gotten in at the beginning and was now the most senior person on staff, while Ellie was a brand-new copyeditor.

James is vibrant, funny, and well liked by everyone. When he seemed to be flirting with Ellie, it was a no-brainer for her—even though I wouldn't exactly say he was her type. Ellie had dated black men before, but she is also an Israeli Jew who steadfastly believed she would marry someone from her own religion. And although Jews come in all colors, finding one with dark skin in the Pacific Northwest was somewhere between futile and impossible. But this difference in faith, and the fact that she and James were about to begin a work-based romance, were not the only two things going against them.

James is West Indian, which means so many things that I had to get out a map and a book on their history, and still Ellie had to explain more to me. The West Indies are a collection of islands in the Caribbean. They are south and east of America, but when Christopher Columbus landed there he thought he had reached Asia. Thus "West" of Europe and "Indies" as in India. Since the mid-1700s most of these Islands have been dependencies and colonies of many European nations, most notably the British, who retained a large collection of the islands in the archipelago until the 1960s. Therefore, many in the region speak English as a first language, and geopolitically, many of these nations are considered a subregion of North America. For these two reasons, the East Coast of America is home to many West Indian people, who are black in color but a mix of many cultures.

One of James's grandfathers was a pale Scottish man with red hair, and a great-grandfather was Chinese. This is not uncommon in the makeup of many West Indian families. There is large British, Asian, and Indian influence throughout the islands, but particularly in Trinidad. James's coloring is dark, but there is also a hint of Asian in his handsome face. He was born in London and raised there until age seven, when his family moved back to Trinidad. James lived in Trinidad for ten years before getting accepted into Columbia University and moving to the United States. There was not one "African" or "American" thing about him when he arrived in New York. Unlike so many immigrants first arriving in this country, though, he was on a fast track for white-collar success, but also slightly unaware of the pitfalls, in love and in work, of what it would feel like to be categorized within an American subculture that was not his.

After college James began an impressive career as a journalist working for some of the biggest newspapers in the United States, and then he began moving west, city by city, before landing in Seattle. By the time he met Ellie, James was more than ready to settle down. Over lunch one afternoon, while the rest of their department was at a meeting, they began the perfect summer romance that James felt responsible to end when September came. He dumped Ellie because he wanted to have children by age forty—only a few months away— and Ellie was thirteen years his junior.

At twenty-six years old, Ellie Gold was not completely against having children, but she didn't fight James too much over the breakup. They both still had tremendous feelings for each other, but she did not want to waste James's time, either—because as it turns out, Ellie, too, understood the repercussions of skin shade in her life. As a Sephardic and Ashkenazi Jew, Ellie has one parent, her mother, who is very light-skinned, and another, her father, who is dark. Born and raised in Israel, her father (whose family came from Spain long before) met her mother (a towhead born in South America) when she moved to Israel at an early age. They had no complications in Israel due to color, as they shared so much else in common: They both spoke Spanish, Hebrew, and English; they both had roots in Israeli culture; and they were both Jewish. They came to the United States doing NGO work for the betterment of Israel before Ellie was born. When Ellie's older brother (by eight years) left for college, they took Ellie, who was a completely Americanized preteen West Coaster by then, on the road. Ellie was interested to see the world and didn't fight them much. She spent the next six years—her teenage years—in Singapore, Tokyo, Hong Kong, and Taiwan.

While living in Asia, Ellie attended Baptist schools. Prayer time and the fact that all her classmates but one were white would begin her personal journey into feeling like an outsider in a group—but it was her after-school experiences that would stay with her forever.

Ellie witnessed the prejudice that existed toward dark-skinned, particularly Indian, people in many of these countries during this time. Ellie's dark-skinned father was often mistaken as Indian, and was sometimes refused service at restaurants. Her family would then leave the establishment and five minutes later Ellie's lighter-skinned mother would then ask for a table and be granted one immediately.

Ethnocentricity, racism, and the prejudices of shade were all part of Ellie's elementary and junior high curriculum.

She didn't discuss any of this intolerance with her dad; rather, he let the lessons speak for themselves. Her parents were moving them around the globe doing their work and her dad was not so caught up in making friends. Their family kept their same cultural practices wherever they lived, and Ellie and her mother were very close and talked about most things. They discussed everything Ellie was feeling at this time, but the memories of the actions Ellie witnessed have stayed with her the most over the years. Therefore, Ellie fully understands the premise of all the questions swirling in my head today.

Ellie didn't spend much time as an adult examining those childhood feelings, but James's desire for children opened her eyes to a deep understanding that she wouldn't want to put her children in the situation she'd experienced—where they would be so different from everyone else. However, she and James were both mad for each other. The love-struck fools continued to go on a platonic date once a week for four months, which officially ended when they attempted to spend a New Year's Eve together as friends. That night, James finally came to terms with the fact that he didn't want to spend his life without her. And Ellie felt the same, even while she feared the possible pitfalls of living as a black and olive/Jewish and heathen/Israeli and Trinidadian American couple.

By this time James had left the company they worked for and Ellie witnessed firsthand how much harder James had to work for jobs than even she did, as an olive-skinned female with fewer degrees and less experience. James had completed a master's degree by this time and still had periods where he was out of work. Stunning statistics were driven home for Ellie during that time. Even during the Clinton-era economic boom, the unemployment rate for young black males was double and, in some parts of the country, triple that of white males.[1] After George Bush's years in office, when America's unemployment rate rose to near Depression-era levels of almost 10 percent, by many accounts more than one-quarter of that figure was reserved for black males. According to *The New York Times*, in 2000, 65 percent of black male high school dropouts in their twenties were jobless, and by 2004, that share had grown to 72 percent—compared with 34 percent of white and 19 percent of Hispanic dropouts. But even when high school graduates were included, half of black men in their twenties were jobless in 2004—up from 46 percent in 2000.[2]

Keep in mind the incredibly high rate of incarceration for black males between twenty and thirty years old—in 1995, 16 percent of black men in their twenties who did not attend college were in jail or prison, and again by 2004, that figure climbed to 21 percent for incarceration, eclipsed only by the fact that by their mid-thirties, six in ten black men who had dropped out of school had spent time in prison. With such statistics, Ellie wondered, who in the black community was actually working? And what would this lack of working males do to this community over many years? The U.S. Bureau of Labor Statistics showed that unemployment in 2009 for blacks, or African Americans, was nearly double that for whites, and there was an even larger discrepancy between blacks and Asians.[3] Ellie found that her experience of being the outsider in the many circles she grew up in couldn't prepare her for just how difficult things could be for an educated black male in the States. NPR.org states that African American men over the age of twenty lead the country's jobless surge with an unemployment rate of 17.1 percent today.[4]

Although Seattle is believed to have the highest interracial couple population in America, Ellie was also concerned about their double minority status, and what this would mean for their children. All of these things furthered Ellie's feelings that life outside of Seattle was not an option for them—a hard reality for her given how important travel had been in her family growing up.

I sit in her apartment while the rain pours outside the floor-to-ceiling windows. Ellie chases the tracks of the raindrops against the windows with her fingers as if they were tears streaming down the life she once saw for herself. She loves James with all her heart and feels lucky to have him, but she was sure that Seattle, Brooklyn, D.C., and Los Angeles were the only places they could live—where their being of different races, different religions, and different heritages wouldn't entirely define every other decision they would make in life.

I feel confused, and moreover a little afraid, when Ellie first pronounces this. I remind her of San Francisco, Atlanta, New Orleans, Miami, and Chicago. But she has stipulations for each of those locales, and it is clear that she's already given this a lot of thought. One city divides black and white Americans by water; another lacks a Jewish community; and some, she feels, are more Southern and Midwestern than I was aware. Ellie is way ahead of me on racial tolerance when it comes to love, and I feel unequipped to discourse with someone who is as liberal-minded as I am but more experienced and well read on the subject. Her willingness and bravery to discuss these potentially embarrassing and hot-button issues at all are what makes me think she might just be the most progressive and evolved woman of my generation whom I personally know.

"Evolved" might seem like the wrong word, except when you consider the cycle of liberalization. First something is taboo, then it becomes chic, but in order for it to become a norm it has to be held up side by side against the norm. Ellie grew up in a home where she witnessed how light and dark were treated compared with one another, and then her own experience in Asia showed her just how hard it is to be the only person of a different color and/or faith than everyone else. Attending college in Iowa state finalized her perspective on how Americans categorize people—into narrow cubbyholes, with little room for people like her who straddle two cultures or, perhaps more to the point, two shades of skin color. Thus, her own experiences brought her an intimate understanding that sharing a life with James was a choice that would affect many other choices—no matter how much my left-leaning, N.Y./L.A., Buddhist ass wanted to believe that her union was nothing but wonderful and righteous. I believe only a personal evolution could allow anyone to stare into the face of race relations when it comes to love in this country and call it out. And Ellie's willingness to do so is finally making me look at my own history of race and culture that I bring with me into my union with Seung. And I wonder how my own experience might be impacting my pending marriage.

✱ WHEN I BEGAN CATHOLIC SCHOOL, AT SIX YEARS

old, I had heard stories about the "race riots" that had taken place in the public high school just one mile away. This was practically an annual event, due to fighting between black, white, and Latino teenagers. Surrounding counties would lend their police forces to stop the spread of violence from erupting in different parts of my town. My family was out of the city by then, living on a small island off the south shore of Long Island. My parents hoped to give us a less urban experience, hoping to allow us to be kids for as long as possible. The suburb they chose was full of first- and second-generation Americans of every possible descent, and most that I knew were blue-collar like us, and hoping to give their kids more opportunity than they had.

I remember getting off the bus in first grade, in my very Irish enclave, and seeing two white kids chase a black boy all the way to the bay. The white boys carried bats. When the black boy reached the end of the turf, he had no option but to jump the wall of a dock and throw himself into the bay. My friend and I hid in the bushes to see what those guys with bats would do. We saw them yelling and swinging while the lone swimmer crossed a quarter mile of ocean, fully clothed, in winter, to a marsh, where a helicopter is rumored to have picked him up. By that time the streetlights were on and that was my cue to go home.

The following year, in second grade, I was wearing a pin on my uniform to denote an Italian Saint Day. Two tiny, Smurf-like girls I hung around asked about my jewelry while we hopscotched on the black-tar parking lot our school called a playground. "You're not Irish? You're a guinea?" one scoffed. The Smurfettes then let out a tirade of slurs about grease and oil and pigs and woppers and other things I didn't understand. My heart began to race. I had an impulse to make this awful feeling I had yet to identify as shame go away. I surmised I could do this by explaining that this was only half of me. The other half was just like them! But I was afraid. Afraid to disown . . . something. My mom, maybe the things I loved about my house, the Italy I imagined—me, even?

I stood paralyzed in my plaid skirt, wondering how this had all turned so ugly so quickly. Specifically wondering where Jesus could be as these little shits taunted me. Wondering what their well-manicured mothers would say if they could see them now. I had no idea their mothers or fathers were the only people who could have taught them these words I had never read in any book. I sat behind my miniature desk the rest of that day, emotionally distraught, while McShort and McVicious threw slanderous notes at me and whispered my tale to others. How sad to call this a rite of passage, but hasn't everyone had some version of this afternoon in grade school? Over something that made you *different?* After school, however, the rawness of where I grew up was primed to show its teeth.

The mafia of two multiplied in just one afternoon to a bunch of Irish girls and two boys they sucked in. Together this green gang of second-graders cornered me outside chapel to "tell me" what else was wrong with being Italian, as they launched into a beating of another kind.

But this wasn't the start of my cultural journey in America. It wasn't even my first experience with prejudice. It was just the first time it was directed at me. So it remains indelible. My family had a short history in this country before this moment when I was about to get my ass kicked for being a child of two cultures that most people would never even notice I am a blend of. Now that the cultural cat was out of the bag, though, today was my turn on the chopping block. The slight difference between me and my entirely white, Catholic, mostly Irish, eight-year-old classmates was laughable if not saddening, forty minutes from Manhattan, in 1977—but where I grew up defined much about my ethnic experience, as I have found it does for most Americans.

I'd love to say that I was inspired to become an actress by Meryl Streep or someone with an academy award or an Ivy League degree.

But really, I was moved to the stage by learning to survive in the alley behind it where I grew up. I scared off my classmates that day with a tool I realized I had while eating gravel beneath them: words.

As soon as the first shove toppled me, I began telling a tale of my twenty-five Irish cousins and another fifty Italian cousins in the public school who fought other white kids as a warm-up for the fights with blacks and Puerto Ricans in the public high school. And that I would unleash both sides of my family on these twerps if they didn't back off right now. I only bled from the knee, from that first push that brought me to the ground, because then the kids dispersed— and I spent the rest of my adolescence making sure I would never be knocked down again.

I was highly aware during the rest of my school years what the dominant culture of any circle I came upon was. I spent my time mastering the art of blending into any group, to avoid the many physical confrontations that recurred for both boys and girls in my 'hood. I became so deft at fitting into other cultures that I took first place in a rodeo among farm-raised girls at a summer camp and was moving to Israel to live in a kibbutz after finishing my predominately Jewish high school. But as I turned seventeen, my mother finally shook me by the shoulders and forbade me to move to the Middle East. She was over my chameleon nature and told me I was Italian! I could go to Italy to live with the exchange student we'd housed a few years earlier, or I could stay home until college began. And, well, the choice was simple.

While living in Rome, I learned a lot about life *in* America. Specifically, that my family's culture had little to do with Italy—ranging from the Italian expressions they used, which are not even in the Italian language, to the food they ate, which has more to do with New York than with any region of Italy. The cultural tidbits I learned at home that I thought were romantic and foreign were mostly a product of the New York ghettos that bastardized them. I surmised the same applied to our Irish traditions. After this eye-opener, it still took a decade of globe-trotting to crystallize the perspective I have today.

The first step was transferring to a university in England after winning a place in a prestigious drama program. On my first day, a student asked what nationality I was. I responded as I always have: Irish and Italian. Her brow crunched and a high-pitched *"Really?"* came out of her, as only a South Londoner can do. I locked my feet onto the ground and bent my knees slightly. This was not in preparation for a ballet move. Ready to utilize that other skill my New York education gave me, I asked, "Why's that?" with a tone intended to feel like a shove.

"I was sure you were American," she said.

This ridiculous moment was the first time it ever occurred to me that being American is a culture of its own. I was so afraid to seem like a philistine—which I was—at my fancy English college that I spent the next year wiping much of that New York edge off my shoulder, for the same reasons I felt at seven years old: I didn't want to denounce or embarrass my people. My American people, that is.

And, I'm proud to say, for the most part I have—let that chip/block/fear go. I traversed most of the globe during my twenties and became such an everywoman that today I am often assumed to be of whatever culture people like most about me—whether that is a place I have lived for a while or one of my cultural backgrounds. But

I always, gently, remind people that I am wholly American. And a product of the opportunities it has afforded me. That is, until I fell in love with Seung.

All that running around the planet must have sealed my fondness for other cultures with a kiss. Few of the men I ever considered spending my life with pledged allegiance to the same flag I do, but none of their mothers had doubts about me with the intensity of my soon-to-be in-laws' family. And in truth, it's not Seung's mother or his father or any of his relatives who've left me so twisted over my desire to share a life with him. Rather, it is the ethnocentricity of all people in my country who want to judge those of us who love with our hearts first, and our skin . . . never.

I have looked at my own parents' racist boundaries on love and my own feelings of being judged when I've been involved with someone whose parents did not want me to date them because of race. I'm quite sure that I have sweated all those feelings out of me—by seeing the world and learning to understand it. So what exactly is possessing me so much that I can't use my clearest head to make decisions about how to move forward with Seung's family?

I think I have to keep listening and stop analyzing to find that answer. At least I hope so.

✳ ELLIE'S CONCERNS ABOUT MOVING FORWARD

with James were further weighted. She was also aware that her father would have the same negative reaction as Seung's family did if she chose to marry outside of her culture and faith. Adding another race onto this would make this union so much harder for him to accept. I believe this stems from the same reason as it does for many Israeli or Korean or for that matter Greek, Croatian, or Belarusian immigrants to this country . . . or those of Armenian descent. Anyone from a country or culture that almost lost their homeland, language, and customs within our parents' or grandparents' lifetime has a heartfelt desire to keep their traditions alive. Knowing this, Ellie waited almost two years before even telling her mother about her relationship with James. When she finally found out, Mom said she would support Ellie if she chose to spend her life with him. Yet she also suggested that they not tell her father unless this union became very serious. Another year went by before Ellie's dad became aware of his daughter's choice.

"My father had never met any of my boyfriends. Bringing James to a family dinner was a very big deal; it meant I intended to marry him." Ellie tells me this as we sit in a waterfront coffee shop, and it feels reminiscent of Seung's experience. I have finally stopped talking about the mess I have made in my own relationship and the exhaustion I feel at such a comparatively early stage in my life with Seung. Ellie continuously reminds me that she is telling me details of the experiences that once caused her so much worry only because they don't come up at all now, ever even, with her family. She is calm as she talks about the anxiety of her decisions—to live with him or not, to tell her parents or not, and perhaps ultimately to give up a relationship with either James or her parents.

When Ellie did finally decide to move in with James, part of their agreement as a couple was that she would tell her father about them and bring James into the fold. Ellie knew her father would be disappointed about this relationship, but it was clearly time for her and James to stand as a couple in the one place they still weren't: her family home. The first meal at her parents' house with James was highly uncomfortable, yet there was no drama.

"There was very little dialogue between me and my father—not that we were exceptionally chatty before this," says Ellie. But the moments of silence were loaded now. And the continuation of them, over the coming years in Ellie's life, would only make them heavier and heavier.

"But you do what you're doing, Diane. You show up and you put the work in and you try to keep talking as much as possible. And it works out. It always works out, honey. The thing you have to shed now is the anxiety and the anger and the fear, because that is yours. And that's the only thing you can control. You are marrying him, and you have to remember why and move your life forward. If you don't trust them, then please trust me when I say they will come around."

Funny, that's not the way I see it happening. I can't imagine that my Habitrail will just knock itself off its paralyzing stand one day and suddenly move forward into the future. And truth be told, that's not how I remember Ellie's path, either.

This is my good friend. I know her story. And I know my opinion of it has its own biases, but now I must ask her if she really and truly remembers it going that smoothly, after she introduced a black atheist from Trinidad as the man she loved most to her father. Ellie takes a moment.

She reminds me that at James's urging she began therapy after they first told her father about their union. She did this to learn how to put her own experiences and awkward feelings about growing up biracial into words. So that she could then begin to separate that experience from her and James's experience and speak to each, independently, with her family.

Which all sounds so wonderful now—but in the years this was happening I remember feeling very frustrated with her. I wanted her to yell at her father and tell him that "conditional love" was not acceptable! And I wanted to tell her mother to fight harder for her daughter's choices. And I wanted James to propose because it was taking a really, really long time to *me* on the outside. This was, of course, before I stepped up to the podium for my own try at *Racial Jeopardy*, where each question you pose has the potential for incremental gain or total loss. I was unaware of the particular finesse needed in many families before an interracial marriage or having mixed-race children can happen . . . and sometimes still afterward.

In fact, Ellie is the person I believe I most owe an apology to because I had such a "right side/wrong side" view of those who didn't immediately support a son or daughter like her when they began dating someone other than what was "expected." But as Seung's parents have become more and more human to me (even as his relatives become more and more caustic), and as each of the families I have asked to counsel me shows me the way to a happy mixed-race marriage with formerly judging parents, I have come to a larger view of what I consider a "pending" postracial America. This would be an America in which we would be less racially minded because this experience and all of my discussions about it have led me to believe that we are still not "post" anything to do with color and class—even in this new century, even after riding the wave of hope and change in 2008.

But I believe we can get there much faster now, with dialogue, for one main reason. Estimates project that the 2010 census will show that today one out of every three Americans is of mixed race or ethnicity. That figure is up 25 percent since the 2000 census, when checking more than one race became an option for the first time. And this percentage is up because of the children of those original seven million Americans who checked more than one box to define their background at the turn of this century.[5] So as each of these Americans grows up and attempts to find a soul mate, the palette to choose from is widening. And therefore, that line that Ellie awakened me to a long time ago, when a trend goes from taboo to chic to the norm, is probably right around its tipping point.

Yet even reconciling my new opinion of Ellie's path to marriage and seeing that it wasn't so slow after all, but rather allowed her to recognize her own experiences, I'm not transposing this information to my situation yet. I assume I'm just not trusting enough to let this "fix itself" over time. And I can't stop thinking about Jennifer and Sonu, who waited seventeen years for her parents to come around. I don't have the patience for that.

I had no patience long before this romantic relationship began. Lack of patience is like a genetic defect in my family. My father was born without any and he passed that flaw on to me and I'm sure I will give it to one of my unsuspecting children. But sitting here with Ellie, I now wonder if this inability to slow down and let this happen naturally is my actual problem. Because I understand what Ellie is telling me. And I believe it to be true. I've also seen from all the couples I've already talked to that punching the "elephant in the room" doesn't work, either. I can't even make myself go that route when I feel super angry. So Ellie is right that time heals the prejudice of love. I should worry less and let my new family find their own way to me.

But I'm no more convinced I'm going to be good at this "holding my tongue and letting others see things for themselves" job than I was when I first interviewed Lisa. Even then, before I had even met a single person in Seung's family and held my first interview/crying confessional over the phone with a complete stranger—who warned me to think about the long haul and the big picture before taking any action—I had no faith I would rise to that challenge.

I can also see that Ellie has this part figured out for a whole other reason, which has brought her a kind of peace I never could have imagined for her. I'm drinking iced coffee rather than hot in this city famous for its brew because Ellie's son Daniel is running in circles around our table. I'd rather miss out on the freshly brewed than possibly hurt this perfect child in any way by accidentally spilling hot liquid on him. Daniel is making me and everyone else in the café laugh out loud as he tries to cheer me up. At three years old, he might be the most delicious thing in this shop, and there is a lot of pastry behind that counter. But I'm getting ahead of myself . . .

So no, Ellie never gave up on James, just like she never gave up on me even when I pushed her hard, just like she didn't give up on her father when his silence ignited her self-doubt. Rather, she and James stayed in the dating stage for five years, working their way through it. James's hopes of having a child by forty were significantly off track when a life-changing piece of advice fell in his girlfriend's lap and it seemed the obstacle blocking their way around the last bend they were stalled behind was removed.

Ellie's older brother had followed in his cultural and familial traditions. He married a faithful Jewish woman and together they had children soon after marriage. On a visit to see Ellie, her brother listened to her latest concerns about where she stood with their parents and their father's continued hope that she would abandon this relationship for something more familiar. And finally her brother gave it to her straight:

"He said, 'You have to decide, Ellie. You have to decide if this is the relationship for you regardless of them, because while you still have a hint of indecision, Dad will continue to angle you toward how they see your life. And until you are clear and firm on what you want, they will continue to fight for what they know they want—even if that is only because they assume it will be easier for you.'"

It seems so simple, but what this credo finally forced Ellie to do was exactly what she is advising me to do now: take ownership of the life she'd found and not wait for anyone else to bless it. She had to say goodbye to the idea of picking a lifelong partner who would please her parents' goals or vision. And in her case, Ellie, too, had to say goodbye to the long-standing idea of the kind of husband she thought she would have—the banker or lawyer the rest of her boarding school classmates married. Do they enjoy a more comfortable life than two artists will probably ever share? Perhaps, but without the fun and energetic spirit she found in James, who has supported her through all of this and then some—whom she did and still does love like no one ever before—what would her life be?

In fact, the first time Ellie went to Trinidad with James, she called me and half-joked that she had found "her people." On this small island, Ellie found a whole country full of people who looked just like her. There has been so much mixing of races over many generations in Trinidad that the bulk of its people look like Ellie. Indian? Or Latin? Brazilian? Or Persian, or some other mix you can't quite put your finger on. But yet, here they are. Finally—people who look just like the girl who always looked different from the rest. And these people all thought Ellie was from Trinidad until she opened her mouth. Her accent was different, but her spirit and color were just like theirs. And in a strange way, Ellie loved James for this, too.

Taking everything into account, Ellie made a conscious decision to marry and become a mother to someone who would be a wonderful hybrid, just like her, again. Which then allowed her parents' disappointment to run its course. It was always clear that Ellie's parents would love her no matter what, that they would be in her life no matter what, but for so many people in these situations the idea of failing your parents often looms larger than the actual act of doing so. After letting go of that fear, Ellie fully embraced the man she had loved for a long time by now, and we both agree that it seemed almost immediate that her family then embraced James as well.

"There was no TV moment. There was no yelling in the beginning, no hugging in the end. We all just kept showing up to do the work and eventually it just worked," says my friend with an ease I envy.

But the thing I realize as the rain lets up for just one moment in this town is that almost everyone I have spoken with speaks to having had this experience. A moment in a relationship where you fully commit to your partner, no matter what the cost with one of your families. There are more dramatic incidents in some paths to this decision (and to the altar), but none of that drama yields the result I'm searching for, because I am hoping to inspire a change of heart. This change is so gradual that it lacks fanfare. It is not only inspirational but also life-changing—if I will let it happen. I just need to find the inner strength, the personal faith, and the divinely inspired patience that I need to *let it happen*.

* AFTER DANIEL GOES TO BED, I HAVE TWO important questions for Ellie about her beautiful wedding—because I'm feeling inspired to get back to mine. There are two images from her union that remain like slow-motion stills of what love and acceptance mean to me. And now I would like to know how they came to fruition.

James proposed and he and Ellie soon married on a floating dock in Lake Union on one of the most beautiful days I've ever seen in the Pacific Northwest. Just as the dock began to float like a lily pad away from the rowing club, Ellie joined all of her invited guests. Not with her father, who was with all of us, but alone Ellie walked to meet her partner.

The image of her walking herself down the aisle (which was really a small hill to a floating barge) was so breathtaking because she had done all the homework to get here. She walked *herself* to this choice and was owning every step of it now as she approached her soon-to-be husband—which made me cry like a baby at how proud I was of her. Proud that she did not hide behind her family's fears or ignore the reality that she herself had lived. Proud that she took the time to feel all the feelings she had about her former life and her future life. When Ellie finally arrived under the chuppah to meet James, next to their female rabbi, in her stunning white dress on beautiful olive skin, she looked like a princess about to become a queen.

"We looked at the sentiment of what is behind a walk down the aisle and wanted to give ourselves to each other. Because this was our own doing. So no one was walking me down the aisle because I was giving myself to this man," says Ellie.

Later, inside the dining hall, the post dinner music trumped even the beauty of the afternoon. James's family flew in from all over the world to enjoy his long-awaited wedding day. And to facilitate the enjoyment, particularly the dancing, this bride and groom hired a twelve-piece steel drum band—whom they also asked to play traditional Israeli wedding songs. At the end of the evening, when I approached the band members to shake their hands and say how wonderful a job they did, they told me how nervous they were to play "Hava Nagila" for the first time in public.

"I was really nervous how this was gonna go off," Ellie says now when I recall this exchange. "I just kept hoping they practiced."

They did. The bandleader told me she also wasn't ever positive how it was going to go. She was so nervous that the entire band sat in the parking lot the night before Ellie's wedding after loading their equipment in and played the song over and over. Well, watching Ellie's extended family moving in one direction and then the other while clapping and holding hands, with James's family doing the same, to Hebrew songs on Caribbean drums is one of the most resounding images I have ever seen at a celebration of love.

✱ I REALLY CAN'T WAIT TO MARRY THE GIANT

Korean, and have my very evolved friend Ellie in attendance—whose brother's advice is now rattling around in my head as I try and decide what it means for me. I cried so much during Ellie's wedding that I was actually mortified in front of other guests, and here I am crying again. Only now I'm trying to make sure I don't freak out Daniel, who is so excited that I am here he has gotten out of bed three times.

When I look at this handsome boy now, I remember the first thing I asked his mother when he was born. What does the child of black, white, olive, Chinese, Spanish, and Scottish parents look like? To which she said, "He just looks like our Daniel. With really Chinese eyes."

Daniel is the poster child for mixed-race marriage. His hair is like chocolate spaghetti that fans out high from his head. His eyes are almond and his lips are pouty. His skin is wonderfully warm and silky. Ellie's holiday card last year was a picture of him drinking milk while a random Mexican woman stood off to the side taking his picture also. I liked it so much because, knowing their family, I was fully aware that the woman in the frame was just another instant fan of Daniel's look and aura, rather than someone they knew. I feel like he is the face of modern America.

Tonight I really don't want to upset this long-awaited child, but I can't stop crying. I don't know if I'm purging all these tears from happiness for Ellie because I finally appreciate all she has done to get here, or because I finally and sincerely feel hope for my own future and children while looking at her son. But Ellie is as patient as ever with me, while she waits for me to find the words to express all that I am feeling.

"I'm thinking about your brother's advice," I mumble between my tears, while balancing a sleepy boy on my lap. Ellie reminds me again that the advice was to fully accept that this was the relationship for her—and to let go of them—and now I'm cutting her off because I can't get my words out fast enough.

I know who my "them" is, and I actually believe I accepted Seung as mine before *them* even existed. I think I'm a little overwhelmed by *them* at the moment, though, and I'm putting my attention in the wrong place. If I follow the pearls in this chain of wisdom, I should just stay committed to whatever Seung and I want for our life together, while I continue to beat back the people pleaser in me who wants to win *them* over, the micromanaging control freak in me who is attempting to change another person's thoughts or behaviors, and that fearful inner child who lives in the doubt room inside me and would rather miss out on things than fail. If I can possibly let go of all that just going on inside me—and think less about *them*—then I should end up answering only to the best me.

As I get all that out and my breath starts to calm, Ellie smiles at me. This causes Daniel to clap his hands and turn around on my lap to wipe my tears and say, "No more crying now."

And I listen to this wise soul.

NOW I THINK I KNOW where Ellie got some other parts of her peace. Aside from her and James doing all of their homework, her life recentered itself with her son. As it also did for everyone else around her.

The universe must have been rewarding James for his patience because Daniel was a gem from the moment he arrived. Ellie and he chose to wait to find out his gender until the delivery room. When their son was born, there was the inevitable question about circumcision from Ellie's parents, as it's is an important rite of passage for Jewish people. Ellie and James had discussed this during the tail end of their pregnancy and decided a circumcision wasn't for them. Ellie's mother gently broached this subject with her daughter while they were still in the hospital postbirth, asking Ellie to reconsider. This new grandma gave all the reasons she and Ellie's father felt it would be a good thing for Daniel. Ellie's father then joined the conversation, and when Ellie told him that her and James's decision was final, her father actually wept. Which is exactly when James entered the room. These new grandparents got their feelings together quickly and left the room to allow the new parents their private time. Ellie refused to tell James what had transpired, saying they could talk about it at home.

When James got together with some of his friends after the birth, they congratulated him and asked when the bris would take place (the name of the ceremony for circumcising babies in the Jewish faith on day eight of life). James was shocked to know that all these guys, many of whom were not Jewish, knew about this ritual. What they said they all knew was that if you marry a Jewish girl and you have a son, you inevitably circumcise about a week later.

James went home and asked Ellie about this, and about what had transpired between her and her parents at the hospital. Ellie explained and James wanted to call his father-in-law immediately. He wanted details of how the mohel (Jewish holy person who does the incision) would handle things, but he was already sure he would accommodate their request. He asked Ellie's father and brother to handle the details because he wouldn't know how to orchestrate this ceremony, but he was willing to allow them this important ritual in

CHAPTER 12.

A KOREAN NIGHT +

AN AMERICAN NIGHT =

A QUELLED FIGHT

"By the powers vested in me—by the Internet—
I now pronounce you husband and wife."
—BARRY LITTMAN, ESQ.

'M IN SEUNG'S hotel room and his mother is dressing me. She has laid out my Korean wedding gown, all four layers of it, in the order she will put them on me. Seung is in the other room with his father, who is dressing him. All four of us are very nervous and excited as two hundred people wait in the lobby below us, about to be bussed to the Friday night dinner and ceremony location for our Korean wedding. Despite the nerves, both of Seung's parents seem to feel pride as they prepare us to make this rite of passage. My mother is on her way over from her hotel room to watch me prepare for a ritual that neither one of us could have possibly imagined would make up part of my wedding.

THE INITIAL REJECTIONS WE got from Seung's father's relatives never changed. And once we embraced that their decisions were out of our control, those decisions stopped affecting our relationship and our wedding. This bump actually taught us an important lesson: A wedding is like a marriage in that you plan the best you can for your life together, deal with whatever presents itself, and move forward from there. And for us, if you're getting married in your late thirties, part of the program is to learn to move forward with as much grace and positive energy as you can. I learned this entirely by Ellie's example. Seung's hurt feelings passed quickly, since he still had so many family members—especially cousins—to celebrate this day with, but I think I actually figured out how to resolve mine before my flight even returned to L.A. from my weekend in Seattle. I took a cue from Ellie because I saw how wonderfully her life with James turned out. I recalled the image of her on that lone walk to her sacred space beside James, where she gave herself to this man in marriage, without the good and the bad that are sometimes mutually exclusive when it comes to family, and how much fuller her life is because of that choice. I want to be like Ellie. As I want to be like Suzanne and Jennifer and Lisa—and I hope like hell Natalia will join us, too, someday soon—on the betrothed side of interracial coupledom. So with a little more therapy—and many long late-night talks with honest old friends as well as brave new ones, who fully healed what ailed me before I reached this room today—I am here. I let go of the impulse to right any supposed wrongs or prove myself to anyone. And I got to invite several more of my friends, too! All of whom I can't wait to see in less than one hour from now, in a wedding gown fit for a Korean princess.

MY *HANBOK* (TRADITIONAL KOREAN GOWN) is a pink and blue silk that starts at my collarbone and gets bigger and bigger as it makes its way to the floor. The bottom layer begins with cotton on top and morphs into tulle at my middle, creating a bell from my waist on downward. The next two layers are of varying lengths, made of brightly colored silk, with hand-sewn flowers in places that no one but Ama and me will ever see. The icing on the cake is a silk topper and a tiny jacket that is regal yet still feels girlish with its gold trim.

I could not possibly have assembled this dress without my soon-to-be mother-in-law's assistance. She bought it for me, but in her typically unobtrusive way she also allowed me to pick it out for myself. Seung and I went to three *hanbok* dressmakers in Koreatown, Los Angeles, before finding our matching attire. The first family-run store was intimate, which made it all the more obvious when the women working there never addressed me directly or even looked me in the eye while I stood before them betrothed to a Korean national. It did not give us a warm or welcoming feeling, so we tried another.

The second store was fancy, with gowns that cost thousands more than my white wedding dress. The women at this shop were excited to dress me, but worried that nothing they had would be long enough for my body and they would therefore have to custom-build a Hanbok for me. Seung did not like the modern take on their designs for an ancient ritual, so off we went to the third boutique. But this was actually a grocery store with millions of dollars in fancy gowns tucked away in the back. Seung knew a Korean couple who'd bought their Hanbok here, and the same day we got the address to this off-the-beaten-path dressmaker, Seung's father called us from Seoul, also recommending the same shop. As I walked past the many kinds of ramen and fresh vegetables in front, I couldn't help but feel as if Jennifer, who married Sonu in the traditional Indian wedding, was with me, since she, too, found her wedding dress in an Indian grocery store in Virginia.

Colors in Hanboks have to do with the age of the bride and groom. Red was too young for me and peach too old. Pink, I would find out only after we settled on one, is also for a young person, but the grocers/dressmakers believed I was twenty-four years old! I know this because a story about a TV actress buying a Hanbok there later appeared in a few local Korean newspapers, and that was the age the stories ran with. When Seung first told Ama that my Hanbok was pink, she was concerned it wouldn't look right on a thirty-six-year-old bride. But now, as she puts the final layer on me, she says in the hushed whisper Ama always speaks in, "It's perfect. You are perfect, Diane." And I wonder what I did right in my life to deserve this woman as my mother-in-law.

My own mother has now arrived and won't stop crying as she looks at me in my fancy garb. Seung's father pats her shoulder to soothe her. They only met each other for the first time last night at a dinner we had for just my family and Seung's. That dinner was one of the more stressful of my life. My parents had a rather harmonious divorce after thirty-five years spent together, but one year later my father's remaining feelings for my mom turned to anger. They have not seen or spoken to each other in four years until this weekend— specifically, until they sat across from each other last night. Which felt incredibly reminiscent of Lisa and Dave's rehearsal dinner.

I knew Seung's parents would, of course, be very reserved and not do much talking throughout this meal. Silence is foreign in my family to begin with, but given the strife between my mother and father I was sure I wouldn't be the only one in my immediate family feeling on edge. But to make things even worse, there is a giant lie that Seung told his parents about me. A lie that anyone in my family could accidentally slip up on over the course of this meal. And I spent the majority of that evening waiting for disaster to happen.

Seung's birthday and mine are only three days apart, which is good luck in Korean culture. However, the fact that I am one year older than him is very bad luck. In fact, it's highly frowned upon. So as not to burden his parents with any more fears beyond my not being Korean, Seung lied to them and told them I was the same age as him. Making me, in fact, three days younger than him. Though I found this charming at the time, I've since realized how likely it is that we'll be caught at some point, though I'm hoping it's not tonight, the night before our wedding.

I have asked Seung two times over the past eighteen months to try and right the wrong of this at opportune times, but he hasn't wanted to. Since the age difference is so inconsequential to us and so paramount to his mother and father, I have trusted that this is cultural and I should leave it alone. However, after having escaped talk of my age, my graduations, my reunions, and the year I was born up to this point so I, too, wouldn't have to lie to his parents, I'm sure tonight will be the night the cat is let screaming and screeching out of the bag. And not by Seung or me.

I huddle my whole family in the entryway of the restaurant of our joint family dinner and point a finger at my mother. I tell her that there is to be no talk of anyone's age, or anyone's birthdays, or any year before 1976, when my youngest brother was born. I warn my mother that our family will be doing most of the talking tonight (which really means her), but that if, by some miniscule chance, Seung's parents lead us into this territory, I will handle it. I then solemnly swear that I'm going to fine any one of them $500 if they blow this. My brothers (you remember them—the ones who made jokes about Koreans eating dogs the very first night they met Seung) then ask if they also have to pretend I'm a virgin. My father's whole body convulses a little, in repulsion at the mere intimation of my having sex, as he storms off and into dinner. My brothers and grandmother follow, but I grab my mom by the arm and whisper to her one-on-one.

I'm serious when I say it is not my grandmother, her eighty-seven-year-old mother, who I'm worried will slip up. It's her—after two cocktails. She not-so-gently reminds me that I'm not the first person on Earth to have a secret from my in-laws and that I should get over myself.

Which seems like stellar advice until two drinks later when she begins a sentence with, "So, the year Diane was born . . . " and I rise up out of my chair like Jesus Christ on Easter morning. Seung's sister, Eun Yi, who has become more and more of my friend over this wedding process, asks my mother if she could show her to the bathroom right now. Feeling surrounded by me and my new sister, my mother still has the audacity to shrug her shoulders at me like, *Whatever! I got it.*

* TODAY, AS MY MOTHER AND SEUNG'S PARENTS head off to meet my father in the lobby for the Korean ceremony, all is calm again. I wave goodbye to them and then, finding myself alone with Seung in his hotel room for the first time in several days, I jump onto his back like a teenager with too much nervous energy. I ask him if he wants to practice this piggyback ride for later tonight. He is so nervous that he forgets I'm not kidding. Seung puts me down and tells me he wants to practice his speech. He also doesn't want me to hear it, so he is pacing and whispering to himself and kinda reminding me of Fred Flintstone after a fight with Wilma. I am trying to calm him down and remind him that it doesn't matter now. We are all in. Seung never really calms down this evening. I, on the other hand, am done worrying.

All of the homework I can possibly do is done. I've passed the baton of running this show over to my "producer" and the production assistants and all the relatives who will help. And I am weightless tonight. Now I just get to have fun with some of my favorite people in the world who have all come so far to help Seung and me enjoy this day.

Along with Cousin Charles, who will be introducing us when we enter the five-thousand-bulb fairy-light tent for our ceremony, Seung's cousin Mike and three of his dearest friends from around the country will emcee the ceremony from a script that we all wrote together. They will explain each of the five chosen rituals that I have learned over my engagement and let the lightness and joy of love permeate these very serious ceremonies.

But first the crowd will enjoy a traditional Korean barbecue. Or so I believe. I am pleasantly unaware that Seung's other two cousins, Brian and Eric, have not yet gotten the food for this dinner to the tent where it is meant to be served in fifteen minutes. This is because I didn't realize, when I asked them to drive the food up here, that today is also the day Korea is playing in the World Cup.

It's no shocker that there is no Korean food in Mammoth. I've hired a friend's mom, who is a terrific caterer in Koreatown, to make all the most popular Korean dishes. She got started in Los Angeles this morning at five o'clock, and a refrigerated truck will be driving her dishes up the mountain tonight. A local caterer is standing by to do nothing but serve the food, pour soju (Korean rice wine, like Japanese sake) for the collective shots we're asking our guests to toast us with, and get all of my rented gear—everything from chairs to flatware—prepared to be bussed to tomorrow's location.

The kicker is that we asked Seung's single, twentysomething cousins to pick up the truck and then the food from Koreatown to reach the caterers by 5:00 PM. Brian and Eric seemed like the perfect candidates for this mission because they speak fluent Korean and would be able to communicate with our friend's mom and translate the Korean symbols on the dishes to the caterers. We didn't take into account the fact that their pride as Korean Americans would lead them to take a three-hour break, while en route, in a local bar to watch soccer. But that's where they are when my producer calls to check up on them. Our event starts at 7:30 PM, and the food finally arrives at 7:29.

When dessert is served, Charles gets up to begin our ceremony and talk about the Chung family's journey to this country. He is wonderfully serious and wonderfully silly. He makes all the male cousins stand up to prove just how big Koreans are and swears this is because of Cheez-Its. He says that all the Chung mothers ate so many of them when first coming to America that the introduction of dairy into their diets made their kids huge. Charles then raises a glass of soju and asks everyone to make a first toast with the words "Kampai!" As hundreds of people drink in their first taste of Korean spirits, the Como (older sister of Seung's father, who flew here from

Hawaii) begins talking heatedly to Charles. It takes a few relatives to confer and confirm, and then translate to Charles before he gets back on the microphone to say:

"Sorry. *'Kampai'* is the Japanese way to say 'cheers.' *'Kum bei'* is the Korean toast. So, let's do another shot, with *'kum bei!'*"

Everyone laughs and takes another drink, while I squeeze Seung's hand just outside the tent. We're waiting to make our entrance and are just out of sight from the guests, but not out of earshot. I tell him, "I knew the relatives would heckle us if we got anything wrong," and I say it with a smile because I know I've gotten all my Korean things right.

Seung and I now step onto the stolen pallets, which are beautifully wrapped in burlap and silk to encompass the mountain and Asian theme of this night. Our parents then join us from their respective tables at opposite ends of this center stage. Seung and I now begin the first of many bows we will make over the next hour. Seung's mother's family jump out of their seats to assist me right from the start. I do almost twice as many "head to the floor bows" as Seung. Our friend Karl (who found me my coach and is also narrating a part of the ceremony) assures all the females present that reciprocity will be served, as Seung will surely be making up for my excess humility tonight over the rest of his life. Seung gives my parents hand-carved geese, as is tradition because they mate for life. I catch ten Jujubes and eight dates in my dress, meaning I will have eighteen children by Seung. At one point I pour Apa and Ama tea, filling their glasses to the brim and watching their faces closely. I expect them to be shocked when they discover I spiked the tea with Crown Royal, but they only laugh, and I wink, and we settle in to enjoy a terrific night together.

The last ritual of the evening involves Seung carrying me around the tent on his back—and then my mother! My mother refuses, though, even after the entire room cheers her on, so I get two piggyback rides. Seung then takes the microphone and does a masterful job on his speech. He thanks his parents for their love and support and for giving him such a rich culture alongside his very American life. He thanks family and friends for making this long trek, and makes me feel like even more of a princess by talking about my quest for this weekend to be wonderful for everyone. After the crowd has been asked to drink soju many, many, many times (and has the option to chase it with either Guinness or chianti, representing my cultural backgrounds), Seung asks everyone to take one more shot before he hands the microphone over to me.

I thank my grandmother particularly. Not just because she flew from New York with my niece on her lap, and then took a five-hour car ride to reach this ten-thousand-foot town, and is here tonight drinking with the best of 'em, but because she is the immigrant of my family and had it not been for her journey I wouldn't be here at all. I explain how my grandmother came to America in 1927 as the youngest of five children from Ireland. I tell how she nearly gave her mother a heart attack when she eloped with an Italian boy from the neighboring ghetto on 125th Street in Manhattan. There are over twenty-five people in this room tonight whom my grandmother held in her arms as children, all of whom witnessed how rich my gram's life has been, as well as my mother's, due to the blend of two cultures in their household.

I then go on to call anybody a punk who cannot hang and drink as well as this octogenarian. I invite my guests to join us for karaoke in a bar we have rented for the evening in the lobby of the hotel where everyone is staying, and encourage them to have a hangover at my actual wedding tomorrow. Because just like at the wedding Seung and I got together at, magical things can happen at the Friday night party before a Saturday night wedding and no one should hold back on my account. And all jokes aside, I now turn to the other immigrants in the room, my new in-laws.

In Korean, I begin the following speech:

"Father and Mother, I am very glad to be here with you and your family and to marry your son tonight. I thank you for accepting me as part of your family, particularly because I know I was not what you imagined for Seung Yong. But your kindness and love have made me feel welcome. I assure you that I love your son very much, and I look forward to learning your culture with him and sharing it with our children. My heart belongs with all of yours now."

My father-in-law weeps openly from my first sentence onward. As does Seung, even though he does not understand most of the Korean words I am using. But, of course, the content of what I say is not what moves him.

* ON SATURDAY MORNING I JUST WANT MY mother and grandmother with me when I get ready for my actual wedding. The two most wonderful hair and makeup artists whom I have come to love over fifteen years in television are here as guests on my big day, and they are spending the morning with us also, making the three of us look babe-a-licious. While they do their magic, I take twenty orchids from last night's centerpieces and cut them to make my own bridal bouquet. I wanted something from my Korean wedding to be part of my American one, and this seems fitting since one comes from every table. I tie the branches of the orchid stems together with extra lace from my wedding gown and my mother's baby bracelet. I then take my deceased best friend's high school graduation ring to bind them all together.

Also from last night I have two hundred "love notes" from all my guests. The last part of a Korean wedding ceremony is a time for elder relatives to give advice to the new couple and usually give money. We took this one step further by putting note cards under every dinner plate and asking the entire group to write their favorite love advice to us in lieu of cash. Some of the cards are funny but most are heartfelt. Barry, our friend and lawyer by day but minister for tonight, will pick his favorite three notes to share with the group as part of our "sermon" on the mountain deck this afternoon. But my friend and bridesmaid Liz, who is responsible for having introduced me to her husband's friend Seung, is late to pick up these note cards. Liz took my advice to heart last night and is so hungover today that she is two hours late to come be my wedding runner. But it's actually kind of good that she's late, because during this delay, I realize I have an uninvited guest with me.

"Who gets their period on their wedding day?" I ask myself in the bathroom as I scrounge around for feminine doodads. I have nothing in this little medicine chest to remedy what I do not want on my wedding gown. So when Liz finally drags herself over, I send her right back out to get tampons. To which she says, "I guess you're not pregnant, then?"

At thirty-six years old and completely engulfed in a hormonal baby fog, I started trying to get pregnant three months ago. I figured even if I were twelve weeks pregnant on this day, I still wouldn't be showing and that was fine by me. Both Seung's mother and mine independently asked us to start trying to conceive from the moment we got engaged. By the time they were my age, they both had children in high school. So they are plenty eager for me to hurry up. But two weeks ago, after I'd peed on ovulation sticks nearly every morning over the last seventy-five days, my maid of honor told me I should just wait until after the wedding now. She felt I had too much on my plate, and conception would never happen this close to game day. Considering I was going to Korea and then Sri Lanka on my honeymoon and would have a hard time keeping track of everything, I chucked the ovulation kit into the drawer two weeks ago. Even though I wasn't trying, I have to admit I am a little sad to see it confirmed that there's still no baby on board.

And then suddenly Liz is back and I am dressed and off we go. First in an elevator, then in the car, and finally in a gondola to the ceremony site where the entire wedding party is gathered. Seung and I do a reveal, where he sees me as his American bride for the first time and the photographers catch every moment of it on film. We have an enormous wedding party—eight men, eight women, two flower girls, plus our minister and two readers. This party of twenty-five, along with the photogs, are my nearest and dearest and we are all laughing so hard while we do a giant photo shoot. And it's just now that I'm realizing how American this entire ritual is. American weddings vary by family and faith and location, but the emotions behind each beat are all thoroughly a part of our culture. Girl wears white dress, while boy wears his very best. A family passes their daughter to a man who will now become her new family. Friends bear witness as the couple make promises for their future to each other. Bread is broken and celebration ensues.

AS EVERYONE IS brought up by gondola, my dad and I are hiding in the kitchen of the facility that's adjacent to our ceremony site. The guests are given champagne at the bottom of the mountain so they can enjoy the ride up that much more. Fifteen minutes later, they're greeted by the five Buddhist monks here today who are chanting wonderful echoes all around them. Once all the guests are seated, the wedding party begins their procession to our altar to the sound of Leonard Cohen's "Hallelujah." The holy men then join Barry in the closest circle around Seung, who waits for me. And I take my daddy's arm as we begin the walk down the aisle.

When I come into the outdoor room, all the sound stops and our guests stand. I can't help but smile when I see Seung. He not only looks so nervous, but he also looks about sixteen years old. I can feel my father's hand shaking as we walk across the rose petals to those same pallets, covered in more burlap and white trim today. My father lifts my veil and he kisses my cheek. I whisper, "Thank you," and wink at him, trying to calm his nerves. But as I let go, I feel light-headed myself. I reach for Seung and, just as he has from the moment I met him, he steadies me.

Seung and I each wrote five things we love most about each other that Barry will read aloud as part of our vows. We did not show these things to each other, and I have been nervous that Seung's stoic nature would make his love seem less romantic than mine. But in the end, three of the five things we each wrote were exactly the same.

Barry says that Seung loves me because I have the strength of a hundred men to get done what is important to me and mine, and secondly, because I know more about Asian culture than he does. Then, that I love Seung because he allows me to be softer and kinder by his example, and that when he picked me up for our first date and I saw he drove a Porsche, I asked him if he was in the Korean Mob. When he whispered back, "Yes," I didn't even care if he was serious. Barry then notes that we also each wrote that we feel like a perfect yin and yang, but that we gave different examples to prove how. We both said that we needed the other at night because I am so cold and he is so warm and together we make each other more comfortable. We both summed up that we loved how the other valued the family we started with and longed for the one we would make together. And we both spoke of knowing ourselves well enough to know when we've met our match. We went about this point in very different ways, which made me giggle spontaneously on the altar, because Seung's version was so much sweeter and more poetic than mine—even though I was considered the writer between us.

Barry passes our rings around to everyone in attendance, in a bird's nest that my maid of honor has secured them in. He asks each guest here today to function as a part of our marriage and help us to honor it. As he then walks us through the five steps of a traditional American wedding, we only get stuck when we can't get Seung's wedding band on his finger. Not because the crowd has abducted it but because his hands are so swollen from the altitude. I put Seung's wedding band on his pinky and assure our assembly that I will see to it later. Barry closes by saying, "By the powers vested in me—by the Internet—I now pronounce you husband and wife." And with a lean in and a big kiss to Seung, The Giant Korean is mine forever.

* AT THE RECEPTION, SEUNG AND I HAVE AN
official "first dance" (trumping our actual first dance at the engagement party where I first met him, when Christine was underneath my
skirt and I pulled on my eyelids to signal him over to me). And then
I have another dance with my dad. Afterward I take my place on the
side of the dance floor we made for ourselves, under a tree where we
hung disco balls, to watch as Seung dances with his mother. I am
wondering if Ama knows that this is a wedding tradition in our country. It clearly doesn't matter because her face is beaming as she looks
up at Seung now. And then I have a little solo dance with my mother,
too, because for as much grief as I have given her for being an untrav-
eled American whose priority has never been learning new things, she
worked hard on making her children good people. Her vicissitude as
a parent is what has allowed me to challenge her on the differences in
our beliefs. And I thank her most for that.

Just before dinner I ask my bridesmaid Leigh to join me in the
bathroom. Leigh is my oldest friend and the only one I could ask to
do this job with me. There is so much material on the bottom of my
gown, making it into the giant fluffy thing that it is, that I don't know
how I'm going to address my need to change a tampon. But with
Leigh holding four feet of white crinoline, I manage to get halfway
there. When I see that the previous one has absolutely no blood, I
gasp. Leigh is trying to comfort me, saying it's not on the dress either,
but that's not what I'm thinking. I am so excited I can hardly breathe.
Leigh had her children long ago and clearly is not as versed in "latching" as I am. I am almost positive that the disappearance of my period
is because it wasn't a period at all. But, trying not to incite a riot of
excitement, I refrain from explaining any of this. When I tell Leigh I

won't be needing another girl product, she comments how funny the mind is—that one could just will her body to stop its normal cycle. And I hug her, really hoping that I have willed my body into something bigger than that.

When dessert is served, my father walks the room with a humidor, handing out Cuban cigars. I purchased them on a recent trip to Dubai and am so thrilled they have survived all the way here. Both Seung and his sister partake in the cigars, but Seung's dad immediately rushes over to him and tells him that he should put it out. He reminds Seung that Korean children do not smoke in front of their parents, as it's disrespectful. But tonight Seung puts his arm around his father and says, "Apa, the Korean night is over. You are an American citizen and so am I, so smoke 'em if you got 'em!" Apa does not get the reference, but he lights up anyway and lets Seung be. (He does, however, insist that Eun Yi put out her cigar on the spot, so I'm guessing this hall pass for Seung to do as he wants won't be carried over after our big day is done.)

My table has had fancy champagne on it all night. The Korean tables have bottles of Crown Royal, and my Irish relatives have blue-label Jameson. My friends are showered in vodka and Seung's are bathed in scotch. And they all collectively drink too much and dance until the proprietors beg us to get on the bus for the thirty-minute ride home. Once we're on, I see strangers making out with each other and two guys I don't know who are heatedly debating the lyrics to a Don Henley song. There is both laughter and vomit on the ride back, which all proves to me that a good time was had by all.

When Seung and I wake in our condo the next morning, I tell him about the mishap with my period and that for all we know it may have been a fetus latching to my uterus on our wedding day. "Fetus" and "uterus" are not words Seung wants to hear after a night of drinking, so he puts his hand out to make it stop. When I press him that we literally may have gotten pregnant on our wedding day, he pats my face, saying, "That's great, honey." Clearly, he ain't buyin' it.

We race out to our breakfast brunch and I sit down with Seung's cousin Dan from Texas. His daughter and Leigh's daughter were our flower girls yesterday, and I am hoping to get some time with their family before they head out. Dan was Seung's childhood idol. He was the first Korean relative whom Seung saw play football and cheer for American sports teams. Dan is charming and the father to three stunning daughters. His wife, Candace, is elegant and kind and indulged me when I asked for just her youngest daughter to walk with my god-daughter for our ceremony. Suddenly, just now this morning, I realize that Candace is American and Caucasian, and a Texan at that. I just now think to ask her if Como (older sister of Seung's father—her mother-in-law) had any issues when she and Dan got married. She says her mother-in-law did not object, but she pauses just long enough that I suspect someone did.

We smile at each other, not sure of what to do from here, as I am just entering a family she has been a part of for over a decade. Only I'm practiced at this kind of conversation by now, and I am about to ask Candace if it was her family who had an objection to her relationship with Dan. And ask her what they did as a couple to keep their relationship safe from the objections of others. All leading up to the bigger discussion about what Candace did to handle her whoever's feelings at the time of her wedding—when I suddenly realize I don't have to ask anymore.

Because I am here. I have my own story of how I arrived at my marriage to someone of a different race when one family was dissenting at the start. Seung is my husband and everyone here at breakfast this morning makes up both our families. Instead of needing to discuss it all, I just smile as Candace explains to her daughter that she can call me Auntie if she likes. And I'm so excited that my family just might look like hers someday (if I'm lucky enough) and that all the turmoil of "how will we survive if one of our families shuns us?" is done. With a wedding band beneath my beautiful engagement ring on my left finger, I have crossed over from she who is looking for advice—to she who has some to give. My path to marriage was not the most treacherous tale of all those I have heard, and I did manage to arrive at my wedding, with more than enough family and friends to support Seung and me. Hopefully all this drama between love and race will end soon. Until then, I am now ready to be to other mixed-race couples what those forthright and loving souls were to me.

* SEUNG CARRIES ME OVER THE THRESHOLD OF our home in L.A. when we return Sunday night, while my roommate from college in England photographs us. She and a dear friend from New York are sleeping over, as are my father and grandmother. It's a packed house on our first night at home. And at six in the morning the next day, my maid of honor, Laurie, does her last duty and sneaks in the side door of my kitchen to bring me a pregnancy test. I run into my bathroom to pee on the stick, and before stepping out to show her the answer, I race into my bedroom to wake Seung. I put the pee-stick right in Seung's face. He wakes to the oh-so-gnarly smell of my morning's first urine one inch from his nose and asks what an "X" means. I adjust the stick so he can see that it is actually a plus sign. For positive. We are pregnant.

I see five things go running across Seung Chung's face. But the one that lasts is total disbelief. He is left frozen, staring at me like, *How the hell did you make that happen, one second after we were married?* Without his having to say a word, I whisper, "You married an Irish girl. What did you expect?"

Other than Laurie and Seung, no one will know our news for the time being. Immediately upon seeing the positive sign, Laurie fills my bag with five more pregnancy tests, warning me that I will not be satisfied with just one. And then she puts three books wrapped in a T-shirt inside also. When I ask what they are, Laurie says everything I need to know about gestation, and that they're hidden in the shirts in case my in-laws are standing next to me in the security line and I'm asked to empty my bags. Holy shit, did I pick the best maid of honor or what?

We're driving to the airport in less than an hour with Seung's parents, who are also flying to Korea. We're not on the same airline as Ama and Apa, and I am so glad because once I'm on the aircraft and buckled in, I am voraciously inhaling *What to Expect When You're Expecting.* Seung, however, is nonplussed. Either he really doesn't believe it, or he is still too high from yesterday's events. Ah, yes, just yesterday, when my life had a whole other focus.

I will only find out months from now that early pregnancy for men is very different from early pregnancy for women, but while sitting in the fancy class to Korea, I decide to take Seung's cue and put the pregnancy on hold till after our honeymoon. Or at least I will try to.

CHAPTER 13.

LET'S TAKE THIS

SHOW ON THE ROAD!

"How many people will be sitting for dinner
at this wedding reception tomorrow?"
—MS. DIANE FARR, AKA MRS. DIANE CHUNG

S EOUL IS UNLIKE any other city I've ever been in. It's as urban
as Hong Kong or New York, but it does not have an island
feel like both of them do, even though most of the real estate is
upward bound. The streets in the city are as quiet as Chicago's—
where people are polite and don't raise their voices. It's also as clean
as Singapore, but the youth here are a dead giveaway that this is
a democracy through and through. Teenagers in Seoul are much
more artistic than almost anywhere else in Asia, reminiscent to me
only of Tokyo. The kids are listening to music I haven't even heard
of and are outfitted like chic, cool pop stars. Animation and video
games take on a whole other level here, so much so that they make
a PlayStation look like Atari.

The twentysomething working people ever on the move in this
sprawling capital are in a hurry like Californians, but are wielding
electronics that put Hollywood to shame. While riding trains around

this city, I'm amazed not only that everyone's phones work *everywhere* here, but that they just have to tilt their heads to hang up the call before making the next one. Chauffeur-driven cars abound, the shopping puts Paris to shame, and I have to wonder aloud if the whole southern half of this peninsula is rich. Seung replies that we're leaving for the countryside tomorrow and I can see for myself. Before we go I ask him to sit with me in a coffee shop and take a moment to just look around. This city is so fast. And so busy. And the most amazing thing about it all is that I can go an entire day without seeing another non-Asian person. Picture yourself walking through a skyscraper-filled environment where everyone is the same race. It's so strange. But the most amazing part is that even though they are not my race, they are so cosmopolitan that they are not intrigued or even remotely interested in the fact that I'm different or Caucasian. This is the most unique mix of the best of both worlds as an ethnophile. All of us souls who run around the world looking to discover a place just before it is "discovered" by the masses will rarely, if ever, be satisfied. Because discovering a new land and culture, before they are either overly interested in you for your tourism dollars or completely over you for what the tourism has done to them, is a tiny window that most of us with a wanderlust may never hit. Well, let me say for the record, I just found mine in Korea.

The next day Seung and I say goodbye to his parents and take off alone on the fast train to Buson, a small city on the southeastern tip of the country that's famous for its film festival and honeymooners and I finally see the rice paddies. The image of terraced land with people squatting low, doing the backbreaking work that constitutes pulling each grain of rice from the ground, swells my heart. It's a visceral feeling I have, seeing this labor that literally looks like God's work in the hot sun. Korea is so uniquely breathtaking, though, because the backdrop to these gorgeous green vistas of tall grasses are mountains. Huge mountains that go on and on across the country. It is not only one of the most dramatic landscapes I've seen in the lower Orient—it packs the punch of a much bigger state. And to think that I am only seeing half the beauty this landmass has to offer because Kim Jong Il sequesters North Korea from the rest from the world.

Seung and I stay in the same hotel where his parents stayed nearly forty years before on their honeymoon. The hotel has changed greatly, but the beach might be exactly the same. We take long walks over rocks and sand and eat terrific food in very local, family-owned restaurants all along the way. We travel to the outdoor daily market and finally, I feel like an alien. It's not because I'm American. Or Caucasian. It's because I have a T-shirt on that the locals don't like. Said T-shirt covers me across my collarbone and to my elbows. It is loose around the middle, but Seung warned me that it was too fitted on my chest when we left our room today. I was sure I already had a gauge on the modesty in this country and didn't agree. However, the *ajimas* (Korean for older women not related to you) who sell their food at the stalls here today are heckling me. I can't understand their words, but their tone is universal. This is furthered when they literally start grabbing their breasts as a gesture to hide mine. I hurry to the next aisle in this market where the sun isn't so bright on my white shirt, hoping maybe the shade will make it all seem like less of a display.

There are miles of dried everything at these food stalls, from seaweed to frogs. The foods and spices are stunning in color and wonderful to see, but even to me, as well traveled as I like to consider myself, some of these things seem too frightening to even think about consuming. My new husband is having a ball, though, buying all kinds of strange-looking stuff to take back to his parents. (At least I hope it's for his parents.) This very distant town feels like a real honeymoon, and Seung and I sleep in and let all the thrill of the wedding go as we begin to fold back into one another.

TWO DAYS LATER when we get back to Seoul, Seung and I begin our many meetings with his relatives. The women I can't wait to meet most are the two daughters of the eldest male of Seung's father's generation, who were raised entirely in America and came back here to South Korea after college. They are the ones who not only married people their grandmother deemed appropriate, but also nursed their father back to health after his stroke. I can't imagine how these women bridged the gap between having been Americanized in their education and life and yet still so traditional in their relationships to family and their major life choices. The younger sister, Judy, is on the East Coast of America right now but when I meet Rita in person, you might guess that I don't hesitate to ask everything I'm wondering.

"I was miserable at first," says Rita, the elder of these two sisters, about leaving the States to come back to Korea as a single twentysomething. "It was really hard. But eventually it did get better." Again, like all the members of our generation in Seung's family, I find Rita to be without pretense. Her husband went to Pepperdine University, and not only has seen every movie ever made, but is a producer and buyer of films in Korea. Rita tells me that she actually knew her husband before the "tea" set up by their families. She had met him at many events in Seoul through mutual friends, and Rita whispered to him at the end of one late-night party, "Don't tell my grandmother that I was here." Everyone laughs at the table and I can't tell if she is kidding or not, but her candor is fantastic nonetheless. She tells me the story of her wedding, perhaps in preparation for the party we're having here later this week. She says it's not an evening of revelry or dancing, and that children in Korea (even grown children like Seung and me, in their late thirties) do not drink in front of their parents.

So it's not just smoking, it's all the devilish calling cards that I was raised on, as an Irish/Italian/New Yorker/American, that are off-limits in front of parents here. Huh. But Rita also says that as soon as her wedding was over, she and her husband had so many laughs and drinks in rapid succession with friends, not far from the ballroom where their families were, that they totally made up for the formal ceremony. So maybe it's not all that different—just the appearance is?

Rita has us meet today at a four-story restaurant in the middle of Seoul that is run by Buddhist monks. The food is family-style and epic with its portions, and we cannot possibly get through it all. It's only that much more unlikely to happen because Rita and I won't stop talking. She tells me that she has opened a private school to teach the many languages she knows to children. I look at her life and wonder if Seung and I could ever live here. Her husband could produce my movies and I could sit at a little-kid desk after filming and really learn this language from Rita. Seung smiles, knowing how I get sucked into every place I visit, wanting to stay for three to five years, but then end up rarely even returning for a visit because my drive to see someplace new is insatiable. But this is Seung's family's homeland. I know I will be back here, and I'm so thrilled that I do like these people. I'm actually very inspired by Rita, and all of Seung's cousins in fact. I find nothing but comfort in every member of our generation in Seung's family. I look forward to my children playing with theirs.

My other most significant meeting with a family member is with a cousin on Seung's mother's side. Ama was only four years old when her mother passed away, and her father remarried and had more children. She, too, is one of eight siblings. I have always found all of Ama's relatives wonderfully humble and kind. This niece of Ama's, who was born and still lives in Korea, is the same, as well as hardworking. She is a manager at the five-star hotel where Seung's parents have put us up for this week, and where our reception will be held tomorrow, on Saturday evening. Today Seung and I, along with his parents, are following this niece, who is also Seung's cousin—I don't know her name, but she is slightly older than me, so they may never tell me her name because I am not supposed to use it. If I speak to her directly, I will call her Un-Nee (like I called my Korean coach—meaning "big sister"). We are all following Un-Nee for a viewing of the room where our reception will be held.

The anteroom before the ballroom is huge. Un-Nee tells me that this is where Seung and I will line up with his mother and father and bow to every guest, one at a time. She then leads us inside to the main room. It looks so tremendous that I'm totally confused. But this cousin sits me down at what is clearly the conclusion of the English portion of this tour, and she speaks at length to Seung's parents in Korean. When she comes back to me, to ask if I like Seoul, I say, "Yes, very much, Un-Nee." She politely giggles like everyone else does when I call them by the appropriate billing. Seung then politely asks her how long she has been working here and without pause adds her given name, something I can't really understand and definitely cannot spell, but the point is, he says her name and all hell breaks loose.

Un-Nee yells at him. And I mean *yells*. She leans over the table and wags a finger in Seung's face also and tells him first in Korean and then in English that he will not use her first name at any time, ever. And that he should learn from me. I'm so embarrassed for Seung I can't even laugh, because she might as well have spanked him. His parents do nothing to defend him because they, of course, are fastidious believers in the vow of respecting an elder—even a cousin just two years his senior whom he has never even met before. In order to change the subject, I ask Un-Nee (hell yeah, I'm not getting that wrong) how many people will be in this giant room tomorrow night.

She doesn't answer my question but rather explains that my in-laws have chosen several buffets for the evening. There will be Korean food, Japanese food, Chinese food, and American food wrapped all the way around the space. It is traditional to have buffets at Korean weddings, and how many different styles of food you serve is a show of success and pride. But even with a forty foot buffet all the way around the room, this room is too big. I point-blank ask Un-Nee, "How many people will be sitting for dinner at this wedding reception tomorrow?"

And I almost fall out of my chair when she says, "Two hundred."

* ON SATURDAY EVENING, I DON MY HANBOK again for my next full-scale reception. At least I am getting to wear this beautiful dress twice. I'm wondering if there are other rituals I will be asked to do tonight, so I ask my mother-in-law, who says, "No rituals tonight. Just speaking and eating."

I'm not really sure what that means, but who cares. I am always up for a party, and I truly love my in-laws. And not just because I didn't have to do one second of planning for this event. On the first day in Seoul they drove us all over town, and on a bathroom break halfway through the day I asked Seung if I should worry about how quiet we all are in the car. I'm hyperconscious of not taking any bonding time away from them and their son because I'm not Korean. And I'm worried that I am already dampening their family conversation because I don't speak the language. Seung laughs at me and says this is the most talking they've all done since he was in high school.

He tells me to think of his parents like grandparents. Like people who really love him but don't have that much in common with him. They just want to be physically near him. And suddenly, I get it. I spend a lot of time with my grandmother. It mostly centers around food, and my telling her all sorts of things she probably doesn't care one iota about, but she listens intently and loves to hear a good drama from me. I think her favorite thing to do with me is cuddle up and watch TV together. So from this day forward I think of Ama and Apa like Seung's grandparents and the entire week goes splendidly. Every day that they take us on a journey, I take a little catnap in the car and they are so happy to see me sleep and know that I am comfortable with them.

Frankly, I am excited to have this night go by so that I can share the news that I am pregnant with Ama tomorrow before we leave on Monday for our actual honeymoon. I wanted to tell them the second I arrived in Seoul, but I've spent five days trying to talk Seung into telling them—at least before we leave Korea. But he is not yet fully on board. He feels that we should go to the doctor and have someone with a title confirm and charge me for my pregnancy results. Seung just doesn't seem to believe this pregnancy is a fact yet, even though I have taken all five pregnancy tests, one every morning, and they've all given the same result.

Today I beg him to let us tell his parents while we are here this week because otherwise we will have to tell them by phone. Seung may want bloodwork to prove this is not a hysterical pregnancy, but he is also aware just how exciting and important this news will be to his mother and father. He has secretly resigned himself that it is indeed happening and now just wants to prolong the unending discussions and daily phone calls it will unleash between him and his parents for nine long months. Finally, with this admission, I tell him "tough noogies," because I've only had an Ama and an Apa for seven days, but I can't keep it from them anymore. We are telling them tomorrow after wedding number three, no matter what.

❋ **I STAND BETWEEN AMA AND SEUNG ON THE** receiving line in the anteroom. I am amazed at how many ten-foot flower arrangements are in this entry room from friends of the Chungs. I meet a woman who is like a mother to Ama or Apa, I can't remember which, and she is quite old but so fashionable. Someone gives her a corsage and she redresses it herself and makes it even hipper. I'm so excited that I'm quasi-related to her. She, being the eldest in the family, gets on our receiving line first. As the guests start coming, I start bowing. I say hello in Korean and touch my heart with two hands as I say, "Diane." And I bow the deepest full-standing bow possible again. I do this for every single guest for almost an hour!

By the time Seung and I walk into the wedding hall, every seat is filled. There is a dais on a stage above the crowd, and I laugh as I realize Seung and I have to go up there. We look like the actual top of a Korean wedding cake. And everyone stares at us as if we really are just dolls and not actually people. And I begin this fantasy in my head that I just married the president of Korea or something and this is just another diplomatic evening I will sit through, where I don't understand anything but I keep smiling to spread goodwill. And I hold on to this character study all night because that's basically exactly how it goes.

We are only sitting for two minutes when Un-Nee's younger brother gets up to a microphone and begins speaking. This cousin, whom I have not met before tonight, is a stand-up comedian. He is handsome and actually looks like Seung but with much better, fantastically mod hair. I'm stunned as I realize he has been called upon to emcee the wedding. He speaks about Seung and me in Korean and throws in some English here and there, I assume for me. He then shows a video of photos set to music of Seung and me through the ages.

This is really sweet. Seung asked me for baby pictures months ago and I didn't think much of it but assumed it was something for our wedding. When it never transpired I forgot all about it. But here they are, and looking so cute in between Seung's same-age photos. And once I reach the adult years, I can't believe that Seung's dad has found more pictures of me on the Internet than even *I've* found of me on the Internet. Seung leans over in mock anger that there are way more pictures of me than of him. And they're great pictures! I want them, too.

After the slideshow a very dapper man is called to the stage. He speaks for a long time and at a certain point Seung looks over at me smiling. He leans in to whisper that this is another Como's husband. This Como is long deceased and the family really loved her. Her husband is an esteemed professor at a university in Seoul. He is the keynote speaker of our event. I am unaware of it still, but there are yet another four speakers lined up to talk. All broken up by the cousin emcee. Wow, that's what Ama meant when she said "eating and talking."

Seung is smiling because this professor is saying exactly what I have been saying to all the people in my life who ask if Seung's culture and mine are very different. For over a year I have been explaining that I see Koreans like the Irish of Asia. They are a small country, separated from their brethren on the same peninsula only by ideals. They are also victims to the whims of a much larger country (in Korea's case, China), which has been kicking their ass for a century. Therefore, they are scrappy. They have a rugged sense of survival, but they also know how to enjoy life. They eat in feasts and many drink till they drop. And the parallels go on and on. And here is a professor saying the same thing to a room full of people in Seoul, using much less colloquial language than I do, but expressing the same sentiment. And I have a little private moment when I feel like all my homework on the way to this marriage was not just about Seung's family. That it is about me, and who I am as this man's wife. And I love my homework. I have never done research on anything—a country, an author, a character—that has failed to inform some part of my personal worldview. As of today I'm sure that all my research about marrying into this family, this culture, and this race will only make me a better wife and a more well-rounded person.

Which is a complete contradiction to my laughing my ass off when I ask Seung what the professor is saying now and he shrugs his shoulders and whispers, "I have no freaking idea." But it's not his words that are cracking me up. It's the shrug of his shoulders that finally causes me to look at the hat on his head, and I burst out laughing.

We drove all over the city of Seoul today—for nearly six hours—chasing down the hats Seung and I are wearing. We drove from relative to relative, I think finally finishing our hunt at this professor's house. These hats are heirlooms, worn during the wedding ceremonies of many of Seung's father's family members. Apa wanted us to have them for tonight. They also came with immense and ornate wraps that would go on the outside of our wedding gowns, but Ama thought they were too dusty for us to wear. My hat is like a colorful pillbox. The base is round and short and black, and there are very colorful things all around it. It wasn't until I put this hat on that my entire ensemble actually seemed like a costume. The look of the entire dress changed with my hat, and now it seems like it belongs to a life other than my own. I wondered like a teenager, in the bathroom of my hotel suite tonight when I pinned my hat in, if Seung would still find me attractive in my "foreign" gear.

And when I looked at Seung for the first time tonight with his hat on, I mostly saw that he was just as worried about me thinking he looked silly. My immediate instinct was to quell that worry of his. I did and never really looked at his hat again. But now as he is whispering to me that he has no idea what's happening at "our" wedding reception, I am worried that I'm about to fall into a fit of laughter that I will never be able to stop. Because as Seung shrugs and let his eyes roll back a bit, his resemblance to Mickey Mouse's friend Goofy can no longer be overlooked. Seung's hat is like a large black beanie on his head, with two long flaps of fabric hanging down the sides that look just like Goofy's ears. It's clearly not just me who saw this image, because as soon as I start laughing, Seung leans into my ear and talks in Goofy's voice to say, "Hey, Minnie Mouse, wanna ditch Mickey and come get married to me in South Korea?"

And now I laugh so hard that I pee my dress a little.

I'm desperate to stop before I pull focus from the speaker, but just then the professor finishes. Now Seung is moving his head and upper body in all sorts of Goofy-like ways and I may just have to excuse myself to the bathroom. Until a waiter comes over and sits down on the floor between us.

The waiter explains that there is a break before the next speaker and now it is time for us to get up, circle the room, and thank the guests for coming. He explains this in English, but both Seung and I are so shocked to have someone say something we can understand, we just stare at him. This causes him to then add, "You guys seemed to have no idea what was going on, so I thought I would just help you out."

Yes, you are right, and thank you! Seung and I whisper this and as we get up to make our rounds, his parents are already on their feet to take us table by table and introduce us. The waiter is totally right.

As we walk, I say my Korean sentences and am met with smiles everywhere. One gentleman even offers me a bottle of green-label scotch, which I have never seen before, that he says he brought for me because I am Irish. When he asks if I would like to do a shot with him, I've already accepted before I remember Rita's words about drinking in front of Seung's parents. I retract my previous statement and Seung steps in to tell me it would be okay to drink with this person. I have to raise an eyebrow, as I also remember for the both of us that I am newly pregnant. In response to which Seung does that Goofy thing with his shoulders again and I can't even speak, I'm trying so hard to stifle a laugh.

Once we return to our raised dinner table for two (having not done any shots), the waiter stays with us—on the floor behind the linens, where no one can see him—and does the Cyrano for us all night. Sometimes he says things that seem so preposterous that we both look down at him to say, *What?* and then I remember to drop my chopstick and pretend we were looking for it because he's not supposed to be up here with us, or specifically down on the floor between our seats.

Then comes the moment when he says, "Now you get up and give your speech, new husband."

Is it any shocker that Seung is not a big fan of public speaking? No less in a room filled with two hundred, of whom he probably only knows fifteen, people, plus thirty staff members, *and* he has to speak in Korean. Seung really just speaks enough Korean to talk logistics with his parents. I always say he does not speak enough of the language to walk into a Korean nightclub and go home with a national. He doesn't get the nuances of the language, nor have enough vocabulary to joke around in it. So as he stands up tonight, my first thought is *He is in trouble now.* But the pauses I hear him take as he muddles his way through this unexpected and impromptu oratorio are the same he does in English. And he seems okay. The softness in his tone is also the same as when he speaks English, which is incredibly disarming, and I see it working in the room. And his mannerisms seem like his own, but in fact, I think they are just a product of our generation and our mutual culture—our American culture, that is.

As I look at my husband, Seung, he still seems like that guy I hit on in a bar—three times before I finally let him kiss me—even as he is dressed up in a silk robe, with a Disney character–like hat on and speaking another language. Seung's persona supersedes his attire, his location, his words and language, and, most important, his race. He is a man made up of many interesting characteristics, precisely because they are a blend of his experiences growing up in D.C., with many friends and a family that loved him. He loves college football with a fervor that always shocks me, and he is a very competitive golfer. He is also a sneaker-head and hip-hop junkie and so well-versed in pop culture that I often wonder where he gets his intel from. But mostly, he really is just my Seung and no longer The Giant Korean. Isn't life funny that I had to come all the way to Korea to see just how American my husband really is? It is well worth the trip for so many reasons, but especially because I go home with him forever after.

* **THE NIGHT BEFORE WE LEAVE FOR OUR** honeymoon, Seung's parents take us to a very fancy restaurant on the top of a mountain in Seoul. They are excited and I am starving. But when we walk into the private room they have secured for the four of us, I see that the table is built into the floor and realize this is a sushi restaurant. Which makes me seem like the biggest pain in the ass because I can't eat raw fish while pregnant. I turn around and look at Seung and say, "Tell them," out loud. He ignores me and sits down.

As Ama and Apa begin ordering food and I have to say no to everything they suggest, I look at Seung again and plead with him to not do this to me. Finally, with a big huff and puff, he says to the room, "So we have some good news." His parents look at him so blankly that it's clear they have no inkling of what he is about to say.

"Diane is pregnant" is immediately met with a giant scream. A scream of happiness, but a scream. Then silence. Then Apa says something in Korean that requires no translation. I know he's just asked, "How pregnant? How far along?"

Having been reading my book on pregnancy I now realize I have to add on the four weeks before I discovered I was pregnant to give the right "gestation week." Instead of saying that I'm five weeks pregnant, which would be right, I add on another four weeks, thinking I have to go back another cycle, and I incorrectly say I'm nine weeks. Both of his parents look down at my belly. Seung starts talking quickly in Korean and it is obvious that they believe I am nine months pregnant. He explains that I'm really about three weeks in and that I discovered it two days after the wedding in Mammoth.

There is no hugging in this family, and since there is so little talking, there's not much more to say after the joyous scream. My new in-laws sit there perfectly happy and thrilled but never say another word throughout dinner. Not one. Because that is their way. It is so completely different from my family, but lovely, too. And I really am getting used to it now.

When we are walking to the car, I say to Seung, "Your mother is going to ask us not to take a honeymoon because she is worried." And he tells me I am being ridiculous. But as Apa opens the door for me to get in the car, Ama shuts it. She looks at me and says, "Please don't go to that island. Please stay here with us and be safe and I will take care of you." And I look at Seung to please, please answer her because I feel so badly that the answer is hell no, I'm not missing my honeymoon!

The next morning, Ama and Apa pick us up at the hotel and drive us to the airport. This week has been so magical because I've really felt like their child. They've given us our own little house at this hotel, along with a phone and spending money. They've thrown us a big party that I did not prepare for or clean up after in any way. We are thanking them profusely, and Ama is crying. She won't stop touching me and I know that my status as a wife to their son has changed. As I step into the line for security, she takes my hand one more time.

"This is the most important job of your life. Please be very careful. With *our* baby, Diane." I bow to my mother-in-law, and then my father-in-law, and then take Seung Yong Chung's hand. With my other hand I rub my belly like a happy Buddha and all the Chungs laugh with me.

"NOT GOOD ENOUGH to love? Who could be so base?" asked Edmund of Edgar in *King Lear* five centuries ago. Prejudice, when it comes to love, is nothing new. How ironic, though, that love could be the last prejudice even mainstream, seemingly progressive families can still teach their children at home in the giant melting pot that makes up America. Most Americans do teach their children that everyone deserves an education, and that, of course, all people have the right to vote and that all children in the sandbox can share your toys no matter what color their hands are as they reach for your shovel. Yet privately, sometime after the sandbox years and around the time children begin dating, this inclusive sentiment becomes altered. In so many homes, parents tell their children, "But you can't *love* one of them." Frankly, the challenges my generation still faces when picking a partner are not only saddening but, when you come right down to it, also unpatriotic.

So dare I say that if you are an American and enjoy all the opportunities this country affords you, then perhaps it is part of your duty to try to value all Americans equally until proven otherwise by their actions—if not all people, everywhere. Because if we had more nationalism in America—about who we are to each other *inside* this country, not just who we are as a superpower *outside* of it—perhaps we wouldn't be looking at one another like members of another team. Particularly since we are all considered to be the same heathen, capitalist breed when we leave these United States.

Race, like nationalism, is a social construct. Divisions based on race are basically lines drawn around a make-believe concept. The division only exists because we allow it to. I firmly believe it would make our country feel more like "one nation, under God, *indivisible,* with liberty and justice for all" if we would universally accept our national heritage for what it is—a culture of its own.

I would argue the simplest place to begin this new paradigm, of culture before color, is with matters of the heart. I am not pretending this is an easy task, because even beyond those with an extremist anti-miscegenation belief, when some American children start dating outside of their race, religion, or culture, many of their loved ones also seem to slip into what I call a Joseph McCarthy coma. Suddenly, otherwise intelligent people believe every value they have imparted to their child is at risk because of a dinner date. The anxiety this coma brings on, of the "outsider on his or her way in," prevents good people from remembering that everyone is someone's child. And that somewhere, everyone has a mother who worries someone will be unkind to her little one. Differences in religious faith, too, seem to allow some people who are fevered in the coma to do terribly uncharitable things to save their child's afterlife—no matter how many souls they crush in this life. And most sadly, the coma removes every fevered person's belief in their own loved ones. It causes parents of all faiths, backgrounds, and skin colors to doubt their children's ability to make good judgments about the character of others—particularly romantic partners—if they choose them without their parentally prescribed blinders on.

But if all parents could see the person whom their son or daughter brings home to love as no more or less than a fellow human being — if not at least a fellow American—and judge them on that criterion, then couldn't we make a difference, one person at a time?

Because after all, our American culture, which England and the Europeans laughed at when we first had the audacity to emerge as a scrappy colony centuries ago, has always been a melting pot of traditions that immigrants have brought ashore with them: English and Irish, Sunni and Shiite, East and West Timorese, Tutsi and Hutu, Indian and Pakistani, and even those born within who have had to learn to coexist— like Red Sox and Yankee fans. All of this wealth of opportunity and culture is what made America a superpower. This is what we intended to share with the world by example: the philosophy of democracy—not just the armed forces behind it.

*   ASIDE FROM MY OWN FAMILY STORY, THE five couples I detail in this book are only one-quarter of the multiethnic and mixed-religion couples I spoke with from the time I started dating Seung until I married him, and those I formally interviewed once I was writing my personal experience for this book. The wonderfully dynamic and beautiful backgrounds of the people who were not included in this book encompassed people and couples as varied as a Vietnamese American war baby from the south and a Dutch South African in New Jersey; a Mormon Philipino who married a Catholic Mexican in Utah; a black Puerto Rican who married a Midwesterner in New York; a half African American and half Caucasian woman who was raised on an American Indian reservation in the Midwest and an English ousted Zimbabwean in Oregon; a Christian Scientist from Texas who married a Chinese woman in California; a Brazilian from Nebraska and a half-black man from Iowa; a black man from Georgia who married a Mexican woman from Arizona (who are both born-again Christians); a Georgian in Wisconsin and a German-Indian from Miami; an Austrian Jewish male who loves a Christian Swedish male (who are having a one-quarter Latin, one-quarter Asian, and half-Caucasian baby by surrogate); two married women and their daughter in Kansas (one who is black, one who is brown, and one who was adopted from China); and a Caucasian sheik man from the East Coast who loved a Caucasian Mormon female from the West Coast—all of whom were willing to share their experiences with me in hopes of aiding another union. And my two heaviest hitters—a Jewish New Yorker who married a Shiite from Iran and raised a family in Arizona, and a Turkish woman who married an Armenian man and raised a family in Texas—are living proof that love can heal even the most difficult pains of the past. Their wonderfully balanced and happy children have since become the proof and truth I hold tightly to as I begin parenting children of a mixed-race background, like theirs.

Sadly, however, many of these original sixteen couples did not stay together. The reasons these unions ended varied, but I often found myself stuck between wondering whether their relationships ended because of the reasons they gave me or if their dissolution was somehow more influenced by the giant problems we discussed concerning their families' disapproval of their relationships. It became hard for me to believe that external pressure from family was not contributing more to these breakups than some of the couples were even aware, because despite the differences in the final blows to these pairings, the initial pokes, jabs, and knockouts were all remarkably the same. So those are the stories I have chosen to share here.

Of those who did continue their unions from this first batch of interviews, I also had two interviewees who never heard from their own parents again after telling them they were marrying outside of their race. I wrestled with myself endlessly over not including these heart-wrenching stories. Without them, I did not feel like I covered the diaspora of mixed-race marriage in America today—but in truth, I haven't even come close anyway.

My personal experience is just my own, and the people I chose to speak to were those I had access to—who were brave enough to let me call them, again and again over a three-year span, only to ask ever more probing questions. All of the couples I interviewed are more or less from the same class and educational background as I am, and those included here are mostly from the more metropolitan coasts of this country, where perhaps the issue of loving outside racial boundaries is less a flashpoint than in more conservative regions of the country. To be sure, there are harder and more challenging stories out there, I know.

But even being privy to some of these stories firsthand, I

ultimately had to decide why I was asking all of these questions. What was my *goal* in amassing this information? As I became more attached to the couples I was interviewing, I developed a deep interest in creating a road map to our kind of marriage. My desire became less and less about wanting to dish on, expose, or dramatize the crossroads between race and love in any one family and let them run wild through these pages. Rather, my goal was to understand the sometimes hostile, often demoralizing experiences we confront when we love outside our race and find a way to survive them. I wanted to learn from a series of long-term partnerships how these people were able to navigate the prejudices so many Americans have been taught at home and come out, in the end, with a solid relationship—with as little, if any, sense of alienation from family or friends.

So yes, there is more information to be considered in the landscape of interracial dating and perhaps even a retort to be made to these pages, but most important, there is a conversation that needs to be had. A conversation that Bill Clinton—several decades ago now—first asked America to begin "about race" and the integration of races in education, in work, and in living together in harmony in this country. He asked this so long ago that I was still a drunken, sexing starlet then, miles away from the advocate of homemade baby food that I am now. As I still saw myself as an individual at that time.

Individualism is a key component in our American ideal. Part of our collective credo is that any member of our society can rise up from their humble beginnings and achieve success—in work or love. But with age and now children, I see myself, foremost, as a member of a *community*—many communities, in fact, that start with my family and branch all the way out to our planet Earth. My quest within these pages has been to rethink the boundaries I and so many others were taught growing up, and find a way to encompass the community that America is now, where no family is any better than anyone else's based solely on the color of their skin, their economic status, or their philosophical, cultural, and religious beliefs.

As I wrote this book, I spent much time worrying about how my words might be misconstrued, misused, misquoted, and otherwise "missed." Ultimately, I decided to take the risk of writing my family's darkest, most embarrassing, sometimes provocative thoughts to track and revere our collective evolution, and to be fully sure I'd eviscerated any prejudiced tendencies I had within my own vernacular.

And I certainly had some schooling to do for myself.

If you recall, my initial thought when I first looked across the room at Seung, at my friend's engagement party, was *That giant Korean guy is cute.* Yes, I saw him as handsome, but I also saw him first and foremost for how he was different from me. For a few months after we began dating, I refused to acknowledge his race in my heavily Caucasian circle of friends because I wasn't sure if commenting on it was racist. And then I worried that treating race with kid gloves was implying that there was something sinister about our differences. So then I put the words "Korean" and "Asian" back into my vernacular— with a vengeance. And they haven't left me since.

And then I had children. When they began school, I again had no idea how to address the plethora of families I met. Not just interracial couples and their children, or children who are different races from both their parents, but families with very different makeups:

same genders, single parents, three- and four-parent homes, children living in temporary foster homes, children being cared for by nannies, children being cared for by nannies who didn't speak English, and children who didn't speak English themselves. And that was just my first week of preschool!

I once again removed every marker from my conversation that might be outdated or unknowingly hurtful. My oldest child is now four years old, and yes, I still have so much to learn—about other families, sure, but also about how to raise my own. I thus began having all the same intimate discussions that I had with interracial, bi-faithful, and multiethnic couples, with individuals who grew up mixed-race between 1973 and 1985. I've been querying these interesting and amazing souls—as adults today—on what choices their parents made that did and didn't work for them as individuals who straddle two or more races. (Can you smell my next book in that sentence?) And from them I am learning everything else I need to know to rewrite my family's creation myth. Yes, the homework I gave in the class that I taught to unwed fifteen-year-old mothers over a decade ago has come back to me now. Because how I see the world today is different from how my family taught it. So I have some reconfiguring of my own mother myth to do.

✳ I NO LONGER FEAR THAT MY CHILDREN'S RACIAL makeup will define them entirely. Now I think of my marriage and family as just one example of where America and the rest of the world are headed in the twenty-first century. Acceptance is becoming a sweeping tide. In fact, the year I married Seung, my then–TV show, *Numb3rs,* was sold to Korea. It went on to become one of its top-rated shows. I noticed this when I was suddenly invited to every foreign press event CBS did for the show. There were actors more well-known on the series than I was, but at a foreign junket, commentators waited to speak specifically to me. And they always wanted to discuss my marriage. In the years that followed, my children became a topic of discussion, too. When my father-in-law first flew to America after my son, Beckett's, birth, he had suitcases full of gifts that Korean fans had dropped off at his office, after our wedding announcement in Seoul listed the name of his company. So in the end, my marriage to Seung has brought me more fans than fewer—especially in the Korean community.

At my fortieth birthday party, surrounded by lots of friends, I was standing on a dance floor (read: coffee table, but you should know this about me by now), when I looked over at my husband, Seung Yong Chung. He was shaking his head at me. We were in Bali, staying in a house with our nearest, dearest, and most adventurous pals, trying to resurrect the life that Seung and I shared as a couple before we became parents.

I was gyrating on yet another piece of furniture, trying to lure Seung over to me because, like I discovered on the first night I met him . . . Seung Yong Chung is an amazing disco dancer. And he never stops smiling when he is dancing. It is magnetic. People all around him are drawn to look at the Giant Korean who can bust a move. And never do I ever fail to point out Seung to a stranger as "the Korean guy over there," but in our own world, in our own life together, I haven't seen him as a Korean or Asian person in a long time. He is just my Seung—who makes me feel like I won the lotto because he has never stopped loving me, no matter how anyone tried to tear us apart.

After enough cajoling, Seung is on this table with me, doing his dance and smiling his big smile. As our friends shout his name and applaud his stellar moves, I know there is nowhere I'd rather be than dancing right beside this man, so happy to be his wife.

ACKNOWLEDGMENTS

EXTRA-SPECIAL THANKS and a big shout-out for Christine Johnson! She not only was with me on all three occasions when I picked up my husband, and watched my kids so I could write, but also read every single draft of this book when no one but she believed that's what it would become. I'm sure a writer is only as good as her circle of honest friends. I'm so lucky to have you, CJ.

And let me tell you about just a few of my smart, awesome, and capable pals—who took their time and their thoughts and bravely hammered them into my head. David Zucker—my first champion, without whom I probably wouldn't have continued to pursue this for so long. Laurie Bailey and Gregg Kavet—whom I've called upon so many times for help that I'm always shocked when they return my phone calls at all. The New Yorkers who always help me get my art on: Daniel Laikand and Devrin Carlson Smith. And the sexy college coeds Jennifer Jacobson and Jessica Sitomer—I love you both, as well as Lauren Iannotti, the smartest editor I've met in magazines. Lest we forget, the only actresses I know who are smarter than they are beautiful: Navi Rawat and Eva Amurri.

To the magical people who literally made this happen: Brooke Slavik, Kirby Kim, Brooke Warner, Abby Weintraub, and Merrik Bush-Pirkle (what a bonus you were!), along with the sorority of smart ladies at Seal. Your support has been palpable even in email. But extra-special love for Kirby Kim and Brooke Warner—he who went round by round with me in the incredibly "White" world of publishing and she who meticulously worked with me until the last moments of her pregnancy, and then still after her water broke!

To the television people who took my words and sold them as a show before they were even out of my personal computer: Peter Tolan, Matt Rice, Adam Biren, Jacob Fenton, Katz, Comer, and the brothers Suddleson. And all the doers on my team who've helped me carve out a pilot from a 120,000-word original document: especially Mike Baum, Jordan Levin, Pete Aranson, Caitlyn McGinty, Michael Thorn, Lindsay Sloane, and the eternally positive and gracious Jon Wax and my friend Terence Carter—without whom I'm sure this would never have even made it into the starting gate.

To the giving friends of mine who introduced me to their friends whom I feel so close to after getting to know their love stories: Candace Edwards, Tal Rabinowitz, Miki Anzai, Karen Barragan, Lisa Ling, Alyssa Walker, Dan Manross, and my perpetually supportive rainmakers—Catherine McCord and Rona Mercado.

To all my couples and multicultural people who were so brave and cool and took hours on end to talk to me and then sometimes write to me and talk more. Especially the super-cool ones I couldn't include. Lorelie and Jesse, Kyle, Camille, Marlene, Monte, David, Barry, and especially Rene and Raleigh, who informed me on so much and allowed me to get to know them so well. I admire you all and feel privileged to share these pages with you. Gamzee, Candy, Rae-Rae, T, Navi, Liz, Jace, and Tella—sorry to have moved you to the next book, but your stories are so wonderful I didn't want them cut by a word or shortchanged at the very end of a long road here. I'm well aware that those of you I've known the longest had the most at risk when I asked you to participate. You get a second helping of thanks for letting me have my way with you.

And please know that I am doing a standing ovation as I type the following names: Lisa (I still can't believe you're a blonde), JJ and Sonu (I still can't believe you are having another!), Suzanne and David (I'm secretly longing to see Suzanne with bad hair and no makeup on), Nat-a-lia (please buy me a $100 breakfast soon, will you?), and Ellie Super-Platinum Gold (after ten years of friendship, I consider us family, girl). I'm going to stop typing now and—applause, applause, applause. I am proud to know you all and blessed by your tenacity. Thank you for all you have shared.

To all the wonderful women who help me with my family, but most especially Sarah Dollear. And those who support me at all I do—Elizabeth Ricin, Ming Chen, King Chong, and everyone at The Cashmere Agency.

And the magical family that made me and Seung who we are and all those who continue to support us after I dropped my pants and told my most intimate stories in hopes of changing things for their grandchildren, godchildren, nieces, and nephew. To my dad, Tommy, and my super-cool grandmother Aileen—both of whom watched my kids so I could complete this work even knowing that I would make fun of them in it. To my brave and outlandish mother, Paddy Farr, who I sometimes think must be made of steel for how much grief I have given her in this lifetime and yet she is still standing tall . . . and even dancing on the table herself now and then. My Chung mother and father, Young Ja and Tae Wha (although we all know I will never call them by those names). It's incredibly hard to be the first person to believe in someone. Thank you first and foremost for taking a leap of faith with me. My friend and sister-in-law, Eun Yi, whose patience and kindness I could not have lived without when I had three children under eighteen months old. And to the hot hussies who originally laughed at all my thoughts about marrying into their culture. Your humor and honesty still resonate with me.

And to my man, my partner, last boyfriend, husband, and baby daddy—Sing, Singy, Chingy, Chingu, Singster, Seung Yong, SYC, president of K-Power, and Apa of my house. I am so lucky to have you as my partner. Remember that night in the bar when you promised me a baby in front of Wes? So funny that we actually have three of them, ain't it?

And to our little rascals: Beckett, Coco, and Sawyer Chung. Your very existence is like having my heart walk around outside of my body. I thank you for all the inspiration you bring me and for allowing me the time away from home—to not lose myself in all of my love for you. Don't ever give up on your dreams, kids. They are life's precious breath.

NOTES

CHAPTER 3.

1. http://www.nytimes.com/2008/06/08/world/asia/08geesehtml?
pagewanted=all

CHAPTER 11.

1. See www.jobbankusa.com/News/Unemployment/unemploy120203a
.html, accessed January 7, 2011.

2. See www.nytimes.com/2006/03/20/national/20blackmen.html,
accessed January 7, 2011.

3. See www.bls.gov/news.release/empsit.t02.htm, accessed January 7,
2011.

4. See www.npr.org/templates/story/story.php?storyId=120351534,
accessed January 7, 2011.

5. See http://articles.sfgate.com/2008-07-21/news/17173099_1_
mixed-race-multiracial-african-american, accessed January 7,
2011; www.npr.org/templates/story/story.php?storyId=120209980,
accessed January 7, 2011; and seattletimes.nwsource.com/html/
localnews/2008210083_biracial280.html, accessed January 7,
2011.

ABOUT THE AUTHOR

© SHOOTS & GIGGLES PHOTOGRAPHY

D IANE FARR is a television actress, TV and magazine writer, and nationally syndicated columnist, and the author of *The Girl Code: The Secret Language of Single Women.* She's best known for her roles as the female lead on CBS's *Numb3rs,* playing Megan Reeves; on the critically acclaimed FX series *Rescue Me,* as firefighter Laura Miles; and most recently as Jill Robinson on Showtime's *Californication.* She contributes to *Glamour, Esquire, GQ, Cosmopolitan, Marie Claire, Jane, Self,* and *O, The Oprah Magazine,* and writes an internationally syndicated column for the *Herald Tribune.* Farr lives in Los Angeles, California, with her husband and three children.